A Layman Investigates Universal Salvation

A Layman Investigates Universal Salvation

Discovering the Truly Good News

PATRICK SEAMUS O'HARA

RESOURCE *Publications* • Eugene, Oregon

A LAYMAN INVESTIGATES UNIVERSAL SALVATION
Discovering the Truly Good News

Copyright © 2021 Patrick Seamus O'Hara. All rights reserved. Except for brief quotations in critical publications or reviews, no part of this book may be reproduced in any manner without prior written permission from the publisher. Write: Permissions, Wipf and Stock Publishers, 199 W. 8th Ave., Suite 3, Eugene, OR 97401.

Resource Publications
An Imprint of Wipf and Stock Publishers
199 W. 8th Ave., Suite 3
Eugene, OR 97401

www.wipfandstock.com

PAPERBACK ISBN: 978-1-6667-3083-8
HARDCOVER ISBN: 978-1-6667-2281-9
EBOOK ISBN: 978-1-6667-2282-6

11/02/21

This book is dedicated to my spiritual father and dearest friend, a man who has shown me by his life the beauty of Christ's love, compassion, and encouragement as he helps me navigate this difficult race called life.

Contents

Permissions ix
Abbreviations xi
Introduction: Journey to an Unknown Land xiii

Part One: Church Councils, Scripture, and Traditions of the Church   1
Part Two: Eastern Orthodox and Roman Catholic Beliefs on Hell   30
Part Three: The Eternity of Hell from the Church Fathers and Scripture   84
Part Four: Using Reason and Intellect to Understand God   133
A Summary–Context Is Everything   155
If This is True, Why Even Bother?   166
Closing Comments and Questions   178

Bibliography   181

Permissions

Scripture quotations from The Authorized (King James) Version. Rights in the Authorized Version in the United Kingdom are vested in the Crown. Reproduced by permission of the Crown's patentee, Cambridge University Press.
Scripture taken from Young's Literal Translation of the Bible under freedom of public domain.
Permission granted by Bloomsbury Publishing Plc for use of The Canons of Constantinople II as compiled by Norman Tanner.
Permission granted by Fr. Aidan Kimel for all quotations taken from his blog site, Eclectic Orthodoxy.
Permission granted by Fr. Silouan Thompson for quotation from The Fifteen Anathemas Against Origen from his site https://silouanthompson.net
Permission granted by CCEL for quotations from the historian Philip Schaff from his Excursus on the Genuineness of the Acts of the Fifth Council.
Permission granted by First Things for quotations from Saint Origen by David Bentley Hart, October 2015.
Permission granted by Harold Drake for quotation from The Emperor as a 'Man of God': The Impact of Constantine the Great's Conversion on Roman ideas of Kingship
Permission granted by Peter Grice for quotation from Clark Pinnock, Hell and the Holiness of God December 20, 2014 from the web site Rethinking Hell
Permission granted by Paul Penley for quotation from When Heaven and Earth Passed Away: Everything Changed.
Permission granted by Greg Kiser for use of Revelation was Written Before 70 A.D.
Permission granted by Gerry Beauchemin for quotation from Hope Beyond Hell
Permission granted by Aaron Welch for quotations from That Happy Expectation
Permission granted by Got Questions for quotations from What Does It Mean That God Is Sovereign?
Permission granted by Concordant Publishing for quotation from Concerning God's Eonian Purpose.
Permission granted by Gorgias Press for quotation from Terms For Eternity by Ilaria E. Ramelli & David Konstan 2013
Permission granted by the web site Joincake for quotation from Ancient Greek Mythology & The Afterlife Explained

Abbreviations

B.Bat.	Bava Batra
CCC	Catechism of the Catholic Church
CLNT	Concordant Literal New Testament
DBHNT	David Bentley Hart New Testament
KJV	King James Bible
NKJV	New King James Bible
NPNF	Nicene and Post-Nicene Fathers
ST I	Summa Theological First Part
ST II	Summa Theological Second Part
SUKK.	Sukkah. A book of the Mishnah and Talmud.
YLT	Young's Literal Translation of the Bible

Introduction:
Journey to an Unknown Land

YOU ARE INVITED TO go on a journey. It is a journey of investigation and discovery. When first presented with the idea of God saving all, I was at initially intrigued, then joyful, then troubled. Especially troubled. What was this new idea of which I had never heard? When I tried to discuss this concept, the reaction of people was negative. Some were quite disturbed.

The genesis of this book was a forty-page paper, presented to me by a friend who appeared quite troubled when I made certain statements wondering about God saving all. A month later, I was offered a nicely bound presentation, filled with commonly accepted reasons telling me why I must believe in eternal hell. What I intended as a short response, based on my initial limited knowledge of the subject, became an intense search, and is now this book. I felt my friend deserved concise answers rather than throwing out a quick Bible verse or philosophical reply. To respond, I had to go to places I had never heard of before, to a land which had been hidden from me by every pastor and priest to whom I had listened. It was necessary to sort through many facets of this controversy, including Christian history, people involved in the controversy, both past and present, and study of the original Greek Bible texts, using as source material scholars far more advanced than I am. To them I am indebted.

It is a monumental act of hubris on my part, a mere layman, lacking in higher educational degrees, to present such a book to the public. Theologians and linguists such as Dr. David Bentley Hart, Dr. Illaria Ramelli, Thomas Talbot, Brad Jersak, and Fr. Aidan Kimel have written quite thoroughly on this subject. The problem is that some of the books by these apologists are written on a doctorate level–difficult to unintelligible to the average lay person. In working through Dr. Hart's latest book, That All Shall Be Saved, I found it necessary to go back and slowly re-read pages several times to get my mind around what he was saying. As reflected in his writing, he is an immense intellect. My hope is to answer my friend's objections in a voice not requiring a PhD to understand. What you will discover in the following pages is a layman doing his own due diligence to try to understand this subject.

These are strictly my own thoughts and opinions, based on my journey of personal study. I have neither the ecclesial authority nor deep scholastic training to make authoritative pronouncements. This is not as a scholastic book. If you desire doctoral level writing, I recommend Dr. David Bentley Hart, Dr. Illaria Ramelli, Eric Reitan, and John Kronen. I write as an ordinary layman sharing with others the things I found and my conclusions. This book is intended as a beginner's level tool for understanding the basis of belief in Universal Salvation. Perhaps it shall be of help to you. I hope you will go to the authors, websites, and blogs I have referenced and follow up with your own investigation. There are links to men whose writings are much more learned than I will ever be on my best day. Read, study, meditate. Above all, pray.

If my investigative findings and thoughts on Universal Salvation create an interest in you and you would like to go deeper, I highly recommend as your next reading Brad Jersak's book, Her Gates Shall Never Be Shut, and Fr. Aidan Kimel's blog site, Eclectic Orthodoxy at https://afkimel.wordpress.com.

Part One

Church Councils, Scripture, and Traditions of the Church

CONSIDERATION OF SOURCE ONE THROUGH SOURCE FOUR OF MY FRIEND'S PAPER

The Fifth Ecumenical Council–Constantinople II

Source One from my friend quotes a blog piece posted at WordPress on April 28, 2016. The writer, Mike Ratcliff, appeals to what is probably the most often used Infernalist[1] objection to apokatastasis[2]–that it has been condemned by the Fifth Ecumenical Council of Constantinople. For millions of believers, this council definitively settles the issue. His post at WordPress brings up a myriad of usual objections and statements which are not true, such as saying that Universalists do not believe in hell. What I found both puzzling, and a bit strange, was to see my friend, a devout Catholic, quoting from man whose religion is considered heresy by traditional Catholics. Ratcliff identifies as a Calvinist, which predisposes him to believe in eternal hell and defend the same.

---

1. In common discussions of this issue online, the term "Infernalist" has been used to describe those who believe in an unending hell of torment.

2. I will use this Greek word in the book to separate it from the American theological movement called Unitarian Universalism which denies that Christ is God.

In Calvinism, mankind is seen as totally depraved, thus worthy only of wrath from God unless God chooses to elect a person unto redemption. Its foundation is found in the musings of Augustine, who, while a saint in the Roman Catholic Church, was nonetheless fallible in his reasoning. In reading historical information about the Orthodox Church, I found that when the translated writings of Augustine were read in Constantinople, the bishops were deeply dismayed at some of his ideas.[3] But by then, it was too late to stop their spread. The ideas of mankind as a "massa damnata," of being "totally depraved" and worthy only of hell, and of original sin, roared through the Western church like flames through gasoline-soaked prairie grass. Such thoughts are contrary to Orthodoxy theology, anthropology, and soteriology.[4]

One interesting discovery in my research has been to find there have been Calvinists who believed apokatastasis to be true precisely because of their belief in the omnipotence of God. God, being all-powerful, will find a way to assure that the Cross of Christ is successful in bringing all to salvation.

I find it odd that some men read the early fathers and yet believe Calvinist theology was taught in the early church. I believe Mike Ratcliff is in error here, but it is an error that I understand, having been in a Calvinist assembly myself for thirteen years. It was only late in life that I was confronted by apostolic beliefs which challenged my comfortable Calvinism and led to my eventual conversion out of Protestantism. Having made this transition, I would like to speak about the differences between Western (Roman Catholic) and Eastern (Orthodox) Christian teaching on salvation. Many people see these systems as being almost twins because we have much in common, but in several important areas, there are stark differences. These differences are important to understand in coming to see from where the teaching of eternal hellfire originated.

It was not until my third year of seminary studies that I became aware of these substantial differences. I learned that in the Roman Empire, the law was everything. Its shadow fell across every aspect of the Roman citizen, making the understanding and application of the law paramount. The Roman citizen thought in terms of the law, and the law, in turn, granted to him certain rights which he might not enjoy in other countries. Augustine was so enamored of Roman law that he transmitted quotations of the Twelve Tables, which have become highly valuable for the modern reconstruction.

---

3. Many Orthodox refer to Augustine as "Blessed Augustine" but will not use the title "saint" due to his errors.

4. Anthropology is the study and understanding of man. Theology is the study and understanding of God. Soteriology is the study and understanding of salvation.

It is understandable that Roman Empire converts to Christianity would gravitate to seeing sin as a legal violation, with specific punishments due for violations of God's law. An entrenched cultural mindset is not easily set aside, even by baptism.

This cultural view imprinted itself on Christianity, aided by the many passages in scripture which appear to treat sin as a legal violation. In the OT, these verses speak of God's law and commandments, and the punishments for breaking them. Trained in the law, the Roman mind would hear these verses and tend to see God as strict Judge, ready to inflict punishment on offenders of His sovereign rule. In Western theology, the language of salvation is retributive. The believer is given certain practices which may be offered as a kind of payment to avoid punishment.[5] The offender who goes to Purgatory is punished until his sins are paid for, and the punishments, some quite dreadful, depend on the severity of the sins which have not be expiated by repentance:

> The soul was whirled about, here and there, by a huge whirlwind, and blown around in the midst of a great abundance of straw, flying like thatch from a roof and destroyed. After it had been worn out this way by the whirlwind, it was thrown into that house I mentioned before and, there, it was subject to such fierce fire that it glowed like a red-hot iron. Then, it was thrown among the poisonous scorpions, which punctured it with their venom, and, afterword, among the wild boars, which took great bites out of it.[6]

In contrast, as I have drawn closer to the Orthodox Church, reading her saints and studying priests who have written sermons, I find the healthy condition of the soul, rather than punishment, is the concern. This view of God as Great Physician and Father Who Heals Us, is much more comforting than the Western view of God as the Sovereign Judge and Mighty Smiter, poised in eternal watchfulness for the slightest infraction of the rules in order to descend in swift punishment.

---

5. In the teaching of the Catholic Church, an Indulgence is "a way to reduce the amount of punishment one has to undergo for sins." The Catechism of the Catholic Church describes an Indulgence as "a remission before God of the temporal punishment due to sins whose guilt has already been forgiven, which the faithful Christian who is duly disposed gains under certain prescribed conditions through the action of the Church which, as the minister of redemption, dispenses and applies with authority the treasury of the satisfactions of Christ and all of the saints."

6. Turner, "Torn Among the Boars:" St. Hildegard's Frightful Vision of Purgatory. Para. 5.

The outworking of these two different views of sin can be seen in the Sacrament of Confession. In the Roman West, the sinner is given a penance after making confession. A penance is defined in legal terms as a canonical punishment, a reparation, or a light penalty for the violation of God's law. Notice the use of legal language. You will not find this in the Orthodox East. When I go to my spiritual director to confess my sins, he gives no penance afterward. Instead, acting as a physician to my soul, he will speak with me about things I should do to heal my soul and further my theosis,[7] making me less prone to fall into sin again. I am given suggestions which are medicinal in nature, such as reading books which deal with the sin am struggling with, certain prayers, or other actions which are designed to aid in my spiritual growth. The view of mankind in Orthodoxy is that man is sick with sin and needs to be healed, not punished. This view can be seen in the early fathers, who called the Eucharist "the medicine of immortality."

This is Christ. He is not a courtroom judge, but the Great Physician, whose judgment is not to condemn, but to discern what treatment will best facilitate our healing. I believe this judgment extends to all who stand before Him after death. What do we need for complete healing? Every human being will need something.

The significance of Roman law cannot be understated. Neither can its effect upon the Western church.

> Today, Roman law is no longer applied in legal practice, even though the legal systems of some countries like South Africa and San Marino are still based on the old jus commune. However, even where the legal practice is based on a code, many rules deriving from Roman law apply: no code completely broke with the Roman tradition. Rather, the provisions of the Roman law were fitted into a more coherent system and expressed in the national language. For this reason, knowledge of the Roman law is indispensable to understand the legal systems of today. Thus, Roman law is often still a mandatory subject for law students in civil law jurisdictions. In this context, the annual International Roman Law Moot Court was developed in order to better educate the students and to network with one another internationally.
>
> German legal theorist Rudolf von Jhering famously remarked that ancient Rome had conquered the world three times:

---

7. Theosis, or deification, is a transformative process whose aim is likeness to or union with God. In Eastern Orthodoxy, this process is considered the primary focus of our lives. We are here temporarily, and should be concerned with getting ready to be with God.

the first through its armies, the second through its religion, the third through its laws. He might have added: each time more thoroughly.[8]

I hope you see how the Western legal view of God's relationship to mankind facilitates the easy transition from God is love to God as judge and eternal hell as a proper punishment. When you have been raised in a society which is built upon law and punishment, it is a small step from there to seeing everything in the Scriptures as being about the same kind of relationship. I cannot remember, in twenty-five years of being in Protestant churches, ever hearing of Christ as the healer of my soul.

In summary of this first point, in the West sin is about a crime committed against God, a sure and fiery punishment if we do not repent, and salvation is a fire escape from condemnation. In the East, sin is about illness of the soul, healing to be found in a loving God who is our Great Physician, and how to use spiritual medicine to become like Christ.

Source Two goes into greater detail regarding the Fifth Ecumenical Council. This council has become the center of increasing debate and interest in recent years due to the ongoing investigation of all events which took place in this council. At the outset of my investigation, I found important information from Papal Encyclicals Online regarding this council:

> The council did not debate ecclesiastical discipline nor did it issue disciplinary canons. Our edition does not include the text of the anathemas against Origen since recent studies have shown that *these anathemas cannot be attributed to this council.*[9]

This is one of several critical observations about this council. Here is another:

> The canon does not specify which of Origen's teachings are condemned, nor do the acts record any discussion of them by the council fathers. Origen is simply included in a list of previously condemned heretics. This is where things get tricky. The others in the list were condemned by previous ecumenical councils and their heresies were well known; but those councils had never condemned Origen. Which teachings of Origen, therefore, did the bishops of the Fifth Council believe to be antithetical to the apostolic faith? We do not know–neither the canons nor the acts of the council tell us. This point needs to be stressed. We must not assume that because the council fathers condemned Origen by name they therefore intended to condemn his teaching on

---

8. "Roman Law," Paragraphs 34 & 42
9. "Second Council of Constantinople"–553 A.D. Lines 16–17.

apokatastasis. The establishment of conciliar dogma requires more than guesswork and conjectural inference. F. Nutcombe Oxenham, 19th century Roman Catholic theologian and translator of Karl Josef von Hefele's monumental A History of the Councils of the Church succinctly states the historical problem and interpretive task:

"Let me say to any who may consider it an important matter to be assured whether Origen was, or was not condemned, by some ancient Synod, two things–(1) That if it could be ever so conclusively proved that 'Origen was condemned' by the Fifth Council, this would afford no evidence whatever that he was condemned on account of his doctrine of restitution, since he held a great many other doctrines much more open to blame than this one. And then (2) Supposing Origen's doctrine of restitution had been 'by itself condemned,' this would be no condemnation of the doctrine of restitution, as now held. e.g. by Mr. Jukes or by Dr Farrar [two 19th century exponents of universal salvation]; since their two doctrines of restitution are in many important points essentially different."[10]

Unfortunately, Constantinople II has become something of an ignorant cudgel which the supporters of eternal hell use in their desire to beat apokatastasis to death and never hear word of it again. Infernalists are ever quick to resort to Constantinople II as their trump card when they have been backed into a philosophical or scriptural corner from which they cannot extract themselves. In addition, most Christians who even know about the ecumenical councils have no idea of the controversy which surrounded this council, the way Emperor Justinian overreached his authority, and how he, without the proper authority of being a bishop in the church, added his own canons to those of the council. I shall deal with Justinian further down the road, but for now, allow me to deal with what is the first of several erroneous statements made in the paper I received from my well-meaning friend. I will answer each one of these errors as best I can, giving in my answers the reasons I believe apokatastasis is truly the Good News of the Gospel. For those who have had a lifetime of programming in Infernalist thinking, reading this will not be easy, and will most likely be rejected out of hand.[11]

10. Kimel, "Did the Fifth Ecumenical Council Condemn Universal Salvation?" Para 4–5

11. I am expecting men like Dr. Edward Feser, Father Lawrence Farley, and other highly educated theologians and philosophers to gleefully attack what I have written, describing my work as puerile and nonsensical. The very idea that God is so loving and just that He will find a way to save all without compromising His justice gets their knickers in a bunch. I promise to be unimpressed, especially by men of learning who

The Ten Anathemas against Origen of 543 were written ten years before the Fifth Ecumenical Council. (We see Justinian had a problematic relationship with Origen and his followers a good time before the council met) They consist of a letter with appended anathemas written by the Emperor Justinian to the Patriarch Menas. Justinian quotes from Origen's De Principiis in order to expose Origen's errors in detail, and he concludes with ten anathemas summarizing the condemned doctrines. The errors condemned in the Ten Anathemas include the following: the preexistence and fall of souls through satiety (kouros) of divine contemplation, and their chastisement through descent into bodies (Anathema 1); the preexistence of Christ's soul (2); the uniting of Christ's body with both his preexistent soul and the divine Word (3); that Christ assumed the form of all the heavenly powers (4); that in the world to come Christ will also be crucified for the demons (7); that the resurrected body will be spherical and immaterial (5); that the celestial bodies (sun, moon, stars, and firmament) are ensouled, reasoning beings (6); that the power of God is limited or that creation is eternal (8); and that a restoration (apokatastasis) of demons and evil human beings will put an end to temporal punishment. (9)

The Fifteen Anathemas of 553 are similar in form to the Ten Anathemas of 543: They, too, consist of a letter from the Emperor Justinian with attached condemnations. In this letter Justinian writes to the council fathers "concerning Origen and his sympathizers," to warn them about the teachings of certain monks of Jerusalem whom he describes as devotees not only of Origen, but also of Pythagoras and Plotinus. Associated with his letter are fifteen anathemas which until recently were commonly appended to the fourteen canons of the Fifth Ecumenical Council, though modern academics assert that these fifteen additional anathemas were not part of the original conciliar decrees. The principal difference between these Fifteen Anathemas of 553 and the Ten Anathemas of 543 lies chiefly in the very particular christology described in anathemas 6–9, 11, and 14 of 553, which correspond to anathemas 2 and 3 of 543 regarding the preexistent soul of Christ. Justinian's anathemas of 543 are directed against specific doctrines taken from Origen's De Principiis, while the subsequent anathemas of 553, although not

---

can't even take the time to study the Greek properly and/or use proper interpretations of the Bible. Following tradition is not holy, especially when it is proven to be wrong–it is lazy! If I, a simple layman, can read, study, and find these things out, they could. For some reason, they don't want to, and when men such as Dr. Hart have proven that eternal hell is a fraud, they run from the debate and instead hurl insults from a distance.

> mentioning Evagrius Ponticus by name, specifically condemn doctrines which appear to be taken from Evagrius' Kephalaia Gnostica.[12]

I note that Emperor Justinian was having problems with the Origenists long before the council met. The council was called specifically to address the Christological issues which came up at the Council of Chalcedon. For some people, Chalcedon settled nothing. The empire was being ripped apart by dissent–even to the point of riots and death–and Justinian could not tolerate this. When he looked to Jerusalem, it was the Origenists who were causing problems, along with those who had rejected the canons of Chalcedon.

In Source Two I was presented with a quote from the New World Encyclopedia. From the very beginning of this article, we see mention of the controversy which caused this council to be convened:

> The Second Council of Constantinople, also known as the Fifth Ecumenical Council, was a meeting of mostly Eastern church leaders convened by Emperor Justinian I from May 5 to June 2, 553. Presided over by Patriarch Eutychius of Constantinople, the council dealt mainly with the emperor's wish to produce a formal condemnation of the allegedly heretical Three Chapters.[13]

Constantinople II was convened to deal with the Three Chapters. It was not intended to deal with the issue of apokatastasis. For clarity regarding the council, I reprint the canons of Constantinople II for your examination:

> I. If anyone will not confess that the Father, Son and holy Spirit have one nature or substance, that they have one power and authority, that there is a consubstantial Trinity, one Deity to be adored in three subsistences or persons: let him be anathema. There is only one God and Father, from whom all things come, and one Lord, Jesus Christ, through whom all things are, and one holy Spirit, in whom all things are.
> II. If anyone will not confess that the Word of God has two nativities, that which is before all ages from the Father, outside time and without a body, and secondly that nativity of these latter days when the Word of God came down from the heavens and was made flesh of holy and glorious Mary, mother of God and ever-virgin, and was born from her: let him be anathema.
> III. If anyone declares that the [Word] of God who works miracles is not identical with the Christ who suffered, or alleges that

---

12. Thompson, "The Fifteen Anathemas Against Origen" Para 21–22.
13. "Second Council of Constantinople." Para. 1

God the Word was with the Christ who was born of woman, or was in him in the way that one might be in another, but that our lord Jesus Christ was not one and the same, the Word of God incarnate and made man, and that the miracles and the sufferings which he voluntarily underwent in the flesh were not of the same person: let him be anathema.

IV. If anyone declares that it was only in respect of grace, or of principle of action, or of dignity or in respect of equality of honor, or in respect of authority, or of some relation, or of some affection or power that there was a unity made between the Word of God and the man, or if anyone alleges that it is in respect of good will, as if God the Word was pleased with the man, because he was well and properly disposed to God, as Theodore claims in his madness; or if anyone says that this union is only a sort of synonymity, as the Nestorians allege, who call the Word of God Jesus and Christ, and even designate the human separately by the names "Christ" and "Son," discussing quite obviously two different persons, and only pretending to speak of one person and one Christ when the reference is to his title, honor, dignity or adoration; finally if anyone does not accept the teaching of the holy fathers that the union occurred of the Word of God with human flesh which is possessed by a rational and intellectual soul, and that this union is by synthesis or by person, and that therefore there is only one person, namely the lord Jesus Christ, one member of the holy Trinity: let him be anathema. The notion of "union" can be understood in many different ways. The supporters of the wickedness of Apollinarius and Eutyches have asserted that the union is produced by a confusing of the uniting elements, as they advocate the disappearance of the elements that unite. Those who follow Theodore and Nestorius, rejoicing in the division, have brought in a union which is only by affection. The holy church of God, rejecting the wickedness of both sorts of heresy, states her belief in a union between the Word of God and human flesh which is by synthesis, that is by a union of subsistence. In the mystery of Christ the union of synthesis not only conserves without confusing the elements that come together but also allows no division.

V. If anyone understands by the single subsistence of our lord Jesus Christ that it covers the meaning of many subsistences, and by this argument tries to introduce into the mystery of Christ two subsistences or two persons, and having brought in two persons then talks of one person only in respect of dignity, honour or adoration, as both Theodore and Nestorius have written in their madness; if anyone falsely represents the holy synod of Chalcedon, making out that it accepted this heretical view by its terminology of "one subsistence," and if he does not acknowledge that the Word of God is united with human flesh by subsistence, and that on account of this there is only one subsistence or one person, and that the holy synod of Chalcedon thus made a formal statement of belief in the single subsistence of our lord Jesus Christ: let him be anathema. There has been no addition of person or subsistence to the holy Trinity even after one of its members, God the Word, becoming human flesh.

VI. If anyone declares that it can be only inexactly and not truly said that the holy and glorious ever-virgin Mary is the mother of God, or says that she is so only in some relative way, considering that she bore a mere man and that God the Word was not made into human flesh in her, holding rather that the nativity of a man from her was referred, as they say, to God the Word as he was with the man who came into being; if anyone misrepresents the holy synod of Chalcedon, alleging that it claimed that the virgin was the mother of God only according to that heretical understanding which the blasphemous Theodore put forward; or if anyone says that she is the mother of a man or the Christ-bearer, that is the mother of Christ, suggesting that Christ is not God; and does not formally confess that she is properly and truly the mother of God, because he who before all ages was born of the Father, God the Word, has been made into human flesh in these latter days and has been born to her, and it was in this religious understanding that the holy synod of Chalcedon formally stated its belief that she was the mother of God: let him be anathema.

VII. If anyone, when speaking about the two natures, does not confess a belief in our one lord Jesus Christ, understood in both his divinity and his humanity, so as by this to signify a difference of natures of which an ineffable union has been made without confusion, in which neither the nature of the Word was changed into the nature of human flesh, nor was the nature of human flesh changed into that of the Word (each remained what it was by nature, even after the union, as this had been made in respect of subsistence); and if anyone understands the two natures in the mystery of Christ in the sense of a division into parts, or if he expresses his belief in the plural natures in the same lord Jesus Christ, God the Word made flesh, but does not consider the difference of those natures, of which he is composed, to be only in the onlooker's mind, a difference which is not compromised by the union (for he is one from both and the two exist through the one) but uses the plurality to suggest that each nature is possessed separately and has a subsistence of its own: let him be anathema.

VIII. If anyone confesses a belief that a union has been made out of the two natures divinity and humanity, or speaks about the one nature of God the Word made flesh, but does not understand these things according to what the fathers have taught, namely that from the divine and human natures a union was made according to subsistence, and that one Christ was formed, and from these expressions tries to introduce one nature or substance made of the deity and human flesh of Christ: let him be anathema. In saying that it was in respect of subsistence that the only-begotten God the Word was united, we are not alleging that there was a confusion made of each of the natures into one another, but rather that each of the two remained what it was, and in this way we understand that the Word was united to human flesh. So there is only one Christ, God and man, the same being consubstantial with the Father in respect of his divinity, and also consubstantial with us in respect of our humanity. Both those who divide or split up the mystery of the divine dispensation of Christ and those who introduce into that mystery some confusion are equally rejected and anathematized by the church of God.

IX. If anyone says that Christ is to be worshipped in his two natures, and by that wishes to introduce two adorations, a separate one for God the Word and another for the man; or if anyone, so as to remove the human flesh or to mix up the divinity and the humanity, monstrously invents one nature or substance brought together from the two, and so worships Christ, but not by a single adoration God the Word in human flesh along with his human flesh, as has been the tradition of the church from the beginning: let him be anathema.

X. If anyone does not confess his belief that our lord Jesus Christ, who was crucified in his human flesh, is truly God and the Lord of glory and one of the members of the holy Trinity: let him be anathema.

XI. If anyone does not anathematize Arius, Eunomius, Macedonius, Apollinarius Nestorius, Eutyches and Origen, as well as their heretical books, and also all other heretics who have already been condemned and anathematized by the holy, catholic and apostolic church and by the four holy synods which have already been mentioned, and also all those who have thought or now think in the same way as the aforesaid heretics and who persist in their error even to death: let him be anathema.

XII. If anyone defends the heretical Theodore of Mopsuestia, who said that God the Word is one, while quite another is Christ, who was troubled by the passions of the soul and the desires of human flesh, was gradually separated from that which is inferior, and became better by his progress in good works, and could not be faulted in his way of life, and as a mere man was baptized in the name of the Father and the Son and the holy Spirit, and through this baptism received the grace of the holy Spirit and came to deserve sonship and to be adored, in the way that one adores a statue of the emperor, as if he were God the Word, and that he became after his resurrection immutable in his thoughts and entirely without sin. Furthermore this heretical Theodore claimed that the union of God the Word to Christ is rather like that which, according to the teaching of the Apostle, is between a man and his wife: The two shall become one. Among innumerable other blasphemies he dared to allege that, when after his resurrection the Lord breathed on his disciples and said, Receive the holy Spirit, he was not truly giving them the holy Spirit, but he breathed on them only as a sign. Similarly he claimed that Thomas's profession of faith made when, after his resurrection, he touched the hands and side of the Lord, namely My Lord and my God, was not said about Christ, but that Thomas was in this way extolling God for raising up Christ and expressing his astonishment at the miracle of the resurrection. This Theodore makes a comparison which is even worse than this when, writing about the acts of the Apostles, he says that Christ was like Plato, Manichaeus, Epicurus and Marcion, alleging that just as each of these men arrived at his own teaching and then had his disciples called after him Platonists, Manichaeans, Epicureans and Marcionites, so Christ found his teaching and then had disciples who were called Christians. If anyone offers a defence for this more heretical Theodore, and his heretical books in which he throws up the aforesaid blasphemies and many other additional blasphemies against our great God and saviour Jesus Christ, and if anyone fails to anathematize him and his heretical books as well as all those who offer acceptance or defence to him, or who allege that his interpretation is correct, or who write on his behalf or on that of his heretical teachings, or who are or have been of the same way of thinking and persist until death in this error: let him be anathema.

XIII. If anyone defends the heretical writings of Theodoret which were composed against the true faith, against the first holy synod of Ephesus and against holy Cyril and his Twelve Chapters, and also defends what Theodoret wrote to support the heretical Theodore and Nestorius and others who think in the same way as the aforesaid Theodore and Nestorius and accept them or their heresy and if anyone, because of them, shall accuse of being heretical the doctors of the church who have stated their belief in the union according to subsistence of God the Word; and if anyone does not anathematize these heretical books and those who have thought or now think in this way, and all those who have written against the true faith or against holy Cyril and his twelve chapters, and who persist in such heresy until they die: let him be anathema.

XIV. If anyone defends the letter which Ibas is said to have written to Mari the Persian, which denies that God the Word, who became incarnate of Mary the holy mother of God and ever virgin, became man, but alleges that he was only a man born to her, whom it describes as a temple, as if God the Word was one and the man someone quite different; which condemns holy Cyril as if he were a heretic, when he gives the true teaching of Christians, and accuses holy Cyril of writing opinions like those of the heretical Apollinarius; which rebukes the first holy synod of Ephesus, alleging that it condemned Nestorius without going into the matter by a formal examination; which claims that the twelve chapters of holy Cyril are heretical and opposed to the true faith; and which defends Theodore and Nestorius and their heretical teachings and books. If anyone defends the said letter and does not anathematize it and all those who offer a defence for it and allege that it or a part of it is correct, or if anyone defends those who have written or shall write in support of it or the heresies contained in it, or supports those who are bold enough to defend it or its heresies in the name of the holy fathers of the holy synod of Chalcedon, and persists in these errors until his death: let him be anathema.

Such then are the assertions we confess. We have received them from

I. holy Scripture, from

II. the teaching of the holy fathers, and from

III. the definitions about the one and the same faith made by the aforesaid four holy synods.

Moreover, condemnation has been passed by us against the heretics and their impiety, and also against those who have justified or shall justify the so-called "Three Chapters," and against those who have persisted or will persist in their own error. If anyone should attempt to hand on, or to teach by word or writing, anything contrary to what we have regulated, then if he is a bishop or somebody appointed to the clergy, in so far as he is acting

> contrary to what befits priests and the ecclesiastical status, let him be stripped of the rank of priest or cleric, and if he is a monk or lay person, let him be anathema.[14]

These are the accepted canons of the council and, look at that! The word apokatastasis is nowhere to be found, is it? So why do people say Constantinople II anathematizes apokatastasis when you cannot find it in the original canons? Because they have been taught for fifteen hundred years to regard this as truth. They are not aware of the entire history of this troubled council and the highly suspect way it was convened.

At this point, I'm sure someone is saying, "But look at the eleventh canon! It specifically condemns Origen's writings." This gets a little deeper into the heart of the matter, doesn't it? To correctly understand what is being condemned, we should look at the fifteen additional canons–the bogus and not accepted canons. Within them we will find the issues for which Origen was anathemized.

1. If anyone asserts the fabulous pre-existence of souls, and shall assert the monstrous restoration which follows from it: let him be anathema.[15]

This first canon is most popularly quoted against apokatastasis, yet it has nothing to do with it if you read the canon carefully. It is based on a premise and conclusion. Premise: there is a pre-existence of souls. Conclusion: there is a "monstrous restoration" (apokatastasis) which follows from the idea of souls pre-existing before being created here on earth.

What Origen taught regarding the pre-existence of souls is not a teaching which is in any way part of apokatastasis. The thoughts expressed in this, and the rest of the anti-Origen canons, are a collection of bizarre theologoumenon[16] by Origen. You will not find his concept of apokatastasis in the writings of the early fathers who taught it. Which leads to another point.

For the first five hundred years of the church, apokatastasis was taught alongside two other teachings–eternal torment, taught primarily in the Roman West, and annihilation–without a single breath of the word "heresy" ever being uttered. For five hundred years! If this teaching is the great heresy modern day Infernalists claim it to be, there would have been a council a long time before Constantinople II. This lack of any council in the first five centuries of the church declares to me that this teaching was simply not an

---

14. Tanner, "Second Council of Constantinople–553 A.D." Para. 20–36
15. Thompson, "The Fifteen Anathemas Against Origen," Para. 1.
16. A theologoumenon is "a theological statement or concept which lacks absolute doctrinal authority." It is commonly defined as "a theological assertion or statement not derived from divine revelation," or "a theological statement or concept in the area of individual opinion rather than of authoritative doctrine."

issue. It was so not an issue that no mention of life after death appears in the Nicene Creed, other than the promise of life in the world to come.

> In the first five or six centuries of Christianity there were six theological schools, of which four (Alexandria, Antioch, Caesarea, and Edessa, or Nisibis) were Universalist, one (Ephesus) accepted conditional immortality; one (Carthage or Rome) taught endless punishment of the wicked. Other theological schools are mentioned as founded by Universalists, but their actual doctrine on this subject is not known.[17]

The four schools teaching apokatastasis did not cease until Emperor Justinian closed them down because he despised the teaching. He did this because the Origenists were causing divisions and trouble in the empire. Justinian associated with these troubles anything the Origenists were teaching, and thus closed off all communications associated with them–including the teaching of apokatastasis–to try to quell the trouble and bring peace.

This is guilt by association. It is the idea that because Origen had strange theories which contradicted orthodox Christianity, and because a strange form of apokatastasis was part of that body of teaching, the whole teaching of apokatastasis must be condemned. Origen's apokatastasis involves the pre-existence of souls and their restoration to a bizarre, pre-existent state. It was not the same teaching of men like St. Gregory of Nyssa. Origen was a Trinitarian, does this also mean the teaching of the Trinity must be wrong, since he is a heretic? If Origen accepted the Nicene Creed as truth, then could the Creed be wrong? If a gentleman by the name of Bob Smith robs a bank, is every Bob Smith a bank robber? Do you see how this works?

Here are the rest of the canons against Origen–canons which, according to Papal Encyclicals Online, are *highly questionable in nature and not counted as part of the original!*

2. If anyone shall say that the creation of all reasonable things includes only intelligences, without bodies and altogether immaterial, having neither number nor name, so that there is unity between them all by identity of substance, force and energy, and by their union with and knowledge of God the Word; but that no longer desiring the sight of God, they gave themselves over to worse things, each one following his own inclinations, and that they have taken bodies more or less subtile, and have received names, for among the heavenly Powers there is a difference of names as there is also a difference of bodies; and thence some became and are called Cherubims, others Seraphims,

---

17. Schaff, The Encyclopedia of Religious Knowledge by Schaff-Herzog, 1908, Volume 12, Page 96. Philip Schaff is a highly respected historian in the Christian faith.

and Principalities, and Powers, and Dominations, and Thrones, and Angels, and as many other heavenly orders as there may be: let him be anathema.

3. If anyone shall say that the sun, the moon and the stars are also reasonable beings, and that they have only become what they are because they turned towards evil: let him be anathema.

4. If anyone shall say that the reasonable creatures in whom the divine love had grown cold have been hidden in gross bodies such as ours, and have been called men, while those who have attained the lowest degree of wickedness have shared cold and obscure bodies and are become and called demons and evil spirits: let him be anathema.

5. If anyone shall say that a psychic condition has come from an angelic or archangelic state, and moreover that a demoniac and a human condition has come from a psychic condition, and that from a human state they may become again angels and demons, and that each order of heavenly virtues is either all from those below or from those above, or from those above and below: let him be anathema.

6. If anyone shall say that there is a twofold race of demons, of which the one includes the souls of men and the other the superior spirits who fell to this, and that of all the number of reasonable beings there is but one which has remained unshaken in the love and contemplation of God, and that that spirit is become Christ and the king of all reasonable beings, and that he has created all the bodies which exist in heaven, on earth, and between heaven and earth; and that the world which has in itself elements more ancient than itself, and which exists by themselves, viz.: dryness, damp, heat and cold, and the image to which it was formed, was so formed, and that the most holy and consubstantial Trinity did not create the world, but that it was created by the working intelligence which is more ancient than the world, and which communicates to it its being: let him be anathema.

7. If anyone shall say that Christ, of whom it is said that he appeared in the form of God, and that he was united before all time with God the Word, and humbled himself in these last days even to humanity, had (according to their expression) pity upon the divers falls which had appeared in the spirits united in the same unity (of which he himself is part), and that to restore them he passed through divers classes, had different bodies and different names, became all to all, an Angel among Angels, a Power among Powers, has clothed himself in the different classes of reasonable beings with a form corresponding to that class,

CHURCH COUNCILS, SCRIPTURE, AND TRADITIONS OF THE CHURCH   17

and finally has taken flesh and blood like ours and is become man for men; [if anyone says all this] and does not profess that God the Word humbled himself and became man: let him be anathema.

8. If anyone shall not acknowledge that God the Word, of the same substance with the Father and the Holy Ghost, and who was made flesh and became man, one of the Trinity, is Christ in every sense of the word, but [shall affirm] that he is so only in an inaccurate manner, and because of the abasement, as they call it, of the intelligence; if anyone shall affirm that this intelligence united to God the Word, is the Christ in the true sense of the word, while the Logos is only called Christ because of this union with the intelligence, and e converso that the intelligence is only called God because of the Logos: let him be anathema.

9. If anyone shall say that it was not the Divine Logos made man by taking an animated body with a rational soul and mind, that he descended into hell and ascended into heaven, but shall pretend that it is the nous which has done this, that nous, of which they say (in an impious fashion) he is Christ properly so called, and that he is become so by the knowledge of the Monad: let him be anathema.

10. If anyone shall say that after the resurrection the body of the Lord was ethereal, having the form of a sphere, and that such shall be the bodies of all after the resurrection; and that after the Lord himself shall have rejected his true body and after the others who rise shall have rejected theirs, the nature of their bodies shall be annihilated: let him be anathema.

11. If anyone shall say that the future judgment signifies the destruction of the body and that the end of the story will be an immaterial psysis, and that thereafter there will no longer be any matter, but only spirit (nous): let him be anathema.

12. If anyone shall say that the heavenly Powers and all men and the Devil and evil spirits are united with the Word of God in all respects, as the Nous, which is by them called Christ and which is in the form of God, and which humbled itself as they say; and [if anyone shall say] that the Kingdom of Christ shall have an end: let him be anathema.

13. If anyone shall say that Christ [i.e., the nous] is in no wise different from other reasonable beings, neither substantially nor by wisdom nor by his power and might over all things but that all will be placed at the right hand of God, as well as he that is called by them Christ [the nous], as also they were in the feigned pre-existence of all things: let him be anathema.

14. If anyone shall say that all reasonable beings will one day be united in one, when the hypostases as well as the numbers and the bodies shall have disappeared, and that the knowledge of the world to come will carry with it the ruin of the worlds, and the rejection of bodies as also the abolition of [all] names, and that there shall be finally an identity of the gnpsis and of the hypostasis; moreover, that in this pretended apocatastasis, spirits only will continue to exist, as it was in the feigned pre-existence: let him be anathema.

15. If anyone shall say that the life of the spirits shall be like to the life which was in the beginning while as yet the spirits had not come down or fallen, so that the end and the beginning shall be alike, and that the end shall be the true measure of the beginning: let him be anathema.[18]

At this point, someone may respond by pointing to the fourteenth canon which specifically uses the word apokatastasis. I remind you that these canons are not considered legitimate, but more than that, let's take the time to think about what is being said here. Do you see the words, "pretended apokatastasis?" If I were to say, "He pretends to be a professional baseball player," you would know there is such a thing as a real professional ball player and the man in question is not one. The pretended is not the real.

This is true of the pretended apokatastasis of Origen. If you read Origen's thoughts, you will see that the ideas expressed in it are entirely unorthodox–all reasonable beings united into one being, all bodies have disappeared, the abolition of all names, and only spirits will continue to exist rather than the full human being, body, soul, and spirit. Anyone who believes in apokatastasis would reject these ideas out of hand as false. Thus, this is indeed a "pretended apokatastasis" and not the real thing, which was taught without condemnation by Saint Gregory of Nyssa and others. It is a bizarre variation of that which St. Gregory of Nyssa and St. Isaac of Syria taught. It is also quite interesting that this same council commended St. Gregory, who was well-known as an open teacher of apokatastasis. This points to the council recognizing the difference between the real thing, which was never condemned, and the bizarre concept of Origen.

Finally, regarding Constantinople II, I found an Excursus on the Genuineness of the Acts of the Fifth Council by the respected historian, Philip Schaff:

> Some suspicion has arisen with regard to how far the acts of the Fifth Ecumenical Council may be relied upon. Between the Roman Manuscript printed by Labbe and the Paris manuscript

18. Thompson, "The Fifteen Anathemas Against Origen," Para. 2–15

found in Mansi there are considerable variations and, strange to say, some of the most injurious things to the memory of Pope Vigilius are found only in the Paris manuscript. Moreover, we know that the manuscript kept in the patriarchal archives at Constantinople had been tampered with during the century that elapsed before the next Ecumenical Synod, for at that council the forgeries and interpolations were exposed by the Papal Legates.

At the XIVth Session of that synod the examination of the genuineness of the acts of the Second Council of Constantinople was resumed. It had been begun at the XIIth Session. Up to this time only two mss. had been used, now the librarian of the patriarchate presented a third ms. which he had found in the archives, and swore that neither himself nor any other so far as he knew had made any change in these mss. These were then compared and it was found that the two first agreed in containing the pretended letter of Mennas to Pope Vigilius, and the two writings addressed by Vigilius to Justinian and Theodora; but that none of these were found in the third ms. It was further found that the documents in dispute were in a different hand from the rest of the ms., and that in the first book of the parchment ms., three quarternions had been inserted, and in the second book between quarternions 15 and 16, four unpaged leaves had been placed. So too the second ms. had been tampered with. The council inserted these particulars in a decree, and ordered that 'these additions must be quashed in both mss., and marked with an obelus, and the falsifiers must be smitten with anathema.' Finally, the council cried out, 'Anathema to the pretended letters of Mennas and Vigilius! Anathema to the forger of Acts! Anathema to all who teach, etc.'[19]

Source 3 from my friend was a summation of all ecumenical councils at the Intratext Digital Library. It adds nothing new to the argument, other than my friend adding bold emphasis to the excerpt she took from a longer paragraph on the council:

> It further anathematized even Origen himself, and Didymus, and Evagrius, and their detestable tenents, who foolishly affirmed that souls were existent prior to bodies, and that upon the death of one body they enter another; that there is an end to the punishment suffered in hell; that demons are going to recover the original dignity of angelic grace which they used to have; that souls are going to be resurrected naked without a

---

19. Schaff, "Excursus on the Genuiness of the Acts of the Fifth Council," Para. 1–2

body; and that the heavenly bodies have souls ; and still other caxodoxical[20] notions.

Except it was only certain theories of his which the council anathematized, and the traditional, that is, the *orthodox* theory of apokatastasis, was not one of them! It is not true to insist that any of the legitimate canons anathematized anyone who says that there is an end to hell. What I am hoping to prove with the many citations I have given is that my friend has fallen into an error of false inclusivity of orthodox apokatastasis with Origen's strange eschatological ideas which were rejected by the church.

Father Aidan Kimel has a wonderful blog site where he answers objections to apokatastasis:

> But Origen's teachings were condemned by earlier local synods, right? Yes, the most noteworthy being the Synod of Alexandria (399 or 400), convened by Patriarch Theophilus. Theophilus identifies the anathematized teachings of Origen in his Synodical Letter, his official account of the proceedings. He states that the synod condemned eight teachings supposedly found in the On First Principles, but Origen's teaching on the restoration of all humanity to God is not named! The Synod of Alexandria was quickly followed by synods held in Jerusalem and Cyprus (under the leadership of St Epiphanius), each subscribing to Theophilus's synodal. Once again, Origen's teaching on apokatastasis is not named. Theophilus apparently also sent the synodal to Pope Anastasius I, who, in a letter to Bishop Simplicianus expresses his strong agreement with the condemnation of Origen. In 402 Epiphanius visited Constantinople to solicit endorsement of the Synodal Letter, but his request was denied. It may also be noted that in their writings on the errors of Origin, neither St Epiphanius nor St Jerome identify Origen's universalist teaching as heterodox. This may come to a surprise until we recall that in the fourth and fifth centuries, St Gregory of Nyssa was never censured–or even criticized–for his evangelical assertion of universal salvation. Christians may have vigorously disagreed with each other about the question of everlasting damnation (St Augustine's opinion is well known); but at no point did this disagreement rise to the level requiring dogmatic definition. John Wesley Hanson summarizes the early Church's tolerance–and in some quarters, we would need to say "acceptance"–of the universalist view:

---

20. Caxodoxical: A false or wrong opinion or opinions; erroneous doctrine, especially in matters of religion; heresy.

> The state of opinion on the subject of universal salvation is shown by the fact that through Ignatius, Irenæus, Hippolytus and others wrote against the prevalent heresies of their times, Universalism is never named among them. Some of the alleged errors of Origen were condemned, but his doctrine of universal salvation, never. Methodius, who wrote A.D. 300; Pamphilus and Eusebius, A.D. 310; Eustathius, A.D. 380; Epiphanius, A.D. 376 and 394; Theophilus, A.D. 400–404, and Jerome, A.D. 400; all give lists of Origen's errors, but none name his Universalism among them. Besides, some of those who condemned his errors were Universalists, as the school of Antioch. And many who were opponents of Origenism were mentioned by Origen's enemies with honor notwithstanding they were Universalists, as Clement of Alexandria, and Gregory of Nyssa.[21]

Source Four lists the fourteen canons specifically against Origen. But there is a problem in the posting I was given. The source given does not even agree with the source used in Source Two! That alone should raise serious questions in the mind of any honest inquirer.

Let's look at the contested quote:

From Source Two: XIV. IF anyone shall say that all reasonable beings will one day be united in one, when the hypostases as well as the numbers and the bodies shall have disappeared, and that the knowledge of the world to come will carry with it the ruin of the worlds, and the rejection of bodies as also the abolition of [all] names, and that there shall be finally an identity of the gnpsis and of the hypostasis; moreover, that in this pretended apocatastasis, spirits only will continue to exist, as it was in the reigned pre-existence: let him be anathema.

From Source Four: XIV If anyone says or thinks that the punishment of demons and of impious men is only temporary, and will one day have an end, and that a restoration will take place of demons and of impious men, let him be anathema.

Anathema to Origen and to that Adamantius, who set forth these opinions together with his nefarious and execrable and wicked doctrine and to whomsoever there is who thinks thus, or defends these opinions, or in any way hereafter at any time shall presume to protect them.

Quite a difference, isn't it? But wait a minute. There are footnotes at the bottom of this page. The footnotes state:

---

21. Kimel, "Did the Fifth Ecumenical Council Condemn Universal Salvation?" Para. 6–7.

> 319 The reader should carefully study the entire tractate of the Emperor against Origen of which these anathematisms are the conclusion. It is found in Labbe and Cossart, and in many other collections.
>
> 320 The text is, I think corrupt, as all events the Latin and Greek do not agree.[22]

Well, well, well! Could it mean that the Greek text, the original language of the canons, was tampered with by Latin translators who realized that the canons needed to support their theological promotion of hell more strongly? I think so! In fact, given some of the wretched Latin translations of Greek, as well as the unfortunate and sad state of clerical dishonesty and corruption which existed in the Latin West, it almost seems to me a foregone conclusion! I think these men had an agenda. I personally think the agenda was to keep the peasants in line by scaring the hell out of them.

You think I'm kidding? Here is Justinian's venomous statement against apokatastasis:

> It will render men slothful and discourage them from keeping the commandments of God. It will encourage them to depart from the narrow way, leading them by deception into ways that are wide and easy. Moreover, such a doctrine completely contradicts the words of our Great God and Savior. For in the Holy Gospel, he himself teaches that the impious will be sent away into eternal punishment, but the righteous will receive life eternal. Thus to those at his right, he says: 'Come, O blessed of my Father, and inherit the kingdom prepared for you from the foundation of the world' [Mt 25:34]. But to those on his left, he says: 'Depart from me, you cursed, into the eternal fire prepared for the devil and his angels' [Mt 25:41]. The Lord clearly teaches that both heaven and hell are eternal, but the followers of Origen prefer the myths of their master over and against the judgments of Christ, which plainly refute them. If the torments of the damned will come to an end, so too will the life promised to the righteous, for both are said to be "eternal." And if both the torments of hell and the pleasures of paradise should cease, what was the point of the Incarnation of our Lord Jesus Christ? What was the purpose of his crucifixion, his death, burial, and resurrection? And what of all those who fought the good fight and suffered martyrdom for the sake of Christ? What benefit

---

22. Schaff, "The Anathematisms of Emperor Justinian Against Origen." Footnotes.

will their sufferings have been to them, if in the 'final restoration' they will receive the same reward as sinners and demons?[23]

In other words, Justinian appears to reason that a true repentance would not be enough, even combined with the movement of the Holy Spirit in a man's heart, to make love of God the sole reason to turn from sin.[24] If you depict a tad of sarcasm in my last sentence, you are correct. But I am not half as bad as Dr. David Bentley Hart in his description of Justinian:

> As for where they came from, the evidence suggests they were prepared beforehand by the vicious and insidiously stupid Emperor Justinian, who liked to play theologian, who saw the Church as a pillar of imperial unity, and who took implacable umbrage at dissident theologies. A decade earlier, he had sent ten similar anathemas of Origen (or what he imagined Origen to have taught) to Patriarch Menas; and on the council's eve he apparently submitted the fifteen anathemas of 553 to a lesser synod of bishops, in hope of securing some kind of ecclesial approbation for them. Or they may instead have been proposed at a synod as much as nine years before. Whatever the case, it was only well after the Fifth Ecumenical Council's close that they were attached to its canons, and Origen's name inserted into its list of condemned heretics. In this way the anathemas 'went on the books,' where they remain: peremptory, garbed in immemorial authority, and false as hell.[25]

Justinian took over an empire which was being torn apart by strive and divisions. The Council of Chalcedon, called to answer the Monophysite controversy, had neither settled the issue for a substantial number of people, nor unified the empire. For Justinian, an empire filled with division and strife between warring factions of believers on both sides of the controversy was a sure way to lose the empire to pagan enemies. A divided kingdom is a weak kingdom. In addition, Justinian, believing himself to be set on the emperor's throne by an act of God, felt he was responsible to God for the unification of the Christian faith by unifying the empire. He went about

---

23. "St. Justinian on Universalism," Para. 1

24. In all fairness to Justinian, it should be noted that St. Maximus the Confessor specifically says that if the fathers broke this silence, it was only after they first discerned the capacity of their listeners. Maximus also says in several passages that the fear of hell helps to keep beginners from sin, while more mature Christians are motivated through love. In one passage regarding "honorable silence," Maximos says he will only share the interpretation that is suitable for both beginners and the advanced. The church fathers knew the foibles of mankind and the ease with which we can justify our sins.

25. Hart, "Saint Origen," First Things, October 2015. Para. 8

unification with a certain bad zeal. Far from obtaining the goal of unity which he desired, the kingdom was rent with continuous strife for decades to come.

> By 538 A.D. he publicly laid down his interest by declaring that he is no longer Chief in Staff for the army but a theologian and that is how his image on the coins should look like. This religious fire in him brought him in trouble with many and he abused his imperial power for his own goals. It is very likely that the evils that he and his wife did (according to his biographer Procopius) were true and that their conscience plagued them every night and in order to squash the inner voice of self-acknowledged guilt, so that they embarked upon a religious overdrive, giving themselves the license to steal from the rich (with a robin-hood-ism rationalization) and give to the ecclesiastical poor in many forms, which included the building-programs of 37 enormous churches throughout the empire.[26]

> Justinian hoped that the public rejection of these supposedly Nestorian writings and their authors would help reconcile the empire's Monophysites with the Council of Chalcedon, which had determined that Christ had "two natures," divine and human, a formula which was seen by many as opening the door to Nestorianism. The council was resisted by Pope Vigilius, who had been brought to Constantinople against his will several years previously, after he refused to condemn the Three Chapters. Vigilius questioned whether the writers in question were truly heretics and feared that their condemnation would weaken Chalcedon and encourage Monophysitism. Vigilius had long resisted the emperor's policy, but after the council concluded, he finally acquiesced, endorsing its findings and formally condemning the Three Chapters.[27]

> If this seems now merely a tale 'of old forgotten far-off things'– an especially pitiful tale of violent disputes between people substantially in agreement–let it be remembered that in the next eighty years after 553 the differences had so undermined the stability of a good half of the empire in the East, as to lose forever to the emperors the loyalty of Egypt and Syria, and reduce the numbers of the Catholics there to a handful, and the

---

26. De Kock and Van Wyk, "538 AD and the Transition from Pagan Roman Empire to Holy Roman Empire–Justinian's Metamorphosis from Chief of Staffs to Theologian." Para. 3.

27. "Second Council of Constantinople," Para. 2.

jurisdictions of Alexandria, Antioch, and Jerusalem to all but nought. These lands were the original strongholds of the Catholic faith, Egypt, Syria, and the rest, names which whatever they now bring to mind do not suggest the triumph of the religion of Christ our Lord. Islam, of course, has for a thousand years and more dominated them. But the break with the Catholic Church, and its destruction in these lands, goes back earlier still, to long before Mahomet was born, to the Monophysite reaction following the Council of Chalcedon. The emperors who, in the two hundred years after Chalcedon, showed such a passionate anxiety over the various pacts by which they sought to end the division, and who treated the opponents of their endeavours with such ferocity, were by no means despots, half-crazy through their determination that all men should believe as they believed about these high mysteries. What prompted them was their realization that a continuation of the division meant the end of their empire and, as we should say now, of civilization.[28]

A continuation of the division meant the end of the empire. It was in this frame of thinking Emperor Justinian acted. In order to get what he wanted, in manner more akin to thugs and bullies than saints, Justinian had Pope Vigilius brought to Constantinople against his will and then imprisoned him in a kind of house arrest until Vigilius acceded to his demands and called the council. Is this truly how the Holy Spirit works? Is violence a proper method for discerning truth, especially in the realm of Christain doctrine?

As I study the many available papers which describe the events leading up to and after Constantinople II, I see Justinian as primarily a politician, using religion to obtain the goals of the Roman Empire. His desire was the return of the empire to its former glory, to be achieved through unity of all religious and civil factions, and the conquering of lost territory. He was out of his place and had no authority to meddle with the workings of an ecumenical council. Yet in order to understand why this happened, we need to understand the mindset of Roman emperors. It is a way of thinking which modern democratic societies would hold in contempt. The genesis of this melding of Christ to the empire begins with the conversion of Constantine.

In an oft-quoted comment, the Christian apologist Tertullian (c. 160-c. 225) pointed out that "Christians are made, not born." Tertullian's intent was to convince those who hated his faith that Christians were not some kind of alien creatures. "We are the

---

28. Hughes, "Constantinople II, 553," Para. 4.

same as you," he wrote, "we used to laugh" at the idea that there really was only one god, not many.

These converts had to learn how to be Christians. The church had a relatively rigorous program for this purpose–several years of supervised instruction and socialization, culminating in an intensive Lenten program of day-long instruction conducted by the local bishop before baptism But as Tertullian's statement also reminds us, these new Christians had grown up as Romans. Although they now believed in one god instead of many, *they continued to be Romans in every other way.* That is to say, they still held the social, cultural, and political views that they had grown up with. To give but one example, even the steadfast Athanasius of Alexandria thought nothing of using the portraits of the emperor to explain how the Christian Son could be honored without loss of the Father's sovereignty (Athanasius, 3.5). In the same way, new Christians continued to think the same way about slavery, patriarchy, and aristocracy. And, especially important for present purposes, they continued to think of the emperor as a sacrosanct individual–not exactly a god, but holier than the rest of us. "The king on earth is the last of gods but first of men," as the goddess Isis explained it to her son Horus in a Hermetic tract. In many instances, it was the church that adjusted to the needs of converts and not vice versa. Nowhere was this more true than when aristocrats started to convert in sizeable numbers during the fourth century

> At roughly the same time that he was humbling himself to the bishops at Arles, Constantine wrote to his vicar in North Africa, Aelafius. In this letter, Constantine referred to himself as the person to whom "the Highest Divinity" (*summa divinitate*) "has committed by his divine nod the government of all earthly things" (*cuius curae nutu suo caelesti terrena omnia moderanda commisit*). In both of these statements, Constantine showed that he did not think adopting Christianity took anything away from the special relationship late Roman emperors were expected to have with divinity.[29]

In terms of effects on Christianity, I have read articles which say that Constantine's conversion was the worst thing that could have happened to Christianity.[30] Justinian's actions were simply a continuation of this Roman belief in the divinely ordained status of the emperor. The bishops of the church, put between a rock and a hard place in how to deal with this, were unfortunate witnesses to how the goals of the empire became the goals of the

---

29. Drake, "The Emperor as a 'Man of God': The Impact of Constantine the Great's Conversion on Roman ideas of Kingship," Para. 1–2 & 12

30. Mickiewiz, "The Worst Thing That Ever Happened to Christianity."

CHURCH COUNCILS, SCRIPTURE, AND TRADITIONS OF THE CHURCH

church. It appears that by the time Justinian took the imperial throne, this melding of the empire and the church into a single body was pretty much complete. Justinian simple pushed it into a higher gear, his actions further establishing the precedent in which the Western empire and the church became united into a single being. And unfortunately, goals of empires always seem to have more to do with power, control, and authority, than the meekness, humility, and love which Christ taught. The actions of the Roman Catholic Church in the succeeding centuries would prove this out.

In doing this, the Christian religion became severely wounded over the next few centuries, until finally it was being used not as Good News, but as a weapon against King Philip IV of France by Pope Boniface VIII, who threatened Philip with eternal hell for not submitting to Boniface's desires. Boniface is the first Roman pope to say such a thing in such a manner, and Philip, quite understandably, tells him to go pound sand. But the damage is done, and this idea of complete submission to the pope as a necessity for one's salvation becomes popular in the Western church. To this day, there are some members of the Roman Catholic Church who insist this is truth, and all outside the boundaries of the Roman Catholic Church, and submission to the pope, are damned.

A final question remains: who then wrote the anathemas and when?

> Over the past century different hypotheses have been advanced, but historians appear to have settled on the following scenario, first proposed by Wilhelm Diekamp in 1899 and more recently advanced by Richard Price in his book The Acts of the Council of Constantinople of 553 (published in 2009): the anathemas were most likely composed by Justinian and his advisors and submitted for approval to the bishops who had come to Constantinople for the council. This probably occurred sometime before the council formally convened on 5 May 553. We do not know how long before the council this meeting took place (days? weeks? months?) nor do we know who attended; but one thing is clear–the Emperor wanted the anathemas cloaked with conciliar authority. We may confidently affirm, therefore, that the 5th Ecumenical Council never officially issued an anathema against apocatastasis. This is not just my private opinion. It is shared by many historians, as well as by Met Kallistos Ware and Met Hilarion Alfeyev.
>
> But let's assume, if only for debate purposes, that the Council did issue the fifteen anathemas. There would still remain the challenging question of interpretation. Not all universalisms are the same! Just as there are both heretical and orthodox construals of, say, the atonement, so there are heretical and orthodox

construals of the universalist hope. There is a critical difference between the apocatastasis of St Gregory of Nyssa–whose name is never mentioned in the anathemas–and the apocatastasis of the 6th century Origenists against whom the anathemas are directed. The views of the latter appear to have been bizarre in many ways. Let me quote a lengthy passage from Met Kallistos Ware:

"There is, however, considerable doubt whether these fifteen anathemas were in fact formally approved by the Fifth Ecumenical Council. They may have been endorsed by a lesser council, meeting in the early months of 553 shortly before the main council was convened, in which case they lack full ecumenical authority; yet, even so, the Fathers of the Fifth Council were well aware of these fifteen anathemas and had no intention of revoking or modifying them. Apart from that, however, the precise wording of the first anathema deserves to be carefully noted. It does not speak only about apocatastasis but links together two aspects of Origen's theology: first, his speculations about the beginning, that is to say, about the preexistence of souls and the precosmic fall; second, his teaching about the end, about universal salvation and the ultimate reconciliation of all things. Origen's eschatology is seen as following directly from his protology, and both are rejected together.

That the first of the fifteen anathemas should condemn protology and eschatology in the same sentence is entirely understandable, for in Origen's thinking the two form an integral unity. At the beginning, so he believed, there was a realm of logikoi or rational intellects (noes) existing prior to the creation of the material world as minds without a body. Originally all these logikoi were joined in perfect union with the Creator Logos. Then followed the precosmic fall. With the exception of one logikos (which became the human soul of Christ), all the other logikoi turned away from the Logos and became, depending on the gravity of their deviation, either angels or human beings or demons. In each case they were given bodies appropriate to the seriousness of their fall: lightweight and ethereal in the case of angels; dark and hideous in the case of demons; intermediate in the case of human beings. At the end, so Origen maintained, this process of fragmentation will be reversed. All alike, whether angels, human beings, or demons, will be restored to unity with the Logos; the primal harmony of the total creation will be reinstated, and once more "God will be all in all" (1 Cor 15:28). Origen's view is in this way circular in character: the end will be as the beginning.

Now, as we have noted, the first of the fifteen anti-Origenist anathemas is directed not simply against Origen's teaching concerning universal reconciliation, but against his total understanding of salvation history–against his theory of preexistent souls, of a precosmic fall and a final apocatastasis–seen as a single and undivided whole. Suppose, however, that we separate his eschatology from his protology; suppose that we abandon all speculations about the realm of eternal logikoi; suppose that we simply adhere to the standard Christian view whereby there is no preexistence of the soul, but each new person comes into being as an integral unity of soul and body, at or shortly after the moment of the conception of the embryo within the mother's womb. In this way we could advance a doctrine of universal salvation–affirming this, not as a logical certainty (indeed, Origen never did that), but as a heartfelt aspiration, a visionary hope– which would avoid the circularity of Origen's view and so would escape the condemnation of the anti-Origenist anathemas."

Many scholars would now question Met Kallistos's identification of the views of Origen with the views of the 6th century Origenists; but his key point stands: the conciliar anathema against apocatastasis does not apply to construals similar to those of St Gregory of Nyssa or St Isaac the Syrian. The universalist hope is, of course, a minority view within Orthodoxy, but being a minority view does not make it heretical. The Orthodox Church has yet to speak its final dogmatic word on this subject.[31]

---

31. Kimel, "A Glimpse into the Enigma that is Fr. Aiden Kimel," Para. 31–36.

Part Two

Eastern Orthodox and Roman Catholic Beliefs on Hell

SOURCE FIVE BEGINS A change in the objections to apokatastasis. From an appeal to Constantinople II, the paper I received turns to pronouncements from within Orthodoxy and Roman Catholicism. This section begins with the Synodikon of Orthodoxy. The Synodikon is read aloud during the Sunday of Orthodoxy in every present-day Orthodox church. The reading itself is part of a larger parcel of Orthodox condemnations of numerous heresies. Upon reading the Synodikon of Orthodoxy, I initially felt it was a strong blow against apokatastasis:

> To them who accept and transmit that there is an end to the torment or a restoration again of creation and of human affairs, meaning by such teachings that the Kingdom of the Heavens is entirely perishable and fleeting, whereas the Kingdom is eternal and indissoluble as Christ our God Himself taught and delivered to us, and as we have ascertained from the entire Old and New Scripture, that the torment is unending and the Kingdom everlasting to them who by such teachings both destroy themselves and become agents of eternal condemnation to others: Anathema! Anathema! Anathema![1]

---

1. This is exactly how the quote was provided to me, but I can't find it anywhere on the Internet after considerable searching. The closest I can come is at Mystagogy Resource Center, The Synodikon of Orthodoxy, Paragraph 48. But even that is different, not only from my friend's quote here, but from other sources as well. As stated, this document has been considerably tampered with over the years, and is not only suspect in its

Initially, this appeared to be an insurmountable obstacle to my hope in apokatastasis, but a bit of deeper investigation turned up some interesting things about this Synodikon. What is the Synodikon?

> The term synodikon is applied to an official definition promulgated by a synod or council, or to a statement which has synodical origin or conciliar authority. The present synodikon was approved and issued by the Synod of 843 which restored the veneration of icons, i.e., it upheld and re-imposed the authority of the Seventh Ecumenical Synod which had fallen into abeyance during the intervening second period of Iconoclasm (815–842). In the manuscripts the titles are various: The Synodikon of Orthodoxy, The Synodikon Confirming Orthodoxy Read on the First Sunday of Great Lent, the synodikon Confirming Orthodoxy, The Synodikon Against All Heresy, and different combination of all the above, In the printed Triodion, the synodikon is titled The Synodikon of the Holy and Ecumenical Seventh Synod for Orthodoxy. Although not entirely correct, we have retained it because the Synod of 843 did not form any new definitions, *but was concerned to proclaim again the authority of the Seventh Council and to re-establish the definition of the Faith propounded there.*[2]

There is a real problem with the quote my friend uses to try to prove her point. It is not from the original Synodikon of 843! It is from a much later addition, which according to Fr. Professor John Louth, had severe political overtones in it. So once again we are treated to the faith being used as political weapon.[3] The website of the Serbian Orthodox Church states the following:

> The text of the Synodikon of Orthodoxy has been much altered over the centuries, chiefly by the addition of material and names that postdate the Restoration of the Icons in 843. This is the case with the text that is printed in the current Triodia. Some of the more zealous contemporary Orthodox even include

---

condemnation of apokatastasis, but of no binding authority as is an ecumenical council.

2. Sanidopoulos John, "The Snynodikon of Orthodoxy," Mystagogy Resource Center. Para. 2

3. Fr. Louth states that the Synodikon itself became an instrument of imperial policy during the Komnene dynasty. Alexios I found his empire impoverished. He remedied this by pillaging the church of its treasures, and needed to do something restore his standing with the Church. The Synodikon was his weapon, and his aim was to present himself, as Photios had seen the emperor, as the source of Orthodoxy

> condemnations of such things as the 'pan-heresy of Ecumenism.'
> *It is probably impossible to reconstruct the original text exactly.*[4]

There is one more thing to realize about the Synodikon. It does not carry authority!

> Among the various elements of Tradition, a unique pre-eminence belongs to the Bible, to the Creed, to the doctrinal definitions of the Ecumenical Councils: these things the Orthodox accept as something absolute and unchanging, something which cannot be cancelled or revised. The other parts of Tradition do not have quite the same authority.[5]

According to this definition, the Synod's original purpose was to confirm what the Seventh Ecumenical Council said in its canons. The Seventh Council was solely concerned with the veneration of icons. In reading the canons of Nicea II, I find no condemnation of apokatastasis by name. The closest we can get is this paragraph from The Decree of the Holy, Great, Ecumenical Synod, the Second of Nicea.

> We detest and anathematize Arius and all the sharers of his absurd opinion; also Macedonius and those who following him are well styled "Foes of the Spirit" (Pneumatomachi). We confess that our Lady, St. Mary, is properly and truly the Mother of God, because she was the Mother after the flesh of One Person of the Holy Trinity, to wit, Christ our God, as the Council of Ephesus has already defined when it cast out of the Church the impious Nestorius with his colleagues, because he taught that there were two Persons [in Christ]. With the Fathers of this synod we confess that he who was incarnate of the immaculate Mother of God and Ever-Virgin Mary has two natures, recognizing him as perfect God and perfect man, as also the Council of Chalcedon has promulgated, expelling from the divine Atrium as blasphemers, Eutyches and Dioscorus; and placing in the same category Severus, Peter and a number of others, blaspheming in various fashions. Moreover, with these *we anathematize the fables of Origen,* Evagrius, and Didymus, in accordance with the decision of the Fifth Council held at Constantinople. We affirm that in Christ there be two wills and two operations according to the reality of each nature, as also the Sixth Synod, held at Constantinople, taught, casting out Sergius, Honorius, Cyrus,

---

4. "Synodikon of Orthodoxy," Lines 1–10.

5. Ware, "The Orthodox Church: An Introduction to Eastern Christianity," Page 191.

Pyrrhus, Macarius, and those who agree with them, and all those who are unwilling to be reverent.[6]

Again, we must insist on asking which fables of Origen did the bishops of the Second Council of Nice believe to be antithetical to the apostolic faith? We do not know–neither the canons nor the acts of the council tell us. This point needs to be stressed. We must not assume that because the council fathers condemned Origen by name, they therefore intended to condemn his teaching on apokatastasis. It is noteworthy that no condemnations of either St. Isaac of Syria or St. Gregory of Nyssa are in the canons. Both these men, and a host of other church fathers, were known supporters of apokatastasis. Surely, if apokatastasis was the problem they would have been anathematized as well. Didn't the council specifically condemn as heretics other men who were long dead? If apokatastasis is a heresy, then Gregory of Nyssa and a host of other saints should have been in that list!

The establishment of conciliar dogma requires more than speculation and conjectural inference. I have already shown A.) The fables of Origen mentioned have to do with his ideas about the pre-existence of souls and the monstrous restoration which follows from them. I have clearly shown what strange ideas of restoration which Origen had, such as balloon-shaped resurrection bodies. apokatastasis is not mentioned here at all, just as in the original and uncorrupted canons of Constantinople II. B.) any condemnation of apokatastasis regarding Constantinople II comes not from the original canons, but from canons now rejected by modern scholarship. The Greek and Roman churches should be embarrassed to death by this. C.) it was Emperor Justinian who entered those anathemas by use of force. This means that until recently, anyone looking at Constantinople II was being deceived by a fraudulent set of canons illegally inserted within the body of the canons. To me personally, this is no small matter!

It is also telling that the council defended Gregory of Nyssa against those who were calumniating him. This is important because St. Gregory of Nyssa was an ardent supporter of the final restoration of all things. His writing makes unmistakably clear his support for apokatastasis. As men who intimately knew church history, council members must have been aware of this! Surely if the condemnation of apokatastasis was in the minds of the bishops of Nicea II, they would have declared him a heretic posthumously. They did not. For me, this is another large strike against the idea of the Orthodox Church declaring apokatastasis heretical by appealing to the canons of the Seventh Ecumenical Council.

---

6. "Second Council of Nicea," Para. 113

If Justinian's additions against Origen, were fraudulent, then the admonitions of Nicea II, in which they declare their support of and belief in all the earlier six councils had taught, cannot legitimately be said to include those canons. The bishops of the time could not have known that these additional canons were fraudulent, but even so, as I have shown, there is no mention directly of apokatastasis in either Constantinople II or Nicea II. It is only a condemnation of the fantastic ideas of Origen regarding the restoration of all things to the pre-existent state of souls prior to creation, which both councils reject, as well as all Christians, then and now.

It appears to me that any declaration that Orthodoxy has officially condemned apokatastasis is at best standing on very shaky grounds, especially considering the corruption of Constantinople II. Understanding this corruption, and the fact that the Catholic Encyclopedia and scholars have both rejected the spurious canons of Justinian, I believe it is past time for the hierarchs of Orthodoxy to convene a council and do what should have been done a long time ago–condemn both Justinian's intrusion into the council and his bogus canons.

"Ah, but you cannot change the canons of a council!" I hear someone reply.

This is apparently untrue also, from this following statement in a paper from St. Vladimir's Theological Seminary:

> As with many other such canons, they may be revoked or modified, formally or informally, in the light of changed circumstances and requirements of the faithful and the Church. In practice, many organizational and institutional canons, even of ecumenical councils, have fallen by the wayside or otherwise been superseded in practice even in the absence of formal decisions to rescind them by a later council.[7]

Such an example of a council being changed or challenged would be the Second Council of Ephesus, also known as the Robber's Council. The Robber's Council was declared null and void. It is my opinion that Constantinople II, convened more for political than theological purposes, brought forth by violence, and intruded upon by a man who had no authority to take part in it, is of the same nature.

A final source I would quote in this regard comes from Fr. Aidan Kimel:

---

7. Ladouceur, "On Ecumenoclasm: Anti-Ecumenical Theology in Orthodoxy," Page 345.

In both The Orthodox Church and "Dogma and Dogmatic Theology," Sergius Bulgakov cites eschatology, among others, as a topic of theology open to dogmatic definition, the implication being that standard Orthodox teaching on the last things–including everlasting perdition–can only be said to enjoy the status of reformable doctrinal propositions. He elaborates upon this claim in his book The Bride of the Lamb, perhaps his greatest work. In the beginning of the section devoted to eschatology, Bulgakov asserts:

"The Church has not established a single universally obligatory dogmatic definition in the domain of eschatology, if we do not count the brief testimony of the Nicaeno-Constantinopolitan Creed concerning the second coming ("He will come again in glory to judge the living and the dead, and His kingdom will have no end"), as well as concerning the resurrection of the dead and the life of the future age. These dogmas of the faith, attested to by the Creed and based on the express promises of the Lord, have not, all the same, been developed by theology. They are considered to be self-evident for the dogmatic consciousness, although that is not, in reality, the case. All the rest, referring to various aspects of eschatology, has not been defined dogmatically; it is an object of dogmatic doctrine that has yet to undergo free theological investigation."

Throughout the history of the Church, bishops and priests have preached the ta eschata, what Bulgakov calls the final accomplishments; but except for the resurrection and parousia of Christ, the Orthodox Church has not seen the need to formally pronounce upon them. The Latin Church has done so, of course–the finality of the particular judgment and the existence of an intermediate purgatorial state being prime examples–but its second millennium dogmas do not carry authority for Orthodoxy.

Note the last sentence of the above quotation: 'it is an object of dogmatic doctrine that has yet to undergo free theological investigation.' Bulgakov believes that authentic dogmas are necessarily supported by intensive study and reflection, argumentation and debate. In their absence, the attempt to bind the conscience is simply an assertion of power and suppression of theological liberty. Consider, for example, the Nicene assertion of the consubstantiality of the Father and the Son in A.D. 325. The use of homoousios was controversial. No one quite knew what it meant or implied, beyond excluding the position of Arius; consequently, the Council Fathers were able to sign the final document and return to their respective dioceses with very different understandings of the Nicene 'dogma.' Formal subscription to the homousion, therefore, was insufficient to expel the Arian subordination of Jesus Christ to the Father. What was needed was deeper reflection and deliberation, subsequently accomplished by Athanasius, Hilary, and especially the Cappadocians. Before the homoousion could be assimilated into the depths of the dogmatic consciousness of the Church, it was necessary for theologians to clarify the meaning of 'of one substance with the Father–which ultimately meant giving it a meaning it did not have in the Nicene definition–and demonstrate its coherence with God's self-revelation in Jesus Christ and his work of salvation. Only then could the homoousion be confirmed by the Second Ecumenical Council in 381 and received into the dogmatic consciousness of the Church. A process like this has not happened with regard to the important eschatological questions, particularly on the teaching of eternal damnation.

Nor will it do, Bulgakov avers, to appeal to a consensus patrum to justify hell, as if the Church has always been of one mind on these questions or that dogmatic resolution has already been achieved:

'If it is maintained that the absence of an ecclesial definition is compensated by the existence of a firm ecclesial tradition, patristic and other, one must call such an assertion inaccurate or even completely erroneous. Aside from the fact that this tradition is insufficient and disparate, the most important thing here is the absence of a single tradition. Instead, we have at least two completely different variants: on the one hand, a doctrine originating in Origen and stabilized in the teaching of St. Gregory of Nyssa and his tacit and open followers; and, on the other hand, a widespread doctrine that has had many adherents but none equal in power of theological thought to those mentioned above. (Perhaps in this group we can put Augustine, the greatest teacher of the Western Church, but the originality of his worldview sets him apart in general, especially for Eastern theology.) As regards both particular patristic doctrines and the systematization of biblical texts, an inquiry that would precede dogmatization has yet to be carried out.'

Note the emphasis on the need for theological examination of and reflection upon the sources of revelation as a precondition for authentic dogmatization. Dogmatic definition requires discernment of the intrinsic connections of a theological proposition to the gospel of Christ and the whole of divine revelation. "Dogmas possess a mutual transparency," Bulgakov writes.

> "They are given not as an external listing, as in a catalog or inventory, but are internally organically tied, so that in the light of one dogma the content and strength of the other is revealed." When done well, theology goes beyond the mere enumeration of propositional truths and grasps the profound coherency of the faith, in all of its life-giving beauty and truth.[8]

My conclusion: A Synodikon is a compilation of the decrees and canons of a particular council. The case of the Synodikon of 843, the conciliar compilation is supposed to be that of the Seventh Ecumenical Council, which as we have shown has no definitive statement regarding apokatastasis in its canons. To say otherwise is A.) dishonest B.) agenda driven, and C.) reading into the council what you wish to see.

The paragraph my friend gave me, claiming to be the Synodikon, appears to have been created by someone who, like some modern theologians, had an intense dislike for the idea of God gratuitously forgiving the whole world. I'm sorry, but I smell a rat. The former bad actions in earlier councils, combined with the way that the Christian faith has often been used more as weapon than Good News, leaves me highly distrustful when I find such contradictions.

There needs to be a truly ecumenical council to discuss this issue and to come to a final and dogmatic declaration regarding this. As of now, there simply is none. Therefore, you cannot say Orthodoxy has a settled definition about the eschatological end of humanity. Those in Orthodoxy who support ideas of eternal damnation are usually converts to Orthodoxy who have come from Western churches, bringing with them some considerable dogmatic baggage, including a very Western view of eschatology which is all about sending sinners to the eternal fire they deserve. As one critic of their beliefs noted, "I am glad they found Orthodoxy. Let us pray now that Orthodoxy finds them." A less charitable writer simply calls them the "Crankydox."

Source Six begins a series of statements which appeal to the Catechism of the Roman Catholic Church. This section is the one in which I unfortunately expect to offend some of my Roman Catholic friends. For this, I do apologize, but I will not gloss over what I, being Orthodox in my theology, see as problematic theological errors in Rome and behavior over the centuries which is more in line with political despots than Christian leaders enlightened by the Holy Spirit.

> Throughout the history of the Church, bishops and priests have preached the ta eschata, what Bulgakov calls the final

---

8. Kimel, "Dogma, Damnation, and the Eucatastrophe of the Jesus Story." Para. 1–7

> accomplishments; but except for the resurrection and parousia of Christ, the Orthodox Church has not seen the need to formally pronounce upon them. The Latin Church has done so, of course–finality of the particular judgment and the existence of an intermediate purgatorial state being prime examples–*but its second millennium dogmas do not carry authority for Orthodoxy.*[9]

This is a charitable statement by Fr. Kimel. The more I have become familiar with the history of the Roman Catholic Church, the more I have come to understand the repugnance of the Protestant Reformers for it. I can honestly say that I struggle to maintain a balance between loving the people in the system and having little respect the way the hierarchy of the system has acted. Between the bad translations of the Scriptures from Greek to Latin, the dogmatic acceptance of Augustine's theologoumenon without so much as an ecumenical council, the Papal Reformation of the eleventh century, after which all non-Latin Christians were condemned to hell by Pope Boniface VIII, and the invention of doctrines not known in the first millennium, my attitude towards the whole religious system is unfortunately at this time less than charitable. I find the Latin Mass and Gregorian Chant beautiful. I find many of their saints noble and worthy of imitation. My distaste for the system is a failure of Christian charity on my part to which I freely admit.

My purpose in the following section is not to trash the Roman Catholic Church, although it will seem like it. I see a fundamental problem with Roman Catholic theology. To correctly understand God, we must be enlightened and guided by the Holy Spirit. People who are thus guided exhibit certain behaviors: moral decency, humility, and charity. Jesus said that you can know a tree by its fruit. The fruit of the Roman Catholic Church over the last one thousand years shows me an institution which morphed from being the Christian church in Rome to the Holy Roman Empire, a political entity with a veneer of Christianity. The hierarchy of the Roman church ran it like an empire and treated all who would not submit to it as enemies. How do I accept a dogma made up out of thin air, such as Indulgences, when these men were killing all who would not submit to Rome? This becomes even more egregious when you realize that all dogmas invented by the Roman church after the schism of 1054 AD would leave the early fathers aghast. They were invented by Rome alone, with no input from the Greek church. Thus, I also sense no reason to assign to them any authority over my theological life.

---

9. Kimel, "Dogma, Damnation, and the Eucatastrophe of the Jesus Story." Para. 3.

There is a peculiar tendency to treat as infallible the writings of the saints, early fathers, and theologians of the church. Therefore, when I am given a quote from a particular Roman Catholic saint, or presented with a canon from the Catechism of the Catholic Church, I am expected to bow in submission. I might be more inclined to do so if it were not for the history of this body and how the hierarchy of it have acted in the last one thousand years. St. Paul spoke of the fact that we all see through a glass darkly in our understanding of God and His dealings with us. There is simply no call to believe that any theologian, no matter how holy, has a perfect understanding of God, unimpeded by personal biases, psychological issues, and cultural norms. Even in Eastern Orthodoxy, which I believe to be the faith which has most purely kept what the apostles taught, one can find a history of questionable behaviors and personal theological opinions among leaders of the church. Such behavior calls for scrutiny of the men and their theological ideas rather than the blind acceptance which has caused so much grief throughout history. I must be obedient to the ecumenical councils. Theologoumenon, on the other hand, are not binding on my conscience. Unfortunately, for most folks it is easier just to go along, especially if you are being threatened with God.

One other thing which puzzles me about the Roman Catholic Church is a kind of schizophrenia regarding Holy Tradition. Roman Catholic apologists strongly defend the use of Holy Tradition in their defense of the faith against sola scriptura Protestantism. Holy Tradition means "this is the way we have believed from the beginning." Thus, when Arius put forth his arguments from scripture against the deity of Christ, the belief which carried the day was found in Holy Tradition. The Holy Tradition of the church from the beginning was that Christ was understood to be God manifest in the flesh. No amount of clever argumentation or scripture twisting from Arias could change what had always been taught. That is Holy Tradition.

Knowing this, why was Holy Tradition not respected in dealing with the issue of apokatastasis? By what authority did Justinian attack this teaching and outlaw it without an ecumenical council being called to discuss it? Why did the church go along with this instead of defending this Holy Tradition which had been taught for over five hundred years? As shown, Constantinople II was about the Three Chapters–nothing else! There is nothing in the canons of the council which explicitly mentions apokatastasis, other than the fraudulent and now rejected canons of Justinian, put in for political reasons. Why did the bishops of the church in Rome meekly submit to this imperial intrusion? Thus, any appeals of any Roman Catholic to Holy Tradition or development of doctrine, especially regarding apokatastasis, fall on my deaf ears as I view what I can only describe as political plotting by a tyrant emperor, along with the submission of bishops who found themselves in an undesirable position–do what the emperor says or lose your head! This exercise of political power and authority did not stop with Justinian. It gathered steam during the eleventh century Papal Reformation of the Roman Catholic Church and presented itself to the world as the Holy Roman Empire, a melding of political and religious power, demanding obedience from all it encountered.

> CCC 1033 We cannot be united with God unless we freely choose to love him. But we cannot love God if we sin gravely against him, against our neighbor or against ourselves: "He who does not love remains in death. Anyone who hates his brother is a murderer, and you know that no murderer has eternal life abiding in him." Our Lord warns us that we shall be separated from him if we fail to meet the serious needs of the poor and the little ones who are his brethren. To die in mortal sin without repenting and accepting God's merciful love means remaining separated from him forever by our own free choice. This state of definitive self-exclusion from communion with God and the blessed is called 'hell.'[10]

Regarding the idea of free choice mentioned in CCC 1033, Thomas Talbot, in his excellent paper on God and the free will of man, addresses this issue with clarity:

> The principal challenge facing any proponent of a free will theodicy of hell is to set forth a coherent account of moral freedom, one that establishes the possibility of someone freely embracing an objective horror forever. And the principal challenge to a coherent account of moral freedom is the seemingly plausible argument that determinism and indeterminism are each incompatible with moral freedom. The best solution to this apparent paradox, I have suggested, is to acknowledge that indeterminism is both a necessary condition of our emergence as free moral agents distinct from God and an obstacle to full freedom and moral responsibility. Add to that the condition of minimal rationality and it seems impossible that anyone rational enough to qualify as a free moral agent would freely embrace an objective horror forever. So even if some become so mired in sin and rebellion that they cannot even experience the bliss of union with the divine nature, God nonetheless has a trump card to play that will guarantee their free submission to him in the end:

---

10. Catechism of the Catholic Church. Article 12, "I Believe in Life Everlasting" IV. Hell.

he need only honor their own free choices and allow them to experience the very horror of separation from the divine nature that they have confusedly chosen for themselves.[11]

Determinism, in philosophy, is the theory that all events, including moral choices, are completely decided by previously existing causes. Determinism is usually understood to preclude free will because it proposes that humans cannot act otherwise than they do. Even if I wish to take a certain course of action, causes external to me will decide the outcome. Indeterminism is the opposite of determinism and is related to chance. It is only when an individual is totally free from any outside force or inner restraint, or free from random chance, can a man be said to be a truly free moral agent. In the issue of salvation, until one sees Christ in all His glory, undeceived by either sin, spiritual or theological lies, psychological or emotional factors, and without any internal or external forces of coercion, only then can one be said to make a truly free will choice.

I find Roman Catholic ideas that sprung up in the latter part of the Middle Ages to be troubling. For instance, the teaching that pagans in African countries are doomed to eternal suffering simply for their lack of submission to the pope. Augustine's earnest insistence that unbaptized babies have a place in eternal fire is equally repulsive. The Roman Catholic Church tried to soften this centuries later by inventing the idea of "Limbus Infantium," a place where such unbaptized infants would spend eternity not in fiery torment, but neither in heaven with Christ. In neither of these examples can we find the possibility of the exercise of a free will to reject Christ. You cannot reject that which you have never heard of.

In the following blog entry, the author draws out from personal experience what Talbot is speaking of when he says that all the soul needs for repentance is a true and clear experience of the horror of separation from God:

> If God had respected my free will, I would still be involved in a panoply of sins so disgusting and heinous that I will not mention them here. Or I would now be long dead and gone from this world. Given the severity of my wickedness and the insanity of my actions, I think probably the latter. Think of the Hippie Movement of the 1960's and imagine every licentious, dirty, and wicked thing that the Movement promoted. That was me, and that was my "free will choice," so to speak. I loved the sins of the flesh, I had declared myself an atheist, and I despised Christians.

---

11. Talbot, "Mercy on All, Free-will Theodicies of Hell" Para. 26

I wanted nothing at all to do with them or their Jesus. That was my free will. Go away God! Go away Christians!

So how did I come to the point of repenting and turning to Christ in sorrow for my sins? Did God overtake and remove my free will, eliciting from me a robotic response of repentance which He desired? Was my will violated in such a manner that I had no choice but to do what I was told?

No, God simply let me run out my string.

There is a saying in the Twelve Steps book of AA which says that you cannot make an addict change until he has hit the bottom and is watching his last bubble of air float to the surface. That is exactly what God did with me, allowing me to, of my own "free will," hit the bottom and realize that all the "fun" I was having was about to kill me. Far from the sense of carnal excitement I felt when I took my first hit of marijuana, my life had become, in four years of unrestrained hedonism, a joyless tedium racked with sorrow and drug-induced psychosis. I was in deep trouble, and I knew it, filled with suicidal thoughts but dreadfully scared of the black void which my atheism said was the ultimate end of man. Of my own free will, I began an intense search for the garden gate which offered escape from this fool's paradise into which I had eagerly dashed. No one had to tell me it was get out or die–and no one was coercing me! I had come to the point that I knew it was the only option left for me. Yet even then, I could have chosen to shake my fist at God and die. I took the choice to live and began my search.

The gate out of my individual hell came in the shape of a cross.

Did God in any way violate my free will? Or did He simply allow me to come to a point where the foolishness, the vanity, and the destructiveness of my choices could no longer be ignored, and the joys of unrestrained hedonism were not worth the price I was paying?[12]

This is the answer to an often-heard objection to apokatastasis: if God saves everyone, it will be against their free-will choice to reject Him, thus making robots out of them. The author shows how all God must do, either here, or in the next life for those who are particularly stubborn or particularly deceived in this life, is to let us experience the consequence of what we have chosen. And as Talbot said, once the mind is cleared of all false visions, deceits, and psychological barricades, only an insane person would choose against his best interest and select eternal torment as his final resting place.

12. Hara, "God's Hand and Our Free-Will." Para. 10–15.

When people say that I have a free will, they mean I have the ability to make choices. But the ability to choose is profoundly different from choice made with a will that is free. This is because the will is not free when it is burdened by internal and external causes which push it in directions contrary to its best interest. My ability to choose is free. My ability to choose that which is in my best interest as a sinner, and even sometimes as a Christian, is most certainly not. St. Paul said in Corinthians that he was a wretched man because he did the things he did not wish to do. Where was the great Apostle's free will if he found himself choosing those things he did not wish to do?

Orthodoxy also has no concept of sin being mortal. The idea of being separated from God forever is rejected. Orthodox teaching on the next life is that all souls are redeemed to God and shall be in His presence forever. Those who repented and began to become like Christ in this life, through the various ascetic struggles designed to conquer the passions, will find His presence to be a delight. Those who rejected Christ and turned to sin in their lusts, will find that same presence a tormenting lake of fire which will chastise and cleanse them. Think of the pillar which went with the Israelites out of Egypt. They found it light and warming, while the Egyptians found it dark and terrifying. Same pillar, different experience. Same Christ, different experience.

Among Orthodox believers, there is considerable debate whether this torment lasts forever. Those of us who believe in apokatastasis understand this tormenting experience to be for restoration, not revenge. Is it a punishment which will not end, or a scourging of love, a chastening by our loving heavenly Father designed to bring the soul to its senses and repentance? The latter belief was held by several people who are saints in the churches of both East and West. Augustine acknowledged that there were a great many who believed in and taught this restoration, which he himself held to at one time before changing his mind.

Source Seven continues with the Roman Catechism, which contains quotes from Matthew 5:22–29:

> CCC 1034 Jesus often speaks of "Gehenna" of "the unquenchable fire" reserved for those who to the end of their lives refuse to believe and be converted, where both soul and body can be lost. Jesus solemnly proclaims that he "will send his angels, and they will gather . . . all evil doers, and throw them into the furnace of fire," and that he will pronounce the condemnation: "Depart from me, you cursed, into the eternal fire!"[13]

---

13. Catechism of the Catholic Church. Article 12 "I Believe in Life Everlasting" IV.

Matthew 5:22–29 indeed gives dire warnings about our behavior on earth and the consequences we shall surely pay if we do not do good. But those who believe in eternal torment appear to skip over verse 26, which says: "Verily I say unto thee, thou shalt by no means come out thence, till thou hast paid the uttermost farthing."

Why would Jesus put such an ending statement to this section? It undermines the idea of punishment being forever. Could it be that His judgment is not unto an eternal punishment, but rather unto a just repayment for evil deeds until justice is satisfied? What act of justice punishes without end? Even the law of God given to us stands against such a thing. The teaching of *lex talionis* in the Bible gives us the ideal to be used for justice: the punishment fits the offense. You do not hang a child for stealing a loaf of bread, as the Puritans in New England did. In like manner, there is no offense against God or man which is worthy of the never-ending torture in which Roman Catholic theologians such as Aquinas and Anselm of Canterbury seem to delight. It appears from verse twenty-six that God, fortunately for us, is much more merciful than we would be in the way He deals with His wayward children.

What is this furnace of fire? Hebrews 12:29 says our God is a consuming fire. The early fathers taught that this fire is the passionate love of God, a burning fire. In what way is this like a furnace? Vine's Expository Dictionary at Blue Letter Bible defines the Greek word kaminos as: A furnace for smelting; for burning earthen ware: for baking bread.

In smelting, the valuable is cleansed of all impurities. It sounds just like the process described in 1 Corinthians 3. The rubbish is burned away, leaving that which is pure. In fact, all three definitions in Vine's describe the furnace as being part of acts of creation, not destruction. The furnace of fire is the smelting furnace of God's fiery and passionate love which, according to the church fathers, burns away our sins, yet leaves us as the pure ore. "If any man's work shall be burned, he shall suffer loss: but he himself shall be saved; yet so as by fire."

The Western understanding of the furnace, where there shall be "wailing and gnashing of teeth," is one of punishment and destruction. The proper view is found in 1 Corinthians 3 is that we are to be "saved, yet so as by fire." I believe this is another example of how the culture of law/punishment has infused itself into the thinking of the Western theological mind. Matthew 13:41–42 as a destructive furnace is not consistent with Vine's description. Smelting is a creative and restorative act. It is not about destroying something forever.

Hell

The paper then goes to Matthew 25:41, in which Jesus tells the wicked to depart from Him into everlasting fire. I cannot tell you how many times I have had this verse thrown in my face as an ultimate response. The only problem is that non-Greek speaking translators have done a disservice to this verse and all who read it by translating the Greek word "aionios" to mean everlasting or eternal. There is a specific Greek word for eternal, which is "adidios." It is used only twice in the NT.

The word aionios comes from the root word "aion," which means "age." This is just one of many places in the Bible where agenda appears to have driven the translation. Infernalists insist the word aionios must always mean "eternal." Dr.Illaria Ramelli, in her massive work on apokatastasis, has argued that the proper understanding of aionios in this passage is "age-long" or "age-lasting."

Young's Literal Translation of the New Testament reads: "Then shall he say also to those on the left hand, go ye from me, the cursed, to the fire, the age-during, (aionios) that hath been prepared for the Devil and his messengers;"

Infernalists will immediately point to Matthew 25:46 in disbelief and say, "So you mean that the life that the righteous get is not everlasting, but only age-lasting?" Yes, that is exactly what it says. Not understanding the Greek language and the use of adjectives, you have been taught to think of this verse as promising eternal life, but the context and the Greek of Matthew 25 will not support this:

> What might the necessary exploration of the question of eternal damnation look like? We begin, as always, with Holy Scripture and specifically with our Lord's parable on the Last Judgment in Matthew 25 (always the first text raised), with careful attention to v. 46 and the semantic range of two critical words—aionion and kolasis. In most English translations aionion is typically translated as "eternal" and kolasis as "punishment": "And these will depart into eternal punishment, but the righteous into eternal life" (RSV). But aionion might also be plausibly rendered "age-during" and kolasis "chastisment":
>
>> And these shall be coming away into chastening eonian, yet the just into life eonian. (CLNT)
>>
>> And these shall go away to punishment age-during, but the righteous to life age-during. (YLT)
>>
>> And these will go to the chastening of that Age, but the just to the life of that Age. (DBHNT)
>
> How then do we decide? Only by in-depth study of the myriad eschatologies of Second Temple Judaism and the New

Testament. This is the kind of research that was unavailable to the patristic and medieval Fathers. It is a complex subject, and definitive answers may be impossible. Most certainly we will be left with probabilities, with each scholar reaching his or her own judgments about the eschatological beliefs of Jesus. Did Jesus believe that the chastisements of Gehenna would be temporary (i.e., for an age)? Did he intend to teach everlasting damnation, or was he simply appropriating popular beliefs to confront his audience with the eschatological urgency of his message and mission? It might even be the case, as David Bentley Hart has recently proposed, that because of the diverse and conflicting imagery used by Jesus in speaking of the final judgment–ranging from metaphors of destruction, exclusion, and imprisonment–the gospels do not permit a definitive determination regarding our Lord's beliefs about the final judgment:[14]

It is important to realize that Matthew chapters 23–25 is a discourse about the end of the Old Covenant age. Matthew 24:3 gives us a time signature which makes this clear.[15] It is not about the end of the world. This is a serious error in translation, one that has made people think for centuries that these chapters are about the end of all time–the end of the world. The Greek word translated world in 24:3 is aion. It *always* means age. A new age began in AD 70. Matthew 25 is speaking of the next in a succession of ages yet to come. How many? We do not know. We know that the Bible speaks of multiple ages to come as in verses like Ephesians 2:7 "That in the ages (aion) to come he might shew the exceeding riches of his grace in his kindness toward us through Christ Jesus."

Another mistranslation is found in Revelation 22:5 "And there shall be no night there; and they need no candle, neither light of the sun; for the Lord God giveth them light: and they shall reign for ever and ever."

But Young's Literal Translation says, "And night shall not be there, and they have no need of a lamp and light of a sun, because the Lord God doth give them light, and they shall reign–to the ages of the ages." (aion ho aion)

The Bible speaks of multiple ages yet to come. I learned to read the Bible as an Anabaptist Fundamentalist with the mistaken pre-millennial idea that there is this age we live in now, and then when Jesus returns, the end of everything. This end begins with the Great White Throne Judgment where the condemned are sent to hell and eternal life is given to the repentant.

14. Kimel, "Dogma, Damnation and the Eucatastrophe of the Jesus Story." Para. 35.

15. And when he is sitting on the mount of the Olives, the disciples came near to him by himself, saying, 'Tell us, when shall these be? and what is the sign of thy presence, and of the full end of the *age*?'

Matthew 24 is one of several passages which is thought to speak of the end of all things. It does not. It is about the end of the age and the transition into the next one.

Seeing this gives us a different understanding of Matthew 25. Matthew 23 to 25 is a discourse of Jesus about the coming horror which would fall upon Jerusalem. Christ is warning those listening: in the coming age do you want to enter judgment for your sins, or blessing for your faith in me? Destruction is coming to Jerusalem at the end of this age. If you wish blessing, then heed me and do what I say to assure yourself of missing the age-lasting chastisement which will come upon all who have acted wickedly. We have no indication of the length of the coming age mentioned in Matthew 24:3, only that the punishment in it, as well as the blessing, will be "age-lasting" (aionios).

The believers remembered His warning. When the Roman troops pulled back from the walls of Jerusalem for a respite, the Christians fled by night to the nearby caves in the Red City of Pella. Those who remained in Jerusalem were slaughtered without mercy. Those who listened are enjoying an age of the bliss of Christ's presence even now, and unto the following ages of ages. Those who did not, are in torment in this age as they are chastened for their sins and brought to repentance.

> So Aquila, while he was in Jerusalem, also saw the disciples of the disciples of the apostles flourishing in the faith and working great signs, healings, and other miracles. For they were such as had come back from the city of Pella to Jerusalem and were living there and teaching. For when the city was about to be taken and destroyed by the Romans, it was revealed in advance to all the disciples by an angel of God that they should remove from the city, as it was going to be completely destroyed. They sojourned as emigrants in Pella, the city above mentioned in Transjordania. And this city is said to be of the Decapolis. (Epiphanius, On Weights and Measures 15)[16]

What happens in the age after the one we are in now? And the age after that? And the one after that? We have no specific information, but we know, based on Revelation 22:5, that this current age is not the final one. Revelation promises us "aion ho aion"–age upon age, one age coming after another until there is a final age, spoken of in 1 Corinthians 15:22, when God becomes all in all.

---

16. "Flight to Pella," Para. 6.

> First Corinthians 15:22 For as in Adam all die, even so in Christ shall all be made alive. 23 But every man in his own order: Christ the firstfruits; afterward they that are Christ's at his coming. 24 Then cometh the end, when he shall have delivered up the kingdom to God, even the Father; when he shall have put down all rule and all authority and power. 25 For he must reign, till he hath put all enemies under his feet. 26 The last enemy that shall be destroyed is death. 27 For he hath put all things under his feet. But when he saith all things are put under him, it is manifest that he is excepted, which did put all things under him. 28 And when all things shall be subdued unto him, then shall the Son also himself be subject unto him that put all things under him, that God may be all in all.

Even though I have diverted from discussing the Roman Catechism, I want to stop and unpack this passage a little before I move on. It speaks of the final age and the end of all things. There are strong indications of Universal Restoration that Infernalists cannot just brush off. My comments are in parenthesis.

First Corinthians 15:22 For as in Adam all die, even so in Christ shall all be made alive. (If all are subject to death by virtue of the action of one man, then reasonably what this means is an equal restoration of that done by Adam, in which all are made alive)

23 But every man in his own order: Christ the first fruits; afterward they that are Christ's at his coming. (Now we see an order of finishing this restoration. This order suggests a succession of ages upon ages until the end is reached. Christ, the Last Adam, is made alive at His Resurrection. Those who are His are next to enter into life at His coming. This shows that there is a separation which takes place between the wicked [tares, bad fish] and the righteous [wheat, good fish]. While the righteous are enjoying the bliss of their good choice while alive, what of the wicked? They enter the smelting furnace of the Lord's fiery love. All that is in them that is wood, hay, straw, that which is worthless, is painfully burned away. This is the next age, the one we are in now, which began with the destruction of Jerusalem.)

24 Then cometh the end, when he shall have delivered up the kingdom to God, even the Father; when he shall have put down all rule and all authority and power. (When does the end come? Infernalists will put all these verses together, making this one final act of God at the end of time. I believe this is wrong.)

25 For he must reign, till he hath put all enemies under his feet. (It cannot end until this happens. All enemies are brought to subjection to Him. Who are these enemies? The next verse gives us a clue.)

26 The last enemy that shall be destroyed is death. (Death is an enemy. It is, in fact, the primary enemy of God, for God did not create all that is with the view that death should be a part of the life which He has created. Death is against life, and life is the very being of God.

The Infernalists will respond by saying that this verse proves their point, because sinners are enemies who must be destroyed. Are we His enemies? No, we are His children–all of us. Even those who have falsely given themselves over to being children of the wicked one by their embrace of sin. Using the analogy of life on earth, even if I give myself over to another family, the blood of my family of origin runs in my veins, and no matter how far I stray from them, I am still ontologically part of the family which brought me to life. The same is true of humanity. God gives life to every person. We are all His children.)

27 For he hath put all things under his feet. But when he saith all things are put under him, it is manifest that he is excepted, which did put all things under him. (This is a picture of subjection, such as a king would exercise over His subjects. Or a father over his family. To say all things indicates everyone and everything. Now how, I ask you Infernalists, are all things under His feet if there exists an eternal hell where throughout eternity sinners will curse God, wish Him dead, and have unfulfilled desire to commit sin? Is that a true picture of submission?)

28 And when all things shall be subdued unto him, then shall the Son also himself be subject unto him that put all things under him, that God may be all in all. (All things subdued unto Him. According to this verse, there is no eternal hell in which the sinner curses God [thus forever continuing in sin] and exists in a state of perpetual rebellion. St. Paul says "when" because there is an unknown amount of time which will be needed to bring even the most hardened sinner to repentance, and to pay the last farthing of justice for the evil deeds done in this lifetime. An eternal hell filled with rebellious sinners is not in any way an example of being "subdued unto Him." If you think it is, then you don't understand basic language and the meaning of words.)

> CCC 1035 The teaching of the Church affirms the existence of hell and its eternity. Immediately after death the souls of those who die in a state of mortal sin descend into hell, where they suffer the punishments of hell, "eternal fire." The chief punishment of hell is eternal separation from God, in whom alone man can possess the life and happiness for which he was created and for which he longs.[17]

17. Catechism of the Catholic Church, Article 12, "I Believe in Life Everlasting" IV. Hell

As I continued my investigation, I discovered there is no such word as hell in the original Greek of the NT text. There are twenty-three verses which are translated hell in the New Testament. Twelve of them use the word Gehenna. This was originally the valley of Hinnom, south of Jerusalem, where the filth and dead animals of the city were cast out and burned. Eleven verses use the word Hades. Blue Letter Bible's Outline of Biblical Usage says of Hades: the name Hades or Pluto, the god of the lower regions; Orcus, the nether world, the realm of the dead; later use of this word: the grave, death, hell.

I cannot think of a more frustrating response to deal with when discussing apokatastasis than that of people changing words to suit their agenda. It is as if red only means red if they want it to, but when defending eternal conscious torment, sometimes red really means green.

This is most egregious when dealing with Infernalists who love to pull out verses which they think prove the tired old saying, "Jesus talked more about hell than anyone else." Jesus didn't speak about hell at all, at least, not in the modern understanding of a place of eternal, burning fire. He spoke about two places which are dishonestly translated in the Bible as hell–Gehenna, and Hades. Gehenna and Hades each have a distinct meaning, and it is not hell as defined by Infernalists.

When confronted, these folks will earnestly say, *"Well, Jesus may not have used the exact word hell, but that's what He meant."* Hogwash! Jesus had a habit of using language in precisely the way it was to be understood. When He said that we must eat His Flesh and drink His Blood, He lost most of His disciples as they turned away in confusion and disgust. He would not have used Gehenna to speak about the next life. Either Sheol or Hades would have been the proper word to use. And none of these words were understood to mean the Medieval understanding of a place where sinners are "immersed in the boiling blood forever, each according to the degree of his guilt." Infernalists can be annoyingly like Humpty Dumpty in Alice's Wonderland: *"When I use a word,"* Humpty Dumpty said, in rather a scornful tone, *"it means just what I choose it to mean–neither more nor less."* And some Infernalists are quite scornful as they explain to you that even if the word Gehenna doesn't directly mean hell, that is what Christ nonetheless intended.

Jesus was speaking to Jews, not to Roman emperors or twenty-first century evangelicals. His language therefore is to be understood in the common understanding of the day, not as we wish to see it, nor as it has been so mangled by punishment-minded clerics laboring under wretched translations of the Scriptures, or with an agenda to fulfill. When Jesus spoke, He expected those listening to Him would understand as Jews. Thus, if He was speaking about the afterlife, He would have spoken in the context of Jewish teaching and understanding at that time and would have spoken about Sheol or Hades, not about the garbage dump of Jerusalem. In addition, whenever errors, corruption of text, or plain old misunderstanding had crept into the public discourse about life and God, He corrected them.[18] He did this elsewhere, yet for such a critical issue as one's eternal destiny, He is strangely silent. I see nowhere He corrects the Jewish understanding of the next life and tells them to beware because there is an eternal hell of fiery torment. No Jew listening to Jesus speak of Gehenna would have thought of Dante's lurid descriptions of the next life for the wicked.

> There are, however, several biblical references to a place called Sheol (cf. Numbers 30, 33). It is described as a region "dark and deep," "the Pit," and "the Land of Forgetfulness," where human beings descend after death. The suggestion is that in the netherworld of Sheol, the deceased, although cut off from God and humankind, live on in some shadowy state of existence.
> While this vision of Sheol is rather bleak (setting precedents for later Jewish and Christian ideas of an underground hell) there is generally no concept of judgment or reward and punishment attached to it. In fact, the more pessimistic books of the Bible, such as Ecclesiastes and Job, insist that all of the dead go down to Sheol, whether good or evil, rich or poor, slave or free man (Job 3:11–19).[19]

> The Hebrew Bible itself assumes that the dead are simply dead— that their body lies in the grave, and there is no consciousness, ever again. It is true that some poetic authors, for example in the Psalms, use the mysterious term "Sheol" to describe a person's new location. But in most instances Sheol is simply a synonym for "tomb" or "grave." It's not a place where someone actually goes.[20, 21]

Augustine referred to ideals in Plato's thinking which he believed were compatible with Christian thinking. The Orthodox Church refers

---

18. Such as in Matthew 5:43: "Ye have heard that it hath been said, thou shalt love thy neighbor, and hate thine enemy. 44 But I say unto you, love your enemies, bless them that curse you, do good to them that hate you, and pray for them which despitefully use you, and persecute you."
19. Rose, "Heaven and Hell in Jewish Tradition." Para. 3–4.
20. Ehrman, "What Jesus Really Said About Heaven and Hell." Para. 7.
21. Another good reference to Jewish beliefs on the afterlife can be found at the Jewish Encyclopedia online at https://www.jewishencyclopedia.com/articles/6558-gehenna

to the Western church as having been corrupted by the Platonic thinking of Augustine in these matters. The Roman Catholic Church states, in its Catechism of the Catholic Church, that all truth, regardless of where it is found, belongs to God, since God is truth and the author of such. Apparently, Augustine had little trouble seeing certain Platonic ideas as truth, and then blending them into Christianity where they didn't belong. The Western church appears to have accepted them without council or question.

> Thus, by examining Augustine's background & training in Greek philosophy & Neoplatonic thought, his interaction with and evaluation of Platonism & Neoplatonism to Christianity in his own writing, and the parallel between Neo-Platonic philosophy & his philosophical theology, it is easy to conclude that his philosophical theology of original sin, free will, and the nature of man was influenced by Neoplatonism.[22]

Part of this Neoplatonic thought had to do with the disposition of the soul after death. There is no doubt in my mind that Augustine's theological musings were deeply influenced by Platonic thought and the memories of his life before conversion.

> The concept of a soul within us that cannot die first became a 'Christian' doctrine at the end of the second century AD. Hell had been taught in Greek philosophy long before the time of Jesus, with Plato (427–347 BC) as the important leader in this thinking.
>
> The teaching of an everlasting place of punishment for the wicked is the natural consequence of a belief in an immortal soul. By the year AD 187, it was understood that life, once we have it, is compulsory; there is no end to it, either now or in a world to come. We have no choice as to its continuance, even if we were to commit suicide to end it.[23]

RECEPTION OF AUGUSTINE IN THE ORTHODOX CHURCH

> The Fifth Ecumenical Council, held in Constantinople in A.D. 553, listed Augustine among other Fathers of the Church,

---

22. Livermore, "Augustine," Para. 46.
23. Fudge, "The Origin of Hell-Fire in Christian Teaching" Para. 1–2

though there is no unqualified endorsement of his theology mentioned (just as there is none for most saints of the Church):

We further declare that we hold fast to the decrees of the four Councils, and in every way follow the holy Fathers, Athanasius, Hilary, Basil, Gregory the Theologian, Gregory of Nyssa, Ambrose, Theophilus, John (Chrysostom) of Constantinople, Cyril, Augustine, Proclus, Leo and their writings on the true faith.

In the acts of the Sixth Ecumenical Council (not yet translated into English), he is called the "most excellent and blessed Augustine" and is referred to as "the most wise teacher." In the Comnenian Council of Constantinople in 1166 he is referred to as "O Agios Augustine"–"Saint Augustine."

Despite these acclamations, most of his works were not translated into Greek until circa 1360 by Demetrios Cydones and some Orthodox Christians identify errors in his theology–especially those in his Triadology which gave rise to the Filioque addition to the Nicene-Constantinopolitan Creed–and regard him as being one of the major factors in the Great Schism between the Church in the East and in the West. Thus, there are those among the Orthodox who regard Augustine as a heretic, although there has never been any conciliar condemnation of either him or his writings.

> Another view is expressed by Christos Yannaras, who described Augustine as "the fount of every distortion and alteration in the Church's truth in the West" (The Freedom of Morality, p. 151n.).[24]

It is interesting to note that some Orthodox theologians point to Augustine's writings as a doctrinal turning point in Christian history. Believers in apokatastasis especially note that prior to Augustine, the church enjoyed a robust teaching of apokatastasis in four theological schools across the empire. Augustine is said to have initially embraced this teaching, then turned against it later in his life. Augustine admitted that there were a "great many" who believed in Universal Restoration. It is also puzzling to see how the Western church embraced his new teachings without so much as a council be called to discuss them. These teachings contradicted what the church had been teaching. I heard David Bentley Hart say in a YouTube video that it is a shame that Augustine didn't die twenty years earlier and save the Christian church a great deal of grief.

I imagine the creation of hell being part of a parcel of erroneous theological novums which gained traction in the West with Augustine and were finally codified and demanded to be believed in by Justinian, who despised Origen and his teachings, especially the idea of a future restoration of all

---

24. "Augustine of Hippo," Para. 4–7 & 10

things and people. Justinian wanted control, and threats of an eternity of torture for misbehavior appear to be his method of insuring that a stupid, illiterate, and sometimes ungovernable populace were kept in line.

> CCC 1037 God predestinates no one to go to hell, for this, a willful turning away from God (a mortal sin) is necessary, and persistence in it until the end. In the Eucharistic Liturgy and in daily prayers of her faithful, the Church implores the mercy of God, who does not want "any to perish, but all to come to repentance."[25]

Here is yet another problem with the Roman Catholic Catechism. The Roman Catholic faith does teach there is such a thing as predestination, yet CCC 1037 above states that this is not so.

A definition of predestination can be found in the Catechism:

> To God, all moments of time are present in their immediacy. When therefore he establishes his eternal plan of "predestination," he includes in it each person's free response to his grace: "In this city, in fact, both Herod and Pontius Pilate, with the Gentiles and the peoples of Israel, gathered together against your holy servant Jesus, whom you anointed, *to do whatever your hand and your plan had predestined to take place.*" For the sake of accomplishing his plan of salvation, God permitted the acts that flowed from their blindness. CCC, 600[26]

In other words, God, who wills the salvation of all, by an act of His same divine Will, nonetheless predestined certain men, such as Herod, Pilate, and Judas, to behave in a manner which guaranteed their eternal ruin. To me this is nonsensical double-talk. If I am a parent and see my toddler under a full head of steam running towards a busy highway, I do not allow her to continue this path if I do not wish her to die. If I do nothing, allowing her to get smeared all over the roadway, and then exclaim that it was not my will that she died, one will immediately see the contradiction between my words and my actions. That would be patent nonsense, and anyone who had witnessed my inaction would gladly testify at a trial so that I might spend the rest of my life in prison for my act of depraved indifference. My inaction is my will. If God permits something to happen in His omniscience, He is predestinating a result take place from that action.

---

25. Catechism of the Catholic Church. "I Believe in Life Everlasting," Hell Article 12 IV.

26. Catechism of the Catholic Church, "Jesus Died Crucified," Article 4, Para. 2

This sort of theological and philosophical folderol regarding God does not work for me. Make up your mind. Either God wills that all shall be saved, or His inaction towards certain sinners predestines they will not be saved by taking no action to bring them to repentance, thus guaranteeing His will that they fail in obtaining salvation. But both statements cannot be true at the same time. And trying to blame this on the free will of man to choose damnation is a weasel clause for people too lazy to think about the ramifications of accepting both of these conflicting ideas at the same time.

It appears there may be some connection between the Christian insistence upon a horrific place called hell and ancient Egyptian and Babylonian (pagan) myths. The Egyptian Book of the Dead is unquestionably one of the most influential books in all history. Containing the ancient ritual to be performed for the dead with detailed instructions for the behavior of the soul in the afterlife, it served as the most important repository of religious authority for some three thousand years. According to the renowned Egyptologist, Dr. E. A. Wallis Budge, the idea of suffering after death was found among the pagan religious teachings of ancient peoples in Babylon and Egypt. Budge said that they portray the next world as having pits of fire for the damned.

> In ancient Babylonian and Assyrian beliefs the 'nether world... is pictured as a place full of horrors, and is presided over by gods and demons of great strength and Fierceness.'–The Religion of Babylonia and Assyria Boston, 1898, Morris Jastrow, Jr., p. 581
> Hell, in the theological sense, has no place in most primitive religions, nor has heaven. The existence beyond death is almost universally thought of as "something between being and not being." The Hebrew Sheol and the Greek Hades are good illustrations of this. There was no thought of dividing the future state into separate and distinct conditions of existence. Even so late a writer as the author of Ecclesiastes declares that "all (men and beasts) go unto one place" (Eccl. iii, 20) and "there is one event to the righteous and wicked" (Eccl. ix, 2). Much confusion and misunderstanding has been caused through the early translators of the Bible persistently ren- dering the Hebrew Sheol and the Greek Hades and Gehenna by the word hell. The simple transliteration of these words by the translators of the revised editions of the Bible has not sufficed to appreciably clear up this confusion and misconception. The popular idea of hell as a place of punishment, either redemptive or rigidly retributive in character, did not come suddenly and full-formed into existence. It is the product of centuries of thinking on the great problem of reward and punishment which, instinctively almost,

man associates with human deeds. In the early Stages the idea seems to have been that the souls of the dead appeared before the divine tribunal. The souls that could present a satisfactory record during their earth life were admitted to the presence and abode of the gods, and the souls that could not present such a satisfactory account were cast out not into a place of torment but into an existence more or less deplorable and wretched.

The main features of hell as conceived by Hindu, Persian, Egyptian, Grecian, and Christian theologians are essentially the same. The Western religious from Roman times through the Middle Ages borrowed the doctrine of eternal torture from the pagan philosophers.[27]

Why is this important? It is so because the religions of paganism, with their gods who are more like human beings than He who is divine love, all appear to have the same theme–an angry and offended deity who will get his revenge. It is important to note that pagan ideas of God were so distorted that they worshiped the sun, the moon, other men, and creatures as God. This points to the Stygian darkness in which man's natural understanding labors. Without divine revelation given directly to us, to understand God in all his glory, beauty, and love, is like a blind man trying to understand the color blue. It is simply impossible–thus leading to the many bizarre ideas about God which exist in pagan mythology, even to this day.[28] With the conversion of Constantine, pagans came into the church baptized in body, but not in their heart or understanding. According to lore, they entered the church because it was the thing to do since Christianity had become the religion of the empire. Apparently, they brought the angry God of paganism in with them.

Since my friend has made an appeal to the Roman Catholic Church as a final authority, it is incumbent on me to show the problems I have with that church and why I am Orthodox in my theology. Why did church at Rome fling itself headlong into the doctrine of hell and embrace it with such gusto, especially in the Medieval Age? And what does this mean considering the indefectibility of the Catholic church? For me, the definition of indefectibility is problematic:

> Imperishable duration of the Church and her immutability until the end of time. The First Vatican Council declared that the Church possesses "an unconquered stability" and that, "built on a rock, she will continue to stand until the end of time"

---

27. "Hell," Page 82
28. Such as the garishly overdecorated elephant god of the Hindus, Ganesh.

(Denzinger 3013, 3056). The Church's indefectibility, therefore, means that she now is and will always remain the institution of salvation, founded by Christ. This affirms that the Church is essentially unchangeable in her teaching, her constitution, and her liturgy. It does not exclude modifications that do not affect her substance, nor does it exclude the decay of individual local churches or even whole dioceses.[29]

> By this term is signified, not merely that the Church will persist to the end of time, but further, that it will be preserved unimpaired in its essential characteristics. The Church can never undergo any constitutional change, which will make it, as a social organism, something different from what it was originally. It can never become corrupt in faith or in morals; nor can it ever lose the Apostolic hierarchy, or the Sacraments through which Christ communicates grace to men.[30]

Beginning with the Filioque, the Roman church has done just the opposite. For centuries, doctrines not known to the early fathers, and opposed by the Orthodox church, have been created out of thin air. The Filioque added to the Creed came from the former pagans of the North, known as the Franks. The Frankish doctrinal intrusion into the Roman church succeeded beyond their wildest dreams on February 14, 1014, when, at the Coronation Mass of Henry II as Emperor of the Holy Roman Empire, Henry had the pleasure of hearing the Creed recited with the Filioque. This was a long-sought victory for the Frankish bishops, who had exasperated the popes of Rome with insistent demands for the Filioque be inserted into the Creed.

In my investigation of history, Western Christianity reads more like a tawdry paperback novel than the actions of men filled with the Holy Spirit and directed by Him to follow the teachings of Christ. The papacy was bought and sold, along with the offices of bishops. Several popes were elevated using simony, and once enthroned, disgraced the office with their immoral sexual behavior. The actions of many of the Christian kings and emperors were more in line with the god of war, Mars, than with Christ, the Prince of Peace. I cannot highly enough recommend Fr. John Romanides book, Franks, Romans, Feudalism, and Doctrine–An Interplay Between Theology and Society, regarding this. This is an excellent writing on the nature of the Frankish attack on the Roman church and the victory of Frankish bishops over two centuries, culminating in the insertion of the Filioque into the Creed. It appears the pagan Franks were somehow unaffected by either

---

29. "Indefectibility," Lines 1–7
30. Gonzales, "The Indefectibility of the Church," Para. 2.

their baptism or the teachings of Christ when it came to lusting after power and a desire to rule over others. One must then ask how we trust such men and their successors in matters of doctrine and dogma?

To say the Roman Catholic Church is essentially unchangeable in her teaching, doctrine, and liturgy appears to me as patently false. You will not find in the early fathers ideas such as Indulgences, Purgatory, Limbus Infantium, the Immaculate Conception, and Papal Supremacy. In addition, the Roman church has instituted mandatory celibacy for priests,[31] the use of unleavened bread in the Eucharist, the withholding of the Eucharist from infant children, baptism by sprinkling, and a host of other inventions which, if honestly looked at, will bring one to admit the Roman church has done anything but remain stable in what the united church of the first millennium taught and practiced. Could it be that the teaching of eternal hell came from spiritually blind pagans and was gradually adopted to the Roman Catholic theological lexicon? I think there may be a strong reason to suspect this, especially when looking at the overall behavior of the Western hierarchy. Men who are filled with and guided by the Holy Spirit do not act in the manner many of these men did. To know and teach truth, one must be filled with, controlled by, and led of the Holy Spirit. A spirit-filled life will show itself by behaviors completely the opposite of many of the Latin hierarchs of history.[32]

The creation of an eternal hell of torment is a perfect storm of combined elements: natural blindness of man, Roman Law Court thinking, seeing God as Revengeful Judge rather than Compassionate Father, and the mistranslation of the Greek in the Scriptures. It is recreating God in our image, which we all are prone to do. It is a fear born of the natural darkness of our minds in which we can only imagine God in terms of power, anger, and dreadful judgment. God behaves like us, getting His revenge on all who dare insult Him. This is how we act when offended, therefore we expect no less from an all-powerful Being.

I was tempted to say this all began with Augustine's wretched and pessimistic anthropology, but it goes back farther than that. It goes all the way

---

31. Canon 13 of the Sixth Ecumenical Council specifically notes the Latin demand of clerical celibacy and vigorously opposes it.

32. Read Russian Orthodox Roman Catholic Relations: A Short History by Vladimir Moss. The history of how Roman Catholics have treated others outside their fold shows me that they were anything but filled with the Holy Spirit of God. Russian Orthodox believers were slaughtered like sheep by Roman Catholic Church. Is this how Jesus taught we are to treat our enemies? Is this how someone filled with the Holy Spirit acts? Our Lord said that we can know a bad tree by the bad fruit it bears. A history of Rome after Charlemagne took over shows a tree, which, while having some very good people in it, bore some rotten fruit.

back to the garden of Eden and the fall. God created man in His image. Adam and Eve were created with the potentiality of becoming gods.[33] We see verification of this in Apostle Peter's epistle where he states that we have been made partakers of the divine nature. What is the divine nature which was lost?

The divine nature is love. God is love. God doesn't just love, He *is* love. Man was created to become a creature of divine love, sharing in the divine nature (but never in the essence of God). It does not take long after the Adam and Eve are expelled from Eden to see the effect of sin on the man's nature. Cain kills Abel. Lamech tells his wives he has killed a young man who merely wounded him. As the Genesis account continues, we see violence and retribution, the very opposite of love, have become the norm of human behavior. The darkness of sin brings man to such a point of continuing violence that God wipes the earth clean by a flood. Man does not love his fellow man. He uses him and kills anyone who objects to being used.

Augustine had a term for it: libido dominandi, the lust to dominate. It is the passion for utter control. The whole world–from family members to the world outside–must submit to our desire for power. For the great majority of men in the world, this lust cannot be lived out to its full desire, precisely because there are other men who will defend themselves from such excursions into their own personal liberty. These men who cannot oppress others became the oppressors of their families–wife beaters, adulterers, coarse, harsh men who in turn raise the next generation of coarse young men who will continue the oppression, beating their wives and terrorizing their families. This sin-borne sickness passes from generation to generation.

For some in history though, strong, powerfully built men with both eloquence and savagery, it was easy to create a mob of degenerates who would form an army by which they preyed upon the less fortunate. Join me and together we shall plunder the world! Unsatisfied to take pleasure in the land in which they were born, the relationships and friendships they had, their libido dominandi sent men like Hannibal, Napoleon, Genghis Khan, and others on vast raiding parties to conquer unseen territories, slaughtering by the millions any innocent men, women, and children they encountered. When Alexander the Great saw the breadth of his domain, he wept, for there were no more worlds to conquer. His lust could find no further outlet.

To conquer, to rule over, to be worshiped and revered (or feared, either will do) is the irresistible siren call to such men. But some would not be content with just earthly rule. In their raging libido dominandi, like many other

---

33. St. Athanasius, De Incarnatione or On the Incarnation 54:3, PG 25:192B–"God became man in order that man might become a god."

demented kings around the world, the caesars of the Roman Empire into which Christianity was birthed, claimed godhood, and demanded worship.

While I wish it were otherwise, the church and the men who ruled in it were not exempt from this temptation.[34] The Christian faith teaches us that the passions of the flesh are an enemy to us and our spiritual growth. The history and behavior of the hierarchs of both East and West shows men who succumbed to the siren song of libido dominandi. If the best of Christian leaders were those who ruled in love, caring tenderly for their flock, and leading them by example, the worst among these men were those who lusted after power and control. For them, the way to motivate the sheep to obedience was with the whip. But how do you whip a people who are not afraid of death because Christ has died and eternal life beckons?

You threaten them with an eternal, fiery hell if they are disobedient to your commands!

To understand the ability of mankind to come up with the idea of a God who tortures His creatures without mercy nor end, it is important to understand the ground into which this seed of thought was planted and nurtured.

The fertile ground of such a diabolical understanding is the natural blindness of man's mind, a blindness that persists unless the Holy Spirit brings light and truth to the soul. Numerous passages of the Bible describe man as spiritually blind, his understanding in darkness, and this state being our natural state because of the fall in the garden:

> Proverbs 2:12 To deliver thee from the way of the evil man, from the man that speaketh froward things; 13 Who leave the paths of uprightness, to walk in the ways of darkness.
> Proverbs 4:19 The way of the wicked is as darkness: they know not at what they stumble.
> Matthew 6:23 But if thine eye be evil, thy whole body shall be full of darkness. If therefore the light that is in thee be darkness, how great is that darkness!
> First John 2:11 But he that hateth his brother is in darkness, and walketh in darkness, and knoweth not whither he goeth, because that darkness hath blinded his eyes.

---

34. http://www.romanity.org/htm/rom.03.en.franks_romans_feudalism_and_doctrine.01.htm. If you look up no other link in this book, go to this one and read the sordid history of Charlemagne and the Frankish bishops who followed him. This one sentence describes perfectly the spiritual and moral darkness in which they acted: "In the time of Pippin of Herestal (697–715) and Charles Martel (715–741), many of the Franks who replaced Roman bishops were military leaders who, according to Saint Boniface, shed the blood of Christians like that of the pagans." Baptism does not automatically make you a saint on earth.

> John 12:35 Then Jesus said unto them, yet a little while is the light with you. Walk while ye have the light, lest darkness come upon you: for he that walketh in darkness knoweth not whither he goeth.

Are you seeing the common theme here? Darkness is our natural spiritual condition. C.S. Lewis nicely described this condition in his book, The Last Battle. A group of dwarfs sit together in a barn. Total darkness keeps them from seeing. They cannot taste properly, so that when Aslan presents them with a banquet of the finest foods, they fancy it to be hay, old turnips, and raw cabbage. The rich red wine they mistake for water from a donkey's trough. Then they turn on each other, each suspecting the other has something better.

The dwarfs are a picture of mankind in our natural state. Surrounded by the good things of God–the beauty of sunsets, the pleasure of taste and smell, the glories of creation, of sight and feeling–rather than understanding that only an all-good and all-loving Creator could make such things, in their darkness men came to think of God as fierce, ruthless, angry, hard to please, and desirous of human sacrifice. It is not long in the history of mankind that we find the most abominable of practices recorded in order to please this false narrative. In fear of failing crops, of lack of rain, or just the general displeasure a powerful and fearful deity, men and women overrode normal natural parental affection and threw their infant children into the fires of the false gods, Baal and Molech.

What but an utter darkness of intellect and spirit would make human beings do such a horrible thing? It is the very same blindness which makes some religious leaders today state that in support of abortion, they are doing the work of the Lord, as if the god they claim to serve is a bloodthirsty fiend of the lowest moral degradation, pleased when innocent children are ripped apart in his name in the most heinous fashion imaginable. This is nothing less than utter spiritual darkness at work–and as Lewis intimated, a darkness which these blind leaders have chosen for themselves in choosing to reject the light of conscience, scripture, and the pleadings of those who see such action as the evil it is.

But let me not stop here, lest you be unconvinced. If mankind by nature had clear understanding the difference between good and evil, why would it be necessary for God to go into such detail in the Old Testament to explain to the Hebrew nation–and by extension, all mankind–that having sex with your family members is wrong, sex with animals is wrong, stealing your neighbors' goods is wrong, and murdering another person is wrong? Today, influenced by two millennia of Christian teaching, we understand these behaviors are an abominable desecration of what we were created to be. The need to give such prohibitions in detail to people who readily behaved in such a manner shows the natural blindness of the human intellect. And even then, warned by God through the prophets, the people of Israel chose to ignore these commands and do what their disordered passions drove them to do, going deeper and deeper into blindness of soul.

This blindness has not only caused mankind to not know the good, but to fail to understand God properly. In spiritual blindness, all manner of strange and bizarre gods were imagined, idols that came with equally vile rituals of appeasement. In addition, Satan–that liar of old–put in man's mind a picture of God as harsh, evil, to be feared, and above all, intent upon doing evil to man in His desire for revenge for our sins. This is the reality of the pagan gods we find throughout history. The pagan god is a creation of the evil one, put into the darkened minds of men, and demanding horrific worship to appease his anger.

Can you see now that in such a state of darkness, it is but a small step from throwing your child into the fire of a false god to describing eternity as a place of grim, eternal torture by a displeased deity who will have his revenge? A god whom you have imagined demands human blood is a god who will have it in the next life also, unless you are very, very sure you have done all you can to make him happy and appease his wrath. Man has recast God in his own image–the image of violence, wrath, and selfishness.

This is the god of the pagans, the false god of our darkened imagination, and under Augustine, this juridical idea of a wrathful deity was laid over the God who, in the greatest act of love ever seen, came to die to redeem all mankind. This angry God became the God of the Western church, a church which in the eleventh century Papal Reformation, led by the now-controlling Frankish bishops, became blinded by the desire for universal rule and power.

My point is that we are not naturally given to spiritual insight. We are blind. And the Frankish bishops, who conquered the Roman church and destroyed Her orthodoxy, are no exception. Modern Roman Catholicism of today is not the church of Rome of the first eight hundred years of Christianity. It is a Frankish crossbreed which has run off the doctrinal rails. This is the reason Holy Orthodoxy has firmly resisted the many theological innovations which have cropped up since the schism of 1054 AD.

This history is the reason I reject anything in the Catechism of the Roman Catholic Church which strays outside the writings of the early fathers of the church, the sacred Scriptures, and the revelation of God in Jesus Christ. If it cannot be found in them, I am under no obligation to believe in it. Not even if some mystic claims the Virgin Mary Herself spoke it. Likewise, if one of the early fathers speaks, and his opinion contradicts what we have been told about God–that God is love–then I have every right to question that truth also. Proper knowledge of God is like a three-legged stool. Divine revelation (the Scriptures), knowledge of God's character (love), and the ecumenical councils. The more I study the history of the Roman Catholic Church, the more I see libido dominandi turning it into a political nation with men of high ambition lusting after the power of the clerical robe. This is what I found when I was digging around in Christian history, and to me it is most disturbing.

AN APPEAL TO THE ATHANASIAN CREED

> The Athanasian Creed is also called Symbolum Quincunque, from the first word, 'Quicunque vult salvus esse.'
>
> Its origin is involved in obscurity, like that of the Apostles' Creed, the Gloria in Excelsis, and the Te Deum. It furnishes one of the most remarkable examples of the extraordinary influence which works of unknown or doubtful authorship have exerted. Since the ninth century it has been ascribed to Athanasius, bishop of Alexandria, the chief defender of the divinity of Christ and the orthodox doctrine of the Trinity (d. 373). The great name of 'the father of orthodoxy' secured for it an almost œcumenical authority, notwithstanding the *solemn prohibition of the third and fourth œcumenical councils to compose or publish any other creed than the Nicene.*
>
> Since the middle of the seventeenth century the Athanasian authorship has been abandoned by learned Catholics as well as Protestants. The evidence against it is conclusive. The Symbol is nowhere found in the genuine writings of Athanasius or his contemporaries and eulogists. The General Synods of Constantinople (381), Ephesus (431), and Chalcedon (451) make no allusion to it whatever. It seems to presuppose the doctrinal controversies of the fifth century concerning the constitution of Christ's person; at least it teaches substantially the Chalcedonian Christology. And, lastly, it makes its first appearance in the Latin Churches of Gaul, North Africa, and Spain: while the Greeks did not know it till the eleventh century, and afterwards rejected or modified it on account of the Occidental clause on the procession of the Holy Ghost from the Father *and the Son*.

> The Greek texts, moreover, differ widely, and betray, by strange words and constructions, the hands of *unskilled translators*.[35]

Once again, we come to the problem of the mistranslation of the Greek into Latin. Philip Schaff, Swiss-born American ecumenical leader and theologian whose works, especially the *Creeds of Christendom* (1877), helped set standards in the United States for scholarship in church history, notes translation problems with the transition from the Greek to the Latin edition, not the least of which is in Verse 43 of the creed which reads in Latin:

Verse 43. "Et qui bona egerunt, ibunt in vitam æternam: qui vero mala, in ignem æternum." (And they that have done good shall go into life everlasting: and they that have done evil, into everlasting fire.)

Schaff notes that in verse 43 that eis aion ous kol seis, ad cruciatus eternos. aion ous. (aionios) does not mean "eternal," which is the erroneous translation of Latin translators, who used instead the Latin words in ignem æternum, which means "in eternal fire."

Based on both the prohibition of the third and fourth ecumenical councils, the suspect nature of this creed in general, and the continual and ubiquitous mistranslation of Greek to Latin, I am confident in rejecting the Athanasian Creed as having any authority in the matter of apokatastasis.

On the same page in which my friend appeals to the Athanasian Creed, her second paragraph launches into a defense of the eternal nature of hell from the light of mere reason. In other words, when one thinks about it, it is reasonable for God to punish the wicked in unending torment. The paragraph is filled with the usual objections and misinformation regarding apokatastasis, including this statement:

"Moreover, if all men were fully convinced that the sinner need fear no kind of punishment after death, moral and social order would be seriously menaced."

This objection is false on two counts: First, no one believing in apokatastasis believes that there is a free pass into heaven for those who have done evil in their lives. This is an outrageous lie which is constantly bandied about by the opponents of apokatastasis. Christ and St. Paul both sternly warned of the dire consequences of evil actions. See my statements in the last part of this book about the consequences of sinful behavior in this life.

The second problem with this idea is that it is observably false. All you must do is look at the world around us to see how threats of eternal hell fire have failed to make mankind walk in fear of doing evil. Some of the worst scoundrels, adulterers, murderers, thieves, and generally immoral louts have been and are even now members of the church, raised in Her

---

35. "The Athanasian Creed." Lines 1–14

arms since childhood, having no doubt heard terrifying stories of the fires of hell awaiting the wicked.

My friend's paper goes on to say:

"Furthermore, reason easily understands that in the next life the just will be made happy as a reward of their virtue." (No problem here) "But the punishment of evil is the natural counterpart of the reward of virtue." (No problem here either. Universalists are all for divine justice!) "Hence, there will be punishment for sin in the next life. Accordingly, we find among all nations the belief that evil doers will be punished after death. This universal conviction of mankind is an additional proof for the existence of hell." (No, not really. Pagan ideas of a punishing God filled with anger, revenge, and eternal sadism are not the foundation for my belief in God. I don't go to unbelievers and their spiritually darkened minds for my theology, no matter how universal and world-wide their thoughts are!)

Eastern Orthodoxy does not see God as an angry judge who is looking to condemn mankind for our offenses against His sovereign dignity. We instead see Him as our loving heavenly Father who administers bitter medicine for the healing of our souls. St. Isaac of Syria described the experience of hell as the love of God experienced as pain by the wicked. It is experienced so because the sinner does not want God–he wants himself. Just as the same bright sunlight which blesses healthy eyes causes pain to those eyes which are diseased, so the love of God is experienced as painful chastisement by the wicked.

THE ETERNITY OF HELL

I will divide my attention here to two different ideas regarding the eternity of hell. First will discuss the idea that the Bible teaches an eternity in hell. After that, I will take the quotes given from the early fathers and show that they are mistranslated.

The first statement under this heading is: "The Holy Bible is quite explicit in teaching the eternity of the pains of hell." This would be true *if* the English translation from the Latin were a correct translation of the Greek. As I have mentioned earlier, it is not. Every verse which appears to threaten "eternal fire" is a mistranslation of the Greek word "aionios"–the fire that lasts for an age. Once again, I am presented by my friend with Matthew 25:46 as *the* proof text proving that the wicked suffer eternally.

Some literal translations of the Greek in Matthew 25:46:

Young's Literal Translation: "punishment age-during."

Rotherham Translation: "age-abiding correction."

Weymouth Translation: "punishment of the ages."

Concordant Literal Translation: "chastening eonian."

eonian, "aionios . . . lasting for an age . . . partaking of the character of that which lasts for an age, as contrasted with that which is brief and fleeting . . . (also used of past time, or past and future as well) Derivation: from G165;" G166 aionios–Strong's Greek Lexicon

Kolasis is defined as chastisement, punishment. . .

In the late 2nd century/early 3rd century, Clement of Alexandria clearly distinguished between kólasis and timoria:

> This important passage is very instructive in the light it sheds on the usage of Greek words. The word from which "corrections" is rendered is the same as that in Hebrews 12:9, "correction" "chastening" (paideia); "chastisement" is from *kolasis*, translated "punishment" in Matt. 25:46, and "punishment" is *timoria*, with which Josephus defined punishment, but a word our Lord never employs, and which Clement declares that God never inflicts.
>
> "The divine nature is not angry but is at the farthest from it, for it is an excellent ruse to frighten in order that we may not sin. Nothing is hated by God."(2) So that even if *aionios* (Matt. 25:46) meant endless duration, Clement would argue that it was used as instruction–to restrain the sinner. It should be said, however, that Clement rarely uses *aionion* in connection with suffering.
>
> Clement insists that punishment in Hades is remedial and restorative, and that punished souls are cleansed by fire. The fire is spiritual, purifying the soul. "God's punishments are saving and disciplinary (in Hades) leading to conversion, and choosing rather the repentance than the death of the sinner, (Ezek. 18:23, 32; 33:11, etc.,) and especially since souls, although darkened by passions, when released from their bodies, are able to perceive more clearly because of their being no longer obstructed by the paltry flesh."[36]

Here is another important distinction which the Latin translators missed because they didn't know Greek. The "kolasis aionion" is an age-lasting instructive chastening, not a punishment in retaliation for evil. The West sees God as deeply offended and determined to avenge His name upon all who have spurned Him. But this is not the Greek of Matthew 25. The Greek of Matthew 25:46 is the age-long chastisement which looks to the restoration of the sinner.

---

36. Hanson, Universalism The Prevailing Doctrine Of The Christian Church During Its First Five Hundred Years. Pages 116–117

In the NT, Jude speaks of an "eternal" fire, the word translated eternal coming from the same word, "aionion" as used in Matthew 25. Here is the literal Greek of Jude 1:7

Jude 1:7 "As Sodom and Gomorrah and the cities about them in like manner to these committing ultra-prostitution, and coming away after other flesh, are lying before us, a specimen, experiencing the justice of fire eonian."

The "eternal" (eonian) fire that burned Sodom went out long ago! The fire of Sodom wasn't eternally lasting & neither is the "eternal fire" or punishment in Matthew 25:41–46. In my opinion, a better understanding of this word is to use it as an adverb. The word eternal as adverb describes the nature of the fire itself–ever-burning. Bible commentaries, catechetical classes, priests and theologians, have all taught this verse means the justice will be eternal. No, it is the fire which is everlasting in its nature and never goes out. It is nothing less than the everlasting fire of God's passionate love.

Considering the Greek word kolasis ("punishment" Matthew 25:46) can refer to a corrective punishment, this should tell the reader of Matthew 25:46 what the possible duration of aionios ("everlasting") is and that it may refer to a finite punishment. Why? Because since it is corrective, it is with the purpose of bringing the person corrected to salvation. Once saved the person no longer has need of such a punishment and it ends. It isn't "everlasting."

When we look to be instructed in areas with which we are unfamiliar, we should look to those who have spent years studying the issue. For me, those who have approached an issue without bias are much more reliable sources than someone who has dabbled in the subject and now thinks he is an expert. Dr. Ilaria Ramelli is an Italian-born historian, academic author, and university professor who specializes in ancient, late antique, and early mediaeval philosophy and theology. Her list of accomplishments is impressive.

> Importantly, the Bible describes the punishments of the judgment as aionia, which does not mean "eternal" unless used in reference to God, as Ramelli extensively evidences. The word aidios unqualifiedly refers to eternity, but the Bible does not use it to describe the punishments of the age. Ramelli instead offers "otherworldy," or "of the age to come," or perhaps "next-wordly" as an adequate translation of aionion when describing the punishment at the judgment. This point receives philological confirmation in a passage in Origen in which he speaks of "life after aionios life." As a native speaker of Greek, he does not see a contradiction in such phrasing; that is because aionios life does

not mean "unending, eternal life," but rather "life of the next age." Likewise, the Bible uses the word kolasis to describe the punishment of the age to come. Aristotle distinguished kolasis from timoria, the latter referring to punishment inflicted "in the interest of him who inflicts it, that he may obtain satisfaction." On the other hand, kolasis refers to correction, it "is inflicted in the interest of the sufferer" (quoted at 32). Thus, Plato can affirm that it is good to be punished (to undergo kolasis), because in this way a person is made better (ibid.). This distinction survived even past the time of the writing of the New Testament, since Clement of Alexandria affirms that God does not timoreitai, punish for retribution, but he does kolazei, correct sinners.[37]

Augustine raised the argument that since aionios in Matthew 25:46 referred to both life and punishment, it had to carry the same duration in both cases. However, he failed to consider that the duration of aionios is *determined by the subject to which it refers*. For example, when aionios referred to the duration of Jonah's entrapment in the fish, it was limited to three days. To a slave, aionios referred to his life span. To the Aaronic priesthood, it referred to the generation preceding the Melchizedek priesthood. To Solomon's temple, it referred to 400 years. To God it encompasses and transcends time altogether.

Thus, the word cannot have a set value. It is a relative term and its duration depends upon that with which it is associated. It is similar to what "tall" is to height. The size of a tall building can be 300 feet, a tall man six feet, and a tall dog three feet. Black Beauty was a great horse, Abraham Lincoln a great man, and Yahweh the Great God. Though God is called "great," the word "great" is neither eternal nor divine. The horse is still a horse. An adjective relates to the noun it modifies. In relation to God, "great" becomes great only because of who and what God is. This silences the contention that aion must always mean forever because it modifies God. God is described as the God of Israel and the God of Abraham. This does not mean He is not the God of Gentiles, or the God of you and me. Though He is called the God of the "ages," He nonetheless remains the God who transcends the ages.[38]

---

37. Ramelli, "The Christian Doctrine of Apokatastasis: A Critical Assessment from the New Testament to Eriugena," Para. 3.

38. Beauchemin, "Hope Beyond Hell: The Righteous Purpose of God's Judgment,"

The confusion over Matthew 25:46, in which Augustine and modern critics believe that aionios must carry the same weight of duration for both the wicked and the righteous, comes from misunderstanding the context of the passage. Jesus is not speaking about the end of the world. His whole discourse in Matthew is about the end of the age. Therefore, He is also speaking about what will happen in the next age. Those who believe that Matthew is about the end of the world are confused because they believe that eternity begins in Matthew 25. Once you grasp that Jesus is referring only to what is to happen in the next age–bliss for the redeemed and chastening correction for the wicked–you will stop being confused by this verse.

I am beginning to think that what we see over the centuries of biblical translation is a profoundly lazy scholarship, if you could even use the term scholarship to define what has been done to the Greek in these passages. There are two ways of reading the Scriptures. One is to let the original words in Greek speak exactly as they mean. Just as in English, red cannot denote black, so aionios cannot denote eternal when that is not the meaning. The other way of reading is to come to the Scriptures with a presupposed agenda and then bend the verses to fit your desired theological outcome. This latter appears to have been the way Western translators have approached their work.

In the year 544 A.D. the emperor Justinian wrote a letter in which he used the term "ateleutetos."

> It is conceded that the half-heathen emperor held to the idea of endless misery, for he proceeds not only to defend, but to define the doctrine. He does not merely say, "We believe in aionion kolasin," for that was just what Origen himself taught. Nor does he say "the word aionion has been misunderstood; it denotes endless duration," as he would have said, had there been such a disagreement. But, writing in Greek, with all the words of that abundant language from which to choose, he says: "The holy church of Christ teaches an endless aeonian (ateleutetos aionios) life to the righteous, and endless (ateleutetos) punishment to the wicked." If he supposed aionios denoted endless duration, he would not have added the stronger word to it. The fact that he qualified it by ateleutetos, demonstrated that as late as the sixth century the former word did not signify endless duration.[39]

Ch.1 21–31

39. Hanson, "Universalism the Prevailing Doctrine of the Christian Church During its First Five Hundred Years." Page 283

An honest inquirer, not someone who is reading with a presupposed agenda, should by now be considering these lexical problems from the standpoint of the original Greek language. The problem we face now is having it ceaselessly drummed into our minds for the last thousand years that the Bible teaches eternal punishment. But the Greek, and the testimony of usage such as mentioned above with Justinian, does not allow for this. The question then becomes what will I do with this new knowledge? Will I ignore it because my church tells me differently? Or is it possible that there has been a long-standing agenda which started with the errors of Augustine and exists up to this present day, an agenda which ultimately presents our loving heavenly Father as a monster?

My friend's paper goes on to insist, "The objection is made that there is no proportion between the brief moment of sin and an eternal punishment."

Indeed, there is not! To show just what darkness the Western theological mind devolved to, let me remind you that for a considerable time, the Roman Catholic Church taught as truth one of Augustine's most wretched errors, that unbaptized babies suffer the pains of eternal hell. By what possible stretch of justice would a loving and just God eternally torment a child innocent from his mother's womb? It was the idea of original sin by which Augustine erroneously declared all people, even children lacking the prerequisites of committing sin,[40] stand guilty of Adam's sin, and are condemned from birth. I find such thinking heinous. To me, it this is evidence the hierarchy of Rome were in some degree of spiritual darkness to accept such an idea and not rebuke Augustine.

Even the Bible does not allow for such a miscarriage of justice. God gave us the great principle of His justice–lex talionis–the punishment is proportionate to the offense. Apparently, Augustine's small and narrow view of mankind forgot about this as he rushed to proclaim all of mankind utterly depraved and worthy of punishment because all share in the guilt of Adam's sin. The Western view of God is filled with descriptions of our relationship to God in purely legal terms such as "guilt," "punishment," "satisfaction," and "substitution." My twenty-five plus years in Protestant churches was a litany of threats from an offended God who was looking for any infraction. My Christian life for years was filled with an underlying fear that perhaps I transgressed some boundary which would put me in torment forever.

After this, my friend's paper states:

---

40. Sin is an act committed with full knowledge of what one is doing, deliberate consent to the act, and is an act lacking in love towards either God or man against whom it is committed.

Again, sin is an offence against the infinite authority of God and the sinner is in some way aware of this, though but imperfectly. Accordingly, there is in sin an approximation to infinite malice which deserves an eternal punishment. Finally, it must be remembered that, although the act of sinning is brief, the guilt of sin remains forever, for in the next life, the sinner never turns away from his sin by a sincere conversion.

This is Anselm of Canterbury's thinking, that sin against an infinite God demands an infinite punishment. Infernalists point to the holiness of God as a reason the punishment for sin must be eternal in nature. But is that a legitimate argument?

> The traditionalist argument often turns to God's holiness as a basis for insisting on eternal conscious torment. For instance, the SBC's 2011 resolution on Hell declares "God must judge the unregenerate because He is a holy God whose judgments are altogether righteous." They then insist that God's judgement of the unregenerate consists of eternal conscious torment. Because God is holy, he must (more on this below) punish those who refuse his salvation with eternal conscious torment. But does the word holy warrant such connections? Graham Ware does not think so:
>
> "First, we need to have a working definition of holy. The word holy, like most Hebrew words comes from a three-consonant root (q-d-sh). The adjectival form, qodesh, usually translated as holy, means set apart, separate, or distinct. The verb form means to set apart or consecrate, the noun forms being holiness/set-apartness or holy or set apart things/people/places, (e.g., the Temple and its implements). But set apart from what? In the Hebraic sense, God is holy because he is distinct from his creation. All of reality is creator or created. God's holiness recognizes him as creator, set apart from all he created.
>
> As I just noted, the same root word was used in different noun forms to refer to the Temple (the holy place), or the objects used in the Temple. These were objects set apart for a specific purpose- the purpose of worshiping God. The basins, ladles, and showbread etc. were not to be used for every day, mundane purposes, but in worship. They were distinct from other objects because of the purpose they were dedicated to, not because of something inherent in them.
>
> This same root also had other forms and usages. For instance, qedeshim refers to shrine prostitutes. Not exactly something we would normally consider under the umbrella of "holy

things." But, in the culture of the Ancient Near East, temple servants (including those responsible for ritual sex acts) were "set apart" for the service of the deity. They did not belong to the mundane, everyday world.

So when we say that God is holy, what do we mean? And how does that holiness relate to our discussions of final punishment? Does God's holiness demand eternal torment? Does it even demand any punishment at all? Or is it simply a marker that God is distinct from everything else in creation?

The traditionalist argument for hell as eternal conscious torment often goes something like this: God is holy, and eternal, and therefore sin against this holy and eternal God has eternal ramifications. God's honor, holiness, and glory have been eternally insulted by each and every sin committed by human beings. Every sin is an eternal act because it is an act of rebellion against the eternal and holy God. Thus, all sin must be punished unendingly and experienced consciously by the offender, because recompense must restore that which was taken away

The idea that sin against God is eternal in nature because it violates his eternal honor and holiness is the invention of Anselm, writing in the 11th century. It is rooted not in Scripture, but in feudal understandings of homage; that homage to one's lord must be done in perpetuity in order to sustain the favor of said lord. Insults to the honor of the lord are punished with consequences which are doled out until the lord's honor is satisfied. Thus, if God's honor is insulted by human sin, argues Anselm, God's honor is not satisfied unless man has suffered eternally for his sin (or someone, namely the God-man, in his place, the basis for satisfaction atonement theory, which was later modified by the reformers to establish penal substitutionary atonement), because God's holiness demands his honor be acknowledged eternally. Pinnock comments on this stating:

> Anselm tried to argue that our sins are worthy of an infinite punishment because they are committed against an infinite majesty. This may have worked in the Middle Ages, but it will not work as an argument today. We do not accept inequality in judgements on the basis of the honor of the victim, as if stealing from a doctor is worse than stealing from a beggar.

This, as noted, belongs to feudal relations between lord/suzerain and serf/vassal. While there are some similarities, the Hebraic understanding of holiness is something quite different. God's holiness does not demand punitive action against those who reject him. Nor does God's holiness demand recognition. It simply is, whether humanity honors that holiness or not. God's holiness delineates him as other than creation. It marks God out as distinct or unique among everything that exists. Nothing is equal to God. Hence the refrain "Holy, Holy, Holy, is the Lord God Almighty, who was, and is, and is to come" (Rev.4:8).[41]

As Thomas Talbott argues, if every sin is infinitely serious, then the idea that we can grade offences collapses. If it is responded that perhaps people experience different levels of punishment in hell, albeit eternally, this still isn't compatible with the logic based on that God's infinity=infinite punishment, as then the punishment is not based solely on God's ontological worth but on the specific nature of the sin. This would then mean that the justice problem (apparently solved by recourse to God's infinite worth) rears its head again, as things aren't totally dependent on this infinite ontological worth, but also the specific nature of the sins. This is in line with what Jesus and St. Paul taught, that all shall be rewarded according to their deeds. Great deeds receive great rewards, while evil deeds are recompensed with punishment that is age-lasting and according to the level of malice in the deeds.

Eastern Orthodoxy does not approach sin as a matter of legal retribution, but of Christ taking on human nature, and by assuming it, healing it. The view of the East is medicinal, not judicial. At Pascha we sing (with considerable joy and enthusiasm) "Christ is risen from the dead. By death He conquered death. And to those in the graves, He granted life." Death is defeated and no longer has power over us. This is the error of Western thinking, that salvation is a matter of justice rather than healing.

THE IMPENITENCE OF THE DAMNED

There is a profoundly annoying habit of certain defenders of eternal conscious torment in which they take ideas which cannot be proven from scripture and attach an air of infallibility to them. This is especially true of the class of people known as Thomists, for whom the musings of St. Thomas Aquinas approach divine inspiration. In debates with Thomists, I sense that once Aquinas is quoted, all opposition is expected to close their books, bow the knee, and issue several deeply sorrowful mea culpas before trotting off to Confession.

Aquinas is especially pleaded in the cause of the inability of the soul to repent after death. This is problematic because it appears to place the

---

41. Ware, "Clark Pinnock, Hell, and the Holiness of God." Neither Clark Pinnock nor the site, Rethinking Hell, endorse Apokatastasis, but this passage on holiness vs eternal punishment is important.

writings of Aquinas on the level of an ecumenical council and give them the same authority as the Scriptures. His thoughts are at best Western theologoumenon, theological ideas done by a man who, while brilliant, was nonetheless expressing personal philosophical thoughts in order to attempt understanding of the One beyond understanding. Our authoritative, and quite limited, understanding of God is found in A.) The Sacred Scriptures as primary and B.) The Holy Tradition of the church as defined in ecumenical councils. The writings of Aquinas do not approach the level of authority of either of these, any more than the musings of Augustine or the Orthodox Synodikon.

My friend now directs her defense of an eternal hell to a Catholic Answers web page in which the author, Karlo Broussard, quotes Aquinas in discussing why he believes the soul cannot repent after death. I will reprint it with my own commentary and questions in response.

> Critics of the doctrine of hell often argue that it's unjust because eternal punishment exceeds the temporal nature of a mortal sin. Why should any sin we commit on earth, in time, require everlasting punishment in hell? It's not proportional.[42]

It is most certainly not proportional! The Bible teaches us the punishment for an offense is to be equal to the offense. (lex talionis) Thus, we do not hang a hungry child for stealing a loaf of bread. Does God give us a moral standard He Himself is not bound to? Christ taught we are to be like our Father in heaven. If mankind has been commanded to give punishments proportional to the offense, is God any less bound by the very law of punishment which He gave to guide our earthly justice?

> St. Thomas Aquinas responded to this objection by saying that the measure of a punishment is not determined by the duration of the fault, but rather by its gravity. And since for Aquinas a mortal sin "in a certain respect is infinite," being committed against God, he concludes that "a punishment that is infinite in duration is rightly inflicted for mortal sin."[43]

Where does Acquinas get such an idea? Perhaps from the musings of Anselm of Canterbury, who produced a similar idea in his work Cur Deus Homo. By the standard of lex talionis, the only sin which would have the gravity of demanding an infinite punishment would be if I could do an infinite killing. In other words, only if I could kill God, the Infinite One, would I deserve a punishment in kind–infinite punishment.

---

42. Broussard, "Why We Can't Change Our Soul After Death." Para. 1
43. Broussard, "Why We Can't Change Our Soul After Death." Para. 2

> There is another conundrum, though: the infinite duration of punishment can be just only if the sinner no longer has the ability to repent and will the good. Aquinas writes:
>
> > There would be no everlasting punishment of the souls of the damned if they were able to change their will for a better will; it would be unjust, indeed, if from the moment of their having a good will their punishment would be everlasting (Summa Contra Gentiles 4.93).
>
> In other words, the infinite duration of punishment due a mortal sin is just only if a person is no longer able to change his will for the better.
>
> So, the question before us is: Is a soul able to redirect its will and choose God as its ultimate end after death?[44]

No, the real question is this: why would God, who wills all be saved, and who has declared in scripture that He will have mercy on all, block, hinder, or in some way make it impossible for a soul to repent after death? All power in the human soul comes from Him, not from ourselves. Outside of Him, we are nothing and can do nothing. The real issue here is, does God withhold from man the power to repent after death? If He does, then He is working contrary to the Bible, which says that it is His will to save all.

> The Catholic Church says no. For example, the Catechism teaches, "there is no repentance for men after death," and bases this teaching on the irrevocable character that man's choice takes on after the soul separates from the body–similar to that of the angels (CCC 393). This is why the Catechism defines hell as the "definitive self-exclusion from communion with God and the blessed" (1033; emphasis added).[45]

You have no biblical point of reference for this, just like there is no point of reference for Indulgences, Purgatory, the Immaculate Conception, Original Sin, etc. This is a theologoumenon, and an incredibly sad one at that. What hope does this give to those who have seen their loved ones die outside the church and outside a relationship with Christ? How does this reflect upon the mercy of God? This seems to me to be the logical fallacy of Appeal to Authority. In other words, because we say so, it is.

> But why does our choice become irrevocable after death? To answer this question, we must first consider why our choices are mutable in this life.

---

44. Broussard, "Why We Can't Change Our Soul After Death." Para.3–6.
45. Broussard, "Why We Can't Change Our Soul After Death." Para. 7

> As human beings, we're hardwired to choose things insofar as we perceive some good in them that will make us happy. We can't help it. Even to ask the question, "Why should I choose what's good?" presupposes a desire for the good; otherwise, why would we ask whether we should choose what's good or not?[46]

Exactly. Now prove to me that this desire for the good somehow ceases after death. In thinking about the idea of an eternal hell, one must say that it continues, for the suffering of hell comes from now seeing the good, wanting it, but being denied it, elsewise there would be no suffering, for the soul would be indifferent to its state of separation from God. Therefore, we can assume that the desire for the good continues after death. But after death, the false goods (lust of the flesh, lust of the eyes, pride of life) are seen for what they are and the true good, Christ in all His beauty, is seen by the soul as the real good.

> Now, all these causes for change in our choices (fleeting passions, a change of habit, and correction of intellectual error) involve the body.[47]

No, they don't. They involve the will. The body is merely an outlet by which the intellect and will can assert what they desire. Aquinas believes that through the various information received in the body, the intellect is brought to change in its outlook and a change of will takes place. But this change of information will most definitely take place when the soul meets God. Aquinas is insisting that only within the realm of bodily information can our will be brought to change its desires. But he has no proof of this other than his belief that the body is necessary for this change in intellect and will to take place.

In the Bible, we see God, who is spirit and has not a body as man, changing His will. He is said to repent. Moreover, we see this ability is not limited to God. Satan was at one time the light-bearer of heaven, the most glorious of the angels. But at some point, his will to serve God turned to rebellion. This is a change of choice to serve God, in a created being that is pure spirit. Aquinas' insistence that a body is necessary for repentance must therefore be mistaken.

What about the prayers for the dead? Of what good are these prayers if the dead cannot repent and turn from their selfishness to surrender to God? And this is critical, because unlike Roman legal thinking, salvation is a change in the ontology of the person, not a declaration of forgiveness

---

46. Broussard, "Why We Can't Change Our Soul After Death." Para. 8–9.
47. Broussard, "Why We Can't Change Our Soul After Death." Para. 17.

which makes everything legally okay. In Roman Catholicism, a man can live a life of disinterest in God and the church, receive the Viaticum, and make heaven because his sins are forgiven by this one legal act. But that does not address the real issue, which is the condition of the soul. If the soul of the person is not in love with God, all these acts have no worth. How will that soul find union with the God whom he ignored all his life and wished nothing to do with? One could live a scandalous life and then make confession on one's deathbed which may well be not an act of love for God, but rather trying to find the door marked "Fire Escape." In other words, if death was not imminent, the soul would not repent. It may well be a false confession, motivated by wrong desires which have nothing to do with an actual change of heart.

Luther objected to the selling of Indulgences as a "get out of hell free" card for souls who had died. You buy the Indulgence and bingo!–God releases the soul. That's not how it works. In Orthodoxy we understand the necessity for a complete ontological change in the person. Therefore, we engage in fasting, prayers, and the sacraments, to change ourselves interiorly in the same way medicine goes into a body and heals it by killing off the disease. A soul that dies in a state of sin and rebellion against God is still sick, and no buying of a thousand indulgences will change that state of being. The soul's very ontological orientation must be changed. That is done either by the ascetic and self-sacrificial life here on earth now, or it happens in a much more painful manner under the scourging of God's restorative correction in eternity.

> It's obvious that fleeting passions and dominating sensitive appetites do. Yet even our cognitive processes involve the body. We use our sensory experience to gather information about something, we use mental images as aids when we're trying to reason with certain concepts, and so forth. This is our mode of knowledge as a rational animal. This being the case, certain passions and the habitual indulgence of sensitive appetites can lead us into intellectual error. Aquinas's teaching on "blindness of mind" as a daughter of lust is an example of this (ST II-II:15:3).
>
> We're now in a position to see why our choice becomes irrevocable after death.
>
> If those things that motivate us to change our course of action are rooted in the body, then it follows that when the body is gone the disembodied soul will no longer be able to change its choice. The soul will be forever fixed on whatever it chose as its ultimate end.[48]

48. Broussard, "Why We Can't Change Our Soul After Death." Para 18–20.

As I have shown from scripture and prayer for the dead, this is not so. Not only this, but how just would it be to fix a soul in a state of separation from God when it had no idea of God? What of the pagans who thought God was found in a tree or was a snake because they had never heard the Gospel? Shall God eternally fix them in their state of ignorance merely because they had the misfortune of being born in the wrong place at the wrong time? To me, this smacks of cold-blooded self-righteousness. I'm saved and you aren't. Too bad for you!

> There is no longer any fleeting passion that can distract the soul. There is no dominating sensitive appetite to pull the will away from what it sets its sight on. The will, therefore, becomes habitually aimed at that which it chose as its ultimate end upon death.[49]

What fleeting passion of the body did God have when He repented of His intentions to destroy Ninevah? What fleeting passions did Satan have to start a war in heaven and get cast out? But more than that, it is patently unfair to take a soul which has never even heard of Christ, the Gospel, or the love of God, and insist this soul has made a free will choice and is set upon that choice forever. What freedom to choose did the pagans in Africa have for fifteen hundred years until the Gospel reached them? Infernalists insist God is just, therefore, to be just, there must be at least one glimpse of Christ in all His beauty and love, unhindered by any outside distraction, event, distortion, or deceit, so the soul can exercise a truly free will to make an objective decision. No decision here on earth is either free or objective due to the internal and external issues which afflict us.

> Also, there is no intellectual error to be made, since the preconditions for erroneous judgments (discursive reasoning with the use of sensation and imagination) are no longer present. The soul's mode of knowledge upon death is very much like that of the angels: what is known is known all-at-once (ST I:68:3).[50]

Exactly! But if the truth is finally known, if all deceit and falsehood are stripped away and Christ is seen in all His glory, kindly tell me how a soul would not at once desire this beauty and love which constantly flows from the throne of grace?

> Rather than hell undermining God's justice, it's actually a manifestation of it. God allows the soul to function in accord with

---

49. Broussard, "Why We Can't Change Our Soul After Death." Para. 21.
50. Broussard, "Why We Can't Change Our Soul After Death." Para. 22.

its nature, which includes the irrevocability of choices without the body. So, if a person dies choosing something other than God as his final end, that choice is irrevocable. It's "locked on," so to speak, to something other than God. And it's locked on forever.[51]

It is a horrendous view of God to say He allows the soul to function in accord with its nature. The whole point of salvation is that the nature of man has been corrupted and cannot function properly. It needs to be healed to return to its original and proper function. If God looked at all of us and decided to let us all function according to our nature, not one single person would ever have been redeemed because the nature of all mankind is corrupted from birth!

Finally, the statement that hell is a manifestation of God's justice is correct–only if it comes to a point of finality. Proper justice should be done to the goal of rehabilitation of the offender. Any punishment that does not seek this end is not justice, it is viciousness under the guise of justice.

Final impenitence is, in the end, a piece of speculation which finds its foundation in scholasticism. Scholasticism is regarded in the Orthodox East as the West trying to define every mystery of God and bring those mysteries into definable terminology. We do not do this in the East. For instance, we have no definition like Transubstantiation. We call the Eucharist the "Divine Mysteries" and leave them mystery. There are many Orthodox who are not particularly enamored of Scholasticism. Writing like this is one reason why.

THE DAMNED ARE CONFIRMED IN EVIL: EVERY ACT OF THEIR WILL IS EVIL AND INSPIRED BY HATRED OF GOD.

My friend's paper continues with additional extracts from Aquinas. In them, Aquinas makes statements which I find considerably disturbing. I try to remember he was a product of his times and the culture of Roman courtroom justice.

> From what has been said it follows that the hatred which the lost soul bears to God is voluntary in its cause only; and the cause is the deliberate sin which it committed on earth and by which it merited reprobation. It is also obvious that God is not responsible for the reprobates' material sins of hate, because by *granting His co-operation in their sinful acts as well,* as by refusing them

---

51. Broussard, "Why We Can't Change Our Soul After Death," Para 23.

every incitement to good, He acts quite in accordance with the nature of their state. Therefore, their sins are no more imputable to God than are the blasphemies of a man in the state of total intoxication, although they are not uttered *without divine assistance.*[52]

The phrase "a soul meriting reprobation" again takes us to the idea of God as Cosmic Courtroom Judge in which He deals with guilt or innocence. This is not the view of the early fathers, who spoke of salvation in terms of sickness and divine healing. The Eucharist was called "the medicine of immortality." In Aquinas' view, which I believe was thoroughly influenced by Augustine's anthropology (man as worthless dung), God looks to find fault as judge. At what point of sin does a soul merit reprobation? How many sins get to the point at which God says, "Okay, I no longer will to save that one. He's toast!" And for what hated of God did the Roman Catholic Church assign babies to hell?

When St. Photius received the Greek translation of Augustine's works, it is said he was horrified at the theological errors in it. It is unfortunate the scholastics in the West spent so much time defending such distasteful theologoumenon rather than correcting Augustine's mistakes. Christianity would have been a lot better had they done the latter.

The next statement is truly shocking to me. Am I really reading the idea that God grants His co-operation in sinful acts and withholds every incitement to good? This makes God in some sense the author of evil, since He grants co-operation rather than inciting in the soul a rejection of evil. Is there any time the Holy Spirit refuses to strike the conscience of the sinner to try to bring about a sense of guilt and repentance, even the most hardened of sinners? You may reply, "After a soul reaches a certain stage, the Spirit of God does not strive anymore with it." In the context of apokatastasis, this means the will of God changes towards the sinner, going from love and a will to save all, to hatred and a will to damn certain souls damned. How is this compatible with the teaching that God is unchangeable and immutable, that is, without passions? This quote seems to say that a sinner can come to a certain point in pursuing evil whereby divine love–the very nature of God–in some manner changes and becomes hatred. God stops being love and becomes something else to the sinner? This is ridiculous!

To say that God acts according to the nature of our state is to condemn all mankind. Remember the man in the discussion of free will, the one immersed in drugs, fornication, and hatred of God? If God had done that with him, or with any of us for that matter, he would still be in his state of sin.

---

52. "Hell." New Advent. Para. 22

No, God most definitely does not act according to the nature of our state. Thanks be to God!

The Orthodox faith has a much better explanation of the relationship of God to the sinner. God, being immutable, does not change. He is ever love, ever mercy, ever long-suffering. It is the sinner's relationship to this ontological reality of divine love which determines how the soul experiences God. For the soul that dies in a state of intoxication with sin, the love of God is experienced as torment. This is the same as the experience of the Egyptian army as they pursued Moses and the Israelites to the Red Sea. The same pillar the Hebrew people experienced as light was darkness to the Egyptians. It is a picture of how the same presence of God can be experienced differently by different people, depending not on the unchangeable God, but by the condition of the person. In apokatastasis, this unchanging love ever continues to be expressed to the sinner until it breaks down even the most hardened of souls.

The same is true of the last part of the quote. Does God truly assist the sinner in uttering blasphemies? Perhaps someone who is more proficient in Aquinas than I am can offer an explanation and clear up something I am missing here. If the will of God is the salvation of all, then to aid the sinner in pursuing wickedness runs contrary to the divine will. I am starting to get a feel for why David Bentley Hart has a certain distaste for Thomists.[53]

One final thing for my Roman Catholic interlocutors. If you are going to insist Aquinas is the final word on theological matters, then you must abandon the Immaculate Conception. Aquinas would have none of it!

In this section on final impenitence, the last appeal is made to the parable of the Rich Man and Lazarus:

> For in death there is no one that is mindful of Thee. He knows too that now is the time for turning unto God: for when this life shall have passed away, there remaineth but a retribution of our deserts. "But in hell who shall confess to Thee?" That rich man, of whom the Lord speaks, who saw Lazarus in rest, but bewailed himself in torments, confessed in hell, yea so as to wish even

---

53. "I was once told by a young, ardently earnest Thomist . . . you know, one of those manualist neo-paleo-neo-Thomists of the baroque persuasion you run across ever more frequently these days, gathered in the murkier corners of coffee bars around candles in wine bottles, clad in black turtlenecks and berets, sipping espresso, smoking Gauloises, swaying to bebop, composing dithyrambic encomia to that-absolutely gone, totally wild, starry-bright and vision-wracked, mad angelic daddy-cat Garrigou-Lagrange. . . ." Hart, "Vinculum Magnumentis," Para. 1. This is just classic Hart in all his glory. Yes, I am a Hartist, and I make no apology for it. I am an admirer of a brilliant mind given to snarky destruction of the indefensible idea of a monster God who torments poor souls which He created for no other reason than their eternal destruction.

to have his brethren warned, that they might keep themselves from sin, because of the punishment which is not believed to be in hell. Although therefore to no purpose, yet he confessed that those torments had deservedly lighted upon him; since he even wished his brethren to be instructed, lest they should fall into the same.[54]

Note again Augustine's Roman courtroom thinking in which he declares that after death God gets His retribution. I cannot help but think that the cultural environment in which Augustine lived deeply influenced his ideas about God just as much as his Platonism.

Notice also what Augustine missed. If you take this as real story and not a parable, the Rich Man had already begun to repent in his torment. He, who formerly was indifferent about others, now begs to have his brothers warned. This is metanoia, a change of mind, which is repentance. How is this possible if Aquinas's postulation of final impenitence is true?

While Augustine took this parable as a real story, as do many who read it, biblically speaking I find a much stronger case to take the symbols in the parable and apply them to national Israel.

The Rich Man symbolizes Israel. How was national Israel rich? Through her special relationship with God as the chosen people. Israel had the riches of God's presence and leading, the Temple, and the relationship they had. The priests were clothed in purple and fine linen. I believe upon hearing these words, the priestly class listening to Christ would have begun to identify with it and take closer notice.

If national Israel was indeed the rich man who fared sumptuously every day, who was the beggar? It was the Gentile nations who had none of the riches of a relationship with God. No temple, no law of God, no prophets, and no true worship. In terms of the true riches, the riches of being God's special and chosen people, they were bankrupt. The crumbs which fell from the rich man's table could be the incidental hearing of the Jewish scriptures or seeing the worship in the Temple from the Outer Court of the Gentiles. These were crumbs, but not the full meal which the Jews enjoyed.

In parable both men die. When we think of death, it is normal to think of the cessation of life in the human body. But in scripture, death connotes something besides that. In Genesis 3 we see Adam and Eve die, but they are still alive. In the Parable of the Prodigal Son, the father says "For this my son was dead, and is alive again . . . " In neither case do we see the cessation of physical life. What we see is separation, Adam and Eve from Paradise, the son from his father's presence. In the parable of the Rich Man and Lazarus,

---

54. "Exposition on Psalms 6," Para. 6.

both men are separated from the condition in which they exist and find themselves in a new condition. Thus they "die" to their old life.

The rich man died to his existence and became poor. He was without all the luxuries and benefits which he had previously enjoyed, and this was a torment to him. This is a picture of Judaism, which no longer enjoys the special covenant relationship with God it once had. National Israel is no longer God's special people. In the Parable of the Wicked Husbandmen, national Israel is cast out of the vineyard (the Kingdom of God) and replaced. These two parables describe the same event. National Israel's covenant with God ended in AD 70 with the destruction of Jerusalem. They are replaced by the church, the nation of the Gentiles. Those who were once beggars for crumbs from God's table now feast upon the riches of Liturgy, Sacraments, and the Word of God.

It is interesting to see how the beggar was brought to Abraham's bosom. He was carried by angels. The word angel means "messenger." Who were the messengers who brought the Gentile nations out of their spiritual poverty and into God's rich and abundant mercy? The Apostles. They brought the message of the Gospel, the Good News of the Resurrection and God's favor, to the ends of the known world, bringing with them the invitation to enter the covenant which began with Abraham. St. Paul says "Know ye therefore that they which are of faith, the same are the children of Abraham." Abraham's bosom is where the covenant father, Abraham, holds his children close to him in a special relationship.

On the other hand, in terms of their covenant with God being destroyed, national Israel was buried in AD 70 when Jerusalem was destroyed by the Roman armies of Titus and the Temple razed to the ground. This burial was confirmed by later attempts to rebuild the Temple being met with disaster and death.

It is beyond my understanding how people can take this parable and make a literal story out of it when they do no such thing with other parables, but instead read them as parables and then try to find the meaning to them. What is being done here by Infernalists is reading the parable through a lens of presupposition. When the words death and torment appear in the parable, the Infernalist mind immediately flips over to thinking that this must be about the eternal hell in which they believe.

Part Three

The Eternity of Hell from the Church Fathers and Scripture

THE NEXT SECTION OF my friend's paper calls upon certain church fathers to support the argument for eternal hell. I find this almost amusing in an odd way. A typical defense of all hellist apologists is to look only to those quotes of the early fathers which support their position while ignoring those church fathers who write against them. This is another onslaught to which I am supposed to raise the white flag of surrender.

    The church fathers, those men who lived in the first several centuries of the developing Christian faith, are important because by reading them, we get an understanding of early Christian belief. Why is this important? Well, to give you a personal example, when I was a Protestant, I simply believed what I was told about Holy Communion. I was taught it was not the very Body and Blood of our Lord, the false doctrine being invented by Emperor Constantine

    But when I discovered the early fathers, I discovered men who lived before Constantine's conversion who believed in the Real Presence, thus voiding this argument. Furthermore, some had been taught directly by the apostles. It was unthinkable that such men, willing to lay down their lives in martyrdom, would distort that which they were taught. They were also the men who hammered out the important doctrines of the faith which we must believe today to be orthodox in our Christianity. At councils such as Nicea and Constantinople I, they issued stout condemnations against heresies about the Trinity, the natures of Christ, and other doctrines vital to correct belief. What they taught shows us how the Scriptures were understood. The importance of these men brought me to leave Protestantism because I simply could not find Protestantism in their writings.

The opening salvo in this section against apokatastasis comes from the website of J. Warner Wallace. Wallace is aggrandized on his website as being a "cold-case detective" of immense ability, yet in his investigation of the Christian faith, it appears his detective skills have rather miserably failed him. He has missed several clues which point to the fact that the Protestant distinctives in which he believes did not exist for sixteen centuries.

Wallace uses the church fathers as an authoritative source to prove the existence of eternal hell, which I find a bit hypocritical. As a Protestant, he would deny their authority in what they wrote about the Eucharist being the very Body and Blood of Christ. I call this an appeal to selective reasoning, i.e., you choose only those things which prove your case and ignore all other arguments which might weaken it. In the same vein of selective reasoning, I find no mention by him of the many fathers who did teach apokatastasis. I challenge his first statement: "The early church fathers, with few exceptions, agree with traditional views descriptions of Hell as a place of eternal, conscious torment."

Few exceptions? Not true, sir! You have no idea about the numbers and/or percentages of people who believed in apokatastasis. The fact that four of six theological schools in the first five hundred years of the Christian faith taught apokatastasis points to this being more than just a fringe belief. Only one school taught eternal conscious torment, and significantly, it was a school of the Latin church. Therefore, it does make sense you would be able to find some early fathers who were trained as Infernalists and be able to source their quotes to try to prove your position. But to make apokatastasis a fringe belief, especially when four schools taught it, is at least dishonest. He has also missed Augustine's confession that a vast number of people in his day taught apokatastasis.

Wallace then makes four points:

1. "Hell is a place of judgment for those who have rejected God and denied Jesus as their Savior." As mentioned elsewhere, Orthodoxy denies this. Hell is not a place; it is a state of being. Saint Pope John Paul the Great stated as much in one of his papal writings.

2. "Hell is a place of separation from God." Wrong again. This is the Western view. Hell is God experienced as torment, because it is being in the very presence of God and not wanting to be there. It is love experienced as torment because of your love for sin. Where in the universe is the place where God is not?

3. "Hell is a place of torment in which the rebellious are in anguish and pain." Well, yes, there is anguish and pain. Sin brings correction. It just doesn't happen to last forever because God is love and God is just. Neither love nor justice would create an eternity of torment.

4. "Hell is a place where the rebellious are tormented forever and are conscious of this torment for all eternity." Not according to the Greek in the Scriptures. Not according to the fact that God is love and God is just. Not according to the very character of God. This is more in line with the pagan ideas of God and the afterlife than it is with the Greek New Testament. Perhaps after Constantine made Christianity the official religion of the Roman Empire, pagan ideas slowly seeped into the theological woodwork, including ancient ideas of eternal torment by angry gods.[1]

Another problem with using the early fathers as a reference is that unless they are speaking in an ecumenical council, the best you can say is their reflections are only a theologoumenon, a privately held understanding or definition. Such thoughts do not have the authority of being sacred scripture, nor a canon of an ecumenical council. Therefore, appealing to them has no weight in the search for truth.[2] They may be, in fact, quite influenced by the culture in which they were developed. For instance, the one theological school which taught eternal torment was a Latin school with its emphasis on crime and punishment.

But there is a more fundamental problem. The writings from which he quotes are not in their original Greek language. What is posted on his site are Western translations, and as mentioned before, many of the linguists who took on the translation of the Greek into Latin were deficient in properly understanding Greek.

> The first proof Wallace offers is from the Epistle of Barnabas: "The way of darkness is crooked, and it is full of cursing. It is the way of eternal death, with punishment." The Epistle of Barnabas (70–130 AD).[3]

---

1. Wallace, "What Did the Early Christians Believe About Hell?" Para. 2.

2. Of course, to be honest about it, this works both ways. Therefore, I must have more than just the quotes of the Fathers on my side. It is my hope that by the time you have reached the end of this book, the weight of the Scriptures, properly interpreted, and the use of reason, especially in discussing what little we know about God, will carry the day.

3. Wallace, "What Did the Early Christians Believe About Hell?" Para. 6.

In what language was the original written? That's right–Greek! With a Google search, I found the original text. From our earlier discussion of the Greek word "aionios" you should realize there could be a problem with the translation of Barnabas from Greek to Latin, and then to the English we read today.

The Greek word which has been translated eternal in Barnabas is the same aionios which Dr. Ilaria Ramelli has noted, does not necessarily mean "eternal." There is a specific word for eternal in Greek. The Greek word for eternal is "adidios." But when you have been taught to translate aionios as "eternal," you follow what you have been taught as an obedient member of the church. It is also interesting to note that in the full English text online, the English translation uses the words "thou" and "thee." I discount the Epistle of Barnabas as being an indelible proof of eternal hell. This is more likely Medieval translation from the Greek–and a bad one.

Researching the next quote, from Ignatius of Antioch, I found more errors in translation. The New Advent translation of Ignatius' letter to the Ephesians reads:

> Do not err, my brethren. James 1:16 Those that corrupt families shall not inherit the kingdom of God. 1 Corinthians 6:9–10. If, then, those who do this as respects the flesh have suffered death, how much more shall this be the case with anyone who corrupts by wicked doctrine the faith of God, for which Jesus Christ was crucified! Such an one becoming defiled [in this way], shall go away into everlasting fire, and so shall every one that hearkens unto him.[4]

This again is not what the Greek text says. It took me a few minutes to figure this out because in my research I was reading the New Advent mistranslation and trying to find it in the Greek text of Ignatius. Only when I went back to my friend's paper did I realize my mistake. The translation in her paper is correct:

> Those that corrupt families shall not inherit the kingdom of God. If, then, those who do this as respects the flesh have suffered death, how much more shall this be the case with anyone who corrupts by wicked doctrine the faith of God, for which Jesus Christ was crucified! Such an one becoming defiled [in this way], shall go away into *unquenchable* fire, and so shall every one that hearkens unto him.

---

4. New Advent, "The Epistle of Ignatius to the Ephesians," Para. 17.

That is exactly what the Greek reads. The Greek word for unquenchable is asbestos! What the translators have done here is to superimpose their own understanding on the text rather than look at the Greek words. Unquenchable does not mean eternal any more than red means green! The New Advent translation of Ignatius isn't even in line with other Latin translations. It is profoundly dishonest to take the word asbestos and say it means eternal.

Hebrews 12:29 For our God is a consuming fire.

The early fathers taught that this unquenchable fire is the passionate love of God. It consumes all which is not like Him, cleansing us and making us pure. It can never be put out, never ended, never stopped. It is a love eternal, and thus is indeed the unquenchable fire. To try to make this the same as eternal punishment is reading into the text what Wallace desires to see and has been trained to see by those who have overseen his conversion to Christianity.

The same is true of the next quote we are given, which is from Second Clement 5:5.

> If we do the will of Christ, we shall obtain rest; but if not, if we neglect his commandments, nothing will rescue us from eternal punishment. ("Second Clement" 5:5)[5]

Once again, the word translated eternal is aionios. By now it should start to be clear there are legitimately serious concerns with any of the quotes from the early fathers used by Infernalists to try to prove eternal conscious torment.

Wallace should also realize something else about the early fathers. These Greek-speaking men had great regard for the writings of the Apostles and St. Paul. If the word aionios in the Scriptures only meant eternal, then there is no way that the teaching of apokatastasis would have hung around Christianity for five hundred years! It would have been early brought to a council, declared a heresy, and done with.

Then there are presuppositions within certain quotes which do not directly mention eternal torment. For instance, this quote from Athenagoras of Athens (175 AD)

> We are persuaded that when we are removed from the present life we will live another life, better than the present one . . . or, if they fall with the rest, they will endure a worse life, one in fire. For God has not made us as sheep or beasts of burden, who are mere by-products. For animals perish and are annihilated.

---

5. Wallace, "What Did the Early Christians Believe About Hell?" Para. 10.

> On these grounds, it is not likely that we would wish to do evil. ("Apology")[6]

Notice there is no direct wording in this quote in which Athenagoras says the fire, or the life lived in it, is everlasting, only that it exists, something with which we Universalists would agree. Wallace is guilty of reading into the text an assumption which he wishes to see to support his position. The nature of the fire is undeclared. It is only said we should not be likely to want to do evil if we understand what is waiting for evil doers–a sure and certain just punishment for our choices.

Another quote in which the author reads into it what he wishes to see comes from Tatian (160AD)

> We who are now easily susceptible to death, will afterwards receive immortality with either enjoyment or with pain. (Ante-Nicene Fathers 1.71)[7]

There is nothing in this quote which suggests eternal suffering. Nothing says the pain is eternal. This is again reading into the text.

There is one more objection I would add to these and other quotes from the early fathers. It is the use of selective arguments chosen to bolster one's position while ignoring others. Mr. Wallace prefers those who defend the idea of an eternal hell of torment while ignoring saints of the church such as Isaac of Syria and Gregory of Nyssa.

From Clement of Alexandria (195AD)

> Titus Flavius Clemens was the first significant and recorded Christian from the church of Alexandria, Egypt. His parents were Greek, and he was raised with a solid, formal Greek education. While he tended to blend Greek and Christian philosophies, his view on the issue of hell was derived from the Scriptures:
>
> "All souls are immortal, even those of the wicked. Yet, it would be better for them if they were not deathless. For they are punished with the endless vengeance of quenchless fire. Since they do not die, it is impossible for them to have an end put to their misery. (From a post-Nicene manuscript fragment)"[8]

This quote is a theologoumenon. These are Clement's personal thoughts, not scripture, and therefore, subject to error, such as in the above quote which declares all souls are immortal. The Bible says otherwise. All

6. Wallace, "What Did the Early Christians Believe About Hell?" Para. 17.
7. Wallace, "What Did the Early Christians Believe About Hell?" Para. 14.
8. Wallace, "What Did the Early Christians Believe About Hell?" Para. 24.

souls are by nature mortal. Only God is immortal. His view on hell was not derived from scripture but from some external source, which was Greek philosophy:

> The concept of a soul within us that cannot die first became a 'Christian' doctrine at the end of the second century AD. Hell had been taught in Greek philosophy long before the time of Jesus, with Plato (427–347 BC) as the important leader in this thinking.
>
> The teaching of an everlasting place of punishment for the wicked is the natural consequence of a belief in an immortal soul. By the year AD 187, it was understood that life, once we have it, is compulsory; there is no end to it, either now or in a world to come. We have no choice as to its continuance, even if we were to commit suicide to end it.
>
> At the end of the 2nd century Christianity had begun to blend Greek philosophy–human speculative reasoning, with the teachings of God's Word. Such words and phrases as 'continuance of being', 'perpetual existence', 'incapable of dissolution' and 'incorruptible' began to appear in so-called Christian writings. These had come straight from Plato, the Greek philosopher, all those years before Jesus. Other phrases used were 'the soul to remain by itself immortal', and 'an immortal nature.' It was taught that this is how God made us. But this idea derives from philosophy, not divine inspiration. There are no such words in the Bible. It was Athenagorus, a Christian, but whose teachings, according to the Encyclopedia Britannica, were strongly tinged with Platonism, who had introduced the teaching of an immortal soul into Christianity. In this way, he paved the way for the logical introduction of eternal torment for immortal, but sinful, souls. This was a hundred years and more after the time of the apostles and came straight from popular philosophy.[9]

Tertullian (197AD)

Quintus Septimius Florens Tertullianus was a Romanized African citizen who was born in Carthage (now Tunisia). He became a Christian and was a powerful and influential apologist for the faith, writing prolifically in defense of the doctrines of orthodoxy:

> These have further set before us the proofs He has given of His majesty in judgments by floods and fires, the rules appointed by Him for securing His favor, as well as the retribution

---

9. Fudge, "The Origin of Hell-Fire in Christian Teaching." Para 1–3.

in store for the ignoring, forsaking and keeping them, as being about at the end of all to adjudge His worshipers to everlasting life, and the wicked to the doom of fire at once without ending and without break, raising up again all the dead from the beginning, reforming and renewing them with the object of awarding either recompense.("Apology" 18:3)

Then will the entire race of men be restored to receive its just deserts according to what it has merited in this period of good and evil, and thereafter to have these paid out in an immeasurable and unending eternity. Then there will be neither death again nor resurrection again, but we shall be always the same as we are now, without changing. The worshipers of God shall always be with God, clothed in the proper substance of eternity. But the godless and those who have not turned wholly to God will be punished in fire equally unending, and they shall have from the very nature of this fire, divine as it were, a supply of incorruptibility. ("Apology" 44:12–13)

Therefore after this there is neither death nor repeated resurrections, but we shall be the same that we are now, and still unchanged–the servants of God, ever with God, clothed upon with the proper substance of eternity; but the profane, and all who are not true worshippers of God, in like manner shall be consigned to the punishment of everlasting fire–that fire which, from its very nature indeed, directly ministers to their incorruptibility. ("Apology" 48:12)[10]

Romanized African citizen–and his writing shows the effect of being Roman. The paragraphs smack of Roman law court language: judgments, rules, retribution, repayment. In describing the judgments of God as proofs of God's majesty, he sounds like the law-imbued Calvinists who say that the damnation of souls shows forth God's power and glory. Oh goody! A God who creates sentient beings for the purpose of damning them forever, and that to show how wonderful, glorious, and powerful He is! Marvelous!

Tertullian's' statement that we shall always be the same as we are now without changing runs contrary to Orthodox eschatology. When I was entered into the Byzantine Catholic Church, I was taught was that in eternity, we will ever be growing in our knowledge of God, yet never exhausting Him because He is infinite and far beyond our ability to ever exhaust. Ever growing and yet never reaching a point of satiation while at the same time being infinitely happy in the presence of and in union with divine love. This is also in line with the Roman Catholic Catechism. Tertullian's statement

---

10. Wallace, "What Did the Early Christians Believe About Hell?" Para. 25–28.

appears to contradict prayers offered for our deceased loved ones. If they cannot change, if they are locked into the state in which they died, then I have been wasting my breath, as have a lot of other Christians from the very beginning of the Christian faith. This is speculation by Tertullian, and until I see this either in scripture or the canons of an ecumenical council, I have every right to reject this idea as merely his opinion, which I believe is wrong.

The second part I dispute goes against directly against scripture. Tertullian condemns all who are not true worshippers of God, but Paul speaks of Gentiles who know not God but who do that which is proper. One would have to assume therefore that not knowing God as Gentiles, they also would have a wrong worship. This comment is fundamentalism at its worst, the kind which says unless you worship in our way or belong to our church, you will burn in hell. In the well-known passage about the Judgment Seat of Christ, where the sheep and goats are separated, we see no such condemnation the wicked. Their condemnation comes because they did not feed the hungry, visit the sick, or clothe the naked. They did not do love. The correctness of their theology is not taken into consideration, although I am sure men like Wallace will try to slide theological precision in the side door to prove that wrong worship is the reason for their condemnation. I have lost count of the number of times I have been told I am going to hell for either an imprecise belief–such as writing this horrible, heretical book on God's immense, universal love–or not belonging to a particular denomination.

Tertullian, in turn, deeply influenced another Early Father quoted by Wallace–St. Cyprian of Carthage:

> An ever-burning Gehenna and the punishment of being devoured by living flames will consume the condemned; nor will there be any way in which the tormented can ever have respite or be at an end. Souls along with their bodies will be preserved for suffering in unlimited agonies . . . The grief at punishment will then be without the fruit of repentance; weeping will be useless, and prayer ineffectual. Too late will they believe in eternal punishment, who would not believe in eternal life ("To Demetrian" 24)
>
> Oh, what and how great will that day be at its coming, beloved brethren, when the Lord shall begin to count up His people, and to recognize the deservings of each one by the inspection of His divine knowledge, to send the guilty to Gehenna, and to set on fire our persecutors with the perpetual burning of a *penal fire*, but to pay to us the reward of our faith and devotion! ("To Thibaris" 55:10)[11]

---

11. Wallace, "What Did Early Christians Believe About Hell?" Para. 35–36.

Both Tertullian and Cyprian were brought up in the Latin-speaking Roman Empire three centuries after Christ. This means their thinking was influenced by Roman law and did not comprehend the way the Jewish mind would have understood the Scriptures. This is no small issue.

> Cyprian was born into a rich, pagan, Berber (Roman African), Carthaginian family sometime during the early third century. His original name was Thascius; he took the additional name Caecilius in memory of the priest to whom he owed his conversion. Before his conversion, he was a *leading member of a legal fraternity in Carthage*, an orator, a "pleader in the courts," and a teacher of rhetoric. After a "dissipated youth," Cyprian was baptised when he was thirty-five years old, c. 245 AD. After his baptism, he gave away a portion of his wealth to the poor of Carthage, as befitted a man of his status.
>
> In the early days of his conversion he wrote an Epistola ad Donatum de gratia Dei and the Testimoniorum Libri III that adhere closely to the models of Tertullian, *who influenced his style and thinking*.[12]

Cyprian was a lawyer. I have no doubt his approach to God was a strictly legal one. In thinking about the Roman mind and its adherence to law, I find it odd that the saints felt no sense of injustice in a punishment which had no purpose and was unequal to the offense committed. Cyprian makes certain statements that I cannot find Christ making, such as his insistence that there is no repentance after death for the wicked. One must ask how he knows this with the surety he has? And when Cyprian says, "to set on fire our persecutors," I hear not Christ on the Cross praying for His killers, but cold, hard revenge with a bit of underlying glee. They are gonna git theirs, brother!

This is, in a sense, understandable. Cyprian, and all the early fathers, were only men. They were fallible in their reasoning as they sought to better understand God. The ecumenical councils, often raucous and filled with dissenting opinions, are proof of this. If truth came easily, the councils would have been united in understanding.

My friend's paper finishes this section with four summary points:

1. Souls live on after the grave. Even those who are assigned to Hell are "immortal," "indestructible," and "abide forever." Those assigned to Hell will be "detained in everlasting fire" for a period of time that is "equally perpetual and unending" as the eternal life of those who are in Heaven.

---

12. "Cyprian," Para. 2–3

2. The rebellious will exist in Hell with an "eternal body, fitted to endure the penalties of sins." They will "burn eternally in fire" and they will never "be consumed." Those tormented in Hell will never "have respite" and their torment will never "be at an end." "Souls along with their bodies will be preserved for suffering in unlimited agonies."

3. Souls in Hell will not be allowed to die or cease to exist. "They would prefer to be annihilated rather than be restored for punishment," but this is not the case. The fire of Hell is an "unquenchable fire." It is "clever" and "burns the limbs and restores them, wears them away and yet sustains them, just as fiery thunderbolts strike bodies but do not consume them."

4. The torment suffered by those in Hell will be incredibly unbearable. It will feel as though "a certain fiery worm which does not die, and which does not waste the body" will continually burst forth from the body "with unceasing pain."[13]

My response:

1. Eastern Orthodoxy rejects out of hand the idea of a separate place called Hell. Numerous liberties have been taken with the Bible to make the grave (Sheol, Hades), the trash dump of Jerusalem (Gehenna), and the place for fallen angels (Tartarus) mean a place of eternal torment. In Orthodoxy, the experience of hell is being in the presence of Christ. It is the love of God experienced by the wicked as torment because they cannot tolerate it, nor do they want it in their fallen state.

2. There is no physical fire in hell, contrary to the lurid Roman Catholic tales from Medieval times. The descriptions of a fire in hell being like a physical fire here on earth would be laughable if it were not for the fact that so many people take them seriously and are terrorized by them. It is unthinkable for God to preserve souls in permanent bodies for reason of a suffering which has no purpose. A punishment which serves no purpose other than to appease the lust of the one punishing is not justice. It is sadism. Those who taught apokatastasis taught that the purpose of the punishment was restoration, not revenge.

3. For souls to not be allowed to die means God wills a perpetual torment for billions of conscious and sentient beings, without respite or purpose. It means He created us, knowing we would fall, with the distinct knowledge of the fall and all its consequences, and willed to go forth with creation anyway because it was His will for most of His creatures

13. "What Did Early Christians Believe About Hell?" Para. 43—46

suffer. What does such a thing accomplish? It may create a certain miscreant pleasure in the hearts of those who are self-assured about their final destiny, but for anyone seriously thinking about the ramifications of such an idea, the only thing we can have would be an unspeakable horror at the idea of a Supreme Being who would create sentient beings for no other purpose than to suffer. And by what revelation does Wallace know the response of the soul when it sees Christ in all His love and beauty? He assumes without any evidence that repentance is denied to those who have died, which puts millions of pagans who never even heard of Christ in the unenviable position of being damned for an uncontrollable accident of birth and location.

4. The descriptions of the unquenchable fire and the worm that does not die come from Jesus's warning to the Jews of the coming destruction of Jerusalem in AD 70. The fire never died in the Valley of Gehinnom, where the trash and dead animal bodies were cast. The worms found a never-ending feast there, giving rise to the idea of the worm that does not die. Perhaps, like Tertullian, the minds of certain theologians found immense joy, along with a sense of self-righteous satisfaction, in assigning their enemies to be forever eaten by worms and tormented by fire. For whatever reason, they have failed to see that Christ was describing the coming destruction which was to fall on national Israel, and which caused Him to weep over Jerusalem.

Wallace finishes by saying that such suffering is something we as sinful and imperfect human beings would not wish on our worst enemy, yet he has no problem with attributing such atrocious behavior to God, whom the Bible describes as love. Are we better than God? Is God less loving than we are? Would His will be an eternal barbecue for the sake of assuaging His offended honor? Are we commanded by Christ to forgive our enemies, but this same behavior does not belong to God, in whom is no shadow of darkness?

SCRIPTURE THAT SUPPORTS THE ETERNITY OF HELL

From a lifetime of listening to pastors and priests give homilies and sermons, then going home to meditate upon and study what they have spoken about, I have come to believe there is no book which is more spoken about and less understood than the Bible. I make no claims of inerrancy for myself. What I am going to share in the next pages are the "ah ha" moments which have made me say "Now wait just a minute here!" about things I was once taught are absolute and unquestionable truths.

One of the greatest problems with understanding the Bible is reading it with a wooden literalism–the idea that every word in the Bible was "God-breathed." As a fundamentalist, I was taught this meant God dictated the Bible word for word, and it is to be understood in that manner. In the year nine hundred ninety-nine, many such literalist Christians sold everything they had because they were sure that the thousand-year reign of Christ was about to end in His return.

There is also the problem of reading the Bible out of context of setting, hearing it not as a first century Jew would have understood it, but overlaying our own understanding on it. In addition, there are the cultural intrusions, such as seeing God as a Roman courtroom judge rather than the loving Father our Lord described. Christians in China during the Cultural Revolution were sure that the Rapture of the church was imminent because of the severe persecutions they were enduring. American Christians have conflated the Kingdom of God with America, giving rise to the idea of Manifest Destiny, which sent our troops all over the world to assure that Americanism was promoted and the American Kingdom, ordained by God, was brought to rule the entire world.

The Bible has several places which speak of God having mercy on all and willing the salvation of all. These verses contradict the verses used by Infernalists to prove an eternal hell. Since both statements cannot be true– i.e., that God is going to torment forever the wicked, but wills to have mercy on all and save all–we know that one or the other of these statements is false. Try as you may, A cannot be B and black cannot be white. Someone is in error. What I am doing here is investigating to find the correct understanding of certain Bible verses.

DIRECT REFERENCES TO THE ETERNITY OF HELL

Dealing with objections to apokatastasis can be like trying to grab an eel. If the early fathers are quoted against eternal torment, Infernalists will flip over to the Bible and carpet-bomb you with verses which prove that God indeed throws people into the fires of torment forever. On the other hand, if you start showing them that you do have a dash of knowledge of the Bible in Greek, quoting scholars such as Dr. Ilaria Ramelli and Dr. David Bentley Hart, they will counter with select quotes from early church saints and fathers which they believe show that the church taught eternal conscious torment from the beginning, along with indignant accusations that the church and the fathers are always right and how dare we not believe them?

Earlier I showed how appealing to certain early fathers comes from taking what they wrote in Greek and completely mistranslating the meaning into Latin. I spoke briefly about the mistranslation of the Greek word aionios to mean eternal. With the beginning of this section of my friend's paper, it is time to really dig into the Greek and find out what has been said. The burden is on me to prove, using the sources I have found, that aionios in no way should be translated as the word eternal.

As I begin discussing the verses from Matthew, I wish to remind you that I am giving only my understanding, based on decades of study and learning. My belief has come from reading books, then checking what they wrote, all the time praying for clarity. I hope that what I share here will create your own investigation. You may have never looked at these verses with the understanding that I will present.

THE GOSPEL OF MATTHEW–MATTHEW 25

In this section of her paper, my friend presents me with numerous quotes from the Gospel of Matthew. Here is the problem I see with using Matthew–it is written to the Jews and the Jewish nation. I believe it has been badly misunderstood, especially Matthew 23–25. The whole book of Matthew, with its various parables and warnings, was given to a specific audience for a specific time–the Jews of the first century. We see this from the very first chapter, where Matthew lists a long genealogy of Jesus' family. Why is this important? It is because the Jews were looking for the Son of David to come as Messianic King to rule and reign over Israel. This genealogy would have meant little to a Gentile reading it, but for the first century Jew, it was important proof of Christ being from the lineage of King David. Being David's son, He was the promised Messiah.

In Matthew, the Messiah is presented to His people, they reject His claims, and a terrible consequence comes from this rejection. Matthew 23–25 discusses this climax in detail, outlining the end of the Jewish age, and the command from Christ to the apostles to go out and offer the kingdom to all mankind. The Jewish people have forfeited their position as the special people of God. The kingdom is given to all people through the church.

Matthew 23 is the beginning of a long discourse in which Christ warns the Pharisees they have squandered the opportunity they had and now face destruction. The setting is the Temple. On the previous day, Jesus has entered Jerusalem on the colt of an ass, the Palm Sunday triumphal entry. He leaves the city, and on the way out, curses the fig tree, saying "may nothing ever grow on you again." This signifies what will happen to Israel. The fig tree is a symbol of national Israel, and God has just placed His curse upon it.

The next morning Christ returns and begins a series of parables which prophesy the coming destruction of Jerusalem. After answering challenges from the Sadducees and Pharisees in chapter 22, Matthew 23:1 says, "Then spake Jesus to the multitude, and to his disciples." He is still in the Temple area. In Matthew 23:1–12, Jesus warns the crowd against behaving like the Pharisees, openly condemning them for their hypocrisy. He then turns to the Pharisees and addresses them directly in some of the harshest language He has used up to this point. They are hypocrites, blind guides, a generation of serpents. Our Lord spares no words in letting them know their true spiritual state. After pronouncing the doom of national Israel in verse thirty-eight, He leaves the Temple.

This sets the stage for Jesus to speak at length on the destruction of Jerusalem. The disciples have understood that some calamity looms in the future. In Matthew 23:36, Jesus sets the time for all that He has been discussing by saying "these things shall come upon this generation." This generation. Not people in America two thousand years later waiting for the Rapture of the church. To properly understand what event Jesus was talking about, and the time in which it was to take place, makes all the difference in the world for proper understanding of the various dire warnings in Matthew.

In Matthew 24:1–3, there is a crucial time indicator people have misunderstood because of a faulty Greek translation. The disciples have made the connection regarding Jesus' prophesy of the destruction of the Temple. They ask when all these things will take place, and when the end of the age will come. Not the end of the world, as is wrongly translated in most Western translations. The end of the age. To think that Jesus is talking about the events which follow as the end of this world has caused a massive misunderstanding of everything in Matthew 24 and 25. Everything spoken of by Jesus from Matthew 24:3 to the end of chapter twenty-five has to do with the destruction of Jerusalem in AD 70, and the end of the age. These events will come upon that generation.

THE PARABLE OF THE TEN VIRGINS:

> Matthew 25: 1 Then the kingdom of heaven shall be likened to ten virgins who took their lamps and went out to meet the bridegroom. 2 Now five of them were wise, and five were foolish. 3 Those who were foolish took their lamps and took no oil

with them, 4 but the wise took oil in their vessels with their lamps. 5 But while the bridegroom was delayed, they all slumbered and slept. 6 And at midnight a cry was heard: 'Behold, the bridegroom is coming; go out to meet him!' 7 Then all those virgins arose and trimmed their lamps. 8 And the foolish said to the wise, 'Give us some of your oil, for our lamps are going out.' 9 But the wise answered, saying, 'No, lest there should not be enough for us and you; but go rather to those who sell, and buy for yourselves.' 10 And while they went to buy, the bridegroom came, and those who were ready went in with him to the wedding; and the door was shut. 11 Afterward the other virgins came also, saying, 'Lord, Lord, open to us!' 12 But he answered and said, 'Assuredly, I say to you, I do not know you.' 13 Watch therefore, for you know neither the day nor the hour in which the Son of Man is coming.

It appears that early Christians, much like those of today, did not think like first-century Jews when reading the Scriptures. For instance, when Jesus speaks of "heaven and earth," he is not speaking of this physical planet, nor the sky above us. Heaven and earth are a reference to the Temple.

> Jews did not always mean "the physical universe" when they spoke of heaven and earth together. In Jewish literature, the Temple was a portal connecting heaven and earth. They called it the "navel of the earth" and the "gateway to heaven" (Jub 8:19; 1 Enoch 26:1). Just like the Mesopotamian Tower in Genesis 11, the Temple connected God's realm to where humans lived.
>
> To reflect this belief, the Jerusalem Temple had been built to look like a microcosm of the universe. We typically overlook how literally true the Temple hymn preserved in Psalm 78:69 is: "He built his sanctuary like the high heavens, like the earth, which he has founded forever." The actual holy place and most holy place inside the Temple building were constructed like earth and heaven. The courts outside represented the sea. I am not making this stuff up.
>
> According to Josephus, two parts of the tabernacle were "approachable and open to all" but one was not. He explains that in so doing Moses "signifies the earth and the sea, since these two are accessible to all; but the third portion he reserved for God alone because heaven is inaccessible to men" (Ant. 3:181, cf. 3:123). The veil between the accessible and inaccessible parts of the Temple was designed to represent the entire material world during Jesus' day. Josephus and Philo agree that the veil was composed of four materials representing the

four elements–earth, water, air, and fire (War 5:212–213; Ant. 3:138–144; Quaestiones in Exodum 2:85, cf. Mos 2:88). Heaven was beyond this material world. It was behind the curtain.

Outside the Temple's microcosm of "heaven and earth," the courts looked like the sea. Numbers Rabbah 13:19 records, "The court surrounds the temple just as the sea surrounds the world." In Talmudic tradition, Rabbis described how the inner walls of the Temple looked like waves of the sea (b. Sukk. 51b, b.B.Bat. 4a). From heaven and earth inside the temple, you looked out at the sea surrounding the world. Why? Ancients believed the earth had one giant land mass surrounded by sea. The temple reflected that cosmology. The accessible section of the Temple and the surrounding courts embodied both the land mass and sea believed to comprise the earth. The Most Holy Place was heaven where God's presence resided.

If we listen to Jesus in First-Century Israel, his prediction of "heaven and earth" passing away sounds like the destruction of Jerusalem and her Temple. The contemporary songs, writers, and architecture all make the connection between Jerusalem's Temple and "heaven and earth." Isaiah used the same language of "heaven and earth" to depict Jerusalem and her citizens in Isaiah 65:17–18.

"For behold, I create new heavens and a new earth and the former things will not be remembered or come to mind. But be glad and rejoice forever in what I create; For behold, I create Jerusalem for rejoicing and her people for gladness."

Isaiah is predicting the eventual reconstruction of Jerusalem after its destruction at the hands of invaders. He uses Hebrew parallelism to equate the creation of "new heavens and a new earth" with the restoration of Jerusalem. So Jesus isn't the first prophet to describe Jerusalem and her temple with grand language describing its theological significance. Jerusalem was the place where people encountered the presence of God on earth. The Temple is where heaven met earth.[14]

The first verse in the Parable of the Ten Virgins establishes the place where this event takes place–the Kingdom of Heaven. Several years ago, I realized that this phrase occurs only in the Jewish Gospel of Matthew. I saw this as having some significance, but I could not figure it out. Now, thanks to my research for this book, I have found the answer. The Kingdom of Heaven in Matthew refers to national Israel, and the Temple is the very heart of the kingdom. It is the kingdom *on earth*.

14. Penley, "When Heaven and Earth Passed Away: Everything Changed." Para. 5–11.

The Kingdom of Heaven is therefore to be seen as the earthly rule of God through the ordained priesthood. More specifically, the Temple, the place where God's presence and rule took place. First century Jews listening would have understood this. The entire discourse which has preceded this has been about Jerusalem, the end of national Israel, and especially the destruction of the Temple. Now, due to atrocious exegesis, much of it contained in virulent anti-Catholic hate literature of the nineteenth century, this has changed. Certain denominations teach a quantum shift in Matthew 24 in which Jesus leaps from focus on the Temple's destruction to an event in the far-off future they call "The Rapture of the church."

At the end of the parable, when Jesus says "I do not know you," I find myself thinking of the Genesis verse, "And Adam knew his wife . . . " It is a word which speaks to the deepest intimacy between husband and wife. In this context I think of national Israel as the bride awaiting her bridegroom. Our Lord offered Himself to Israel as the Bridegroom. But when she fails to obtain the Holy Spirit, symbolized by oil, Christ will no longer know her as His bride. His bride is now the Gentile/Jewish church of all nations, who obtained the Holy Spirit at Pentecost. Jesus is prophesying that He will no longer know Judaism as His bride with the ceremonial and Mosaic laws which went with her. To make this into a plea for sending people into eternal hell at the end of the world is an egregious misunderstanding of the context–the destruction of Jerusalem–in which Christ was speaking.

The same must be true in some manner of the second parable given, the Parable of the Talents, which begins at verse 14 of Matthew 25. Since the theme which was begun in Matthew 25:1 is the destruction of the Temple, we should assume Jesus is teaching about the same event under another parable to give emphasis and to clarify. Verse 30 is the end of this parable. There is no time indicator showing that the weeping and gnashing of teeth lasts forever. This is, again, reading into the text.

MATTHEW 25:31–46 JUDGMENT OF THE NATIONS

The next appeal from my friend is this discourse in which we see Jesus separating the sheep from the goats. According to Infernalists, Jesus rewards the sheep, who fed the hungry, clothed the naked, and cared for the poor, with eternal life. The wicked, those who did not care for the needy, are rewarded with eternal destruction.

Verse 46 ends this discourse regarding the destruction of Jerusalem and the warnings to His listeners, many of whom would be alive to experience all that He had warned about. For those who believe in an eternity of fire and torment, this section is frequently referred to as an absolute proof text which discredits any attempt to defend apokatastasis.

Most Christians regard this passage as having to do with the end of all things because of the use of the phrase ". . .end of the world. . ." in Matthew 24. Christ returns, He judges all mankind, and that's a wrap, folks! For most Christians, this section refers to the end of all things, the Last Judgment, and then eternity with God or in hell. It is interpreted as meaning this because the word eternal appears in the text.

In understanding words and their meanings, root words establish the meaning of their derivatives. The word colorful is an adjective that has to do with color. It has nothing to do with being bitter. Let's take the Greek root word "aion," which means "age," and replace it with the word "eternal" to see how that works.

> Matthew 13:22 Now he who received seed among the thorns is he who hears the word, and the cares of this eternal (aion) and the deceitfulness of riches choke the word, and he becomes unfruitful.
> Romans 12:2 And do not be conformed to this eternal, (aion) but be transformed by the renewing of your mind, that you may prove what is that good and acceptable and perfect will of God.
> First Corinthians 2:8 Which none of the princes of this eternal (aion) knew: for had they known it, they would not have crucified the Lord of glory.
> Galatians 1:4 Who gave himself for our sins, that he might deliver us from this present evil eternal, (aion) according to the will of God and our Father
> Matthew 13:39 The enemy that sowed them is the devil; the harvest is the end of the eternal; (aion) and the reapers are the angels.
> Matthew 13:40 As therefore the tares are gathered and burned in the fire; so shall it be in the end of this eternal. (aion)

I hope by now you can see how ridiculous a wrong translation of aion sounds in the examples above. In every case, if you put the word "age" in those verses, they now make sense. Jesus and Paul speak of the end of the age. Age is the one and only meaning of aion, therefore, we must give strong weight to it carrying the same meaning in its derivatives such as aionios.

In Revelation, we see mention of ages yet to come. First let's look at a mistaken translation from the KJV: Revelation 22:5 "There shall be no night there: They need no lamp nor light of the sun, for the Lord God gives them light. And they shall reign forever and ever."

And now the literal Greek from the YLT: "Revelation 22:5 and night shall not be there, and they have no need of a lamp and light of a sun, because the Lord God doth give them light, and they shall reign–to the ages of the ages."

Do you sense the difference between these two interpretations? In the KJV interpretation you see eternity as one flat plane of existence rather than ever-changing ages upon ages. In the YLT, one age comes and goes, to be followed by another and yet another. To me, this is a significant mistranslation, one of many I have found over years of studying the Bible.

First Timothy 1:17 "Now unto the King eternal, immortal, invisible, the only wise God, be honour and glory for ever and ever. Amen." (KJV)

This is even more horrendous. This is not what the Greek says at all! Once again, I present for you the Greek wording of 1 Timothy 1:17 with the proper literal translation:

First Timothy 1:17 "And to the King of the ages, the incorruptible, invisible, only wise God, is honor and glory–to the ages of the ages! Amen." (YLT)

The KJV reading makes God eternal, rather than the King over all the ages. No ages exist, He is just the eternal King. It is a description of His being rather than of His rulership over the ages to come, (to the ages of ages). In the KJV interpretation you continue to see eternity as one flat plane of existence rather than ever-changing ages upon ages.

Here is another mistranslation: Titus 1:2 "In hope of eternal life, which God, that cannot lie, promised before the world began" (KJV)

Titus 1:2 "Upon hope of life age-during, which God, who doth not lie, did promise before times of ages." (YLT)

Chronos aionios. Times of ages. That's a whole lot different than before the world began. And this is the problem we face over and over in the New Testament. Men making erroneous translations because they were taught erroneous translations by men who were taught erroneous translations. We are reading a thousand years of erroneous translations which have become accepted as correct when they are not!

The same is true with 1 Corinthians 2:7. The word aionios is translated "world" in this verse with absolutely no rhyme or reason other than the prejudice (one might rather uncharitably also say stupidity) of the translators.

First Corinthians 2:7 "But we speak the wisdom of God in a mystery, even the hidden wisdom, which God ordained before the world unto our glory:" (KJV)

First Corinthians 2:7 "But we speak the hidden wisdom of God in a secret, that God foreordained before the ages to our glory," (YLT)

You may ask why this is important. It is because we have stopped thinking of God's dealing with His creation as a series of epochs, or ages, and think of it instead as timeline divided into two parts: creation of Adam and Eve to now, and after the present time, eternity. No ages, no epochs of existence before Adam, and none to come after death. If there are no ages, then eternity becomes all there is after death with no possibility of moving through one age to another age. There is no idea of one age ending and another age beginning in which God deals with the unrepentant in a manner which will bring them to repentance. We are assured by Infernalists that all one gets is this life, and then the next, with no hope of change if you have failed to repent in this life. This is how Matthew 25:46 is viewed by those who insist it is the end of the world and the final Judgment.

The same is true of Matthew 24:3, another frequently mistranslated verse which uses "aion." The mistranslation of this verse at the beginning of Christ's discourse on the destruction of the Temple has led millions to think that the verses following are about the end of the world.

Matthew 24:3 "And as he sat upon the mount of Olives, the disciples came unto him privately, saying, Tell us, when shall these things be? and what shall be the sign of thy coming, and of the end of the *world*?" (aion) (KJV)

From this error, certain Christians have created a fantasy called "the Rapture of the church" and "the Great Tribulation" which they think are yet to come before the end of the world. Problem–that is not what it says in Greek! The word translated as "world" is "aion" and it never means "world." It always means age. The discourse found in Matthew 24 and 25 is about the end of the age. This age ends, according to Matthew 24:2, when the Temple in Jerusalem is razed to the ground by the Roman troops of Titus in AD 70.

The Bible is an important document in the life of the Christian. We are urged to read it, memorize portions of it, and take it to heart its commands. But if the translation is wrong, are we then really reading and understanding God's intent? If in a conversation I say to a translator, "Please tell him I am his friend." and the translator says in Arabic, "He wants to kill you," did the true message come across? How is the Bible any different?

In such an important guide for our lives as the Bible, and for what little understanding we have of the immortal, invisible, incomprehensible God, would you not think the wording used in this book would be carefully chosen? There does exist a specific Greek word which means eternal–aidios–found in only two verses of scripture:

> Romans 1:20 Ever since the creation of the world his invisible nature, namely, his eternal (aidios) power and deity, has been

clearly perceived in the things that have been made. So they are without excuse;

Jude 1:6 And the angels that did not keep their own position but left their proper dwelling have been kept by him in eternal (aidios) chains in the nether gloom until the judgment of the great day;

If eternal punishment was meant in all verses such as Matthew 25:46, then why was this word, which is specific in meaning eternal, not used? More than that, why did Jesus not use it in each case where He instead used aionios?

A much more important foundation for the proper understanding of aionios is the Septuagint. The Septuagint (also known as the LXX) is a translation of the Hebrew Bible into the Greek language. The name Septuagint comes from the Latin word for "seventy." The tradition is that 70 (or 72) Jewish scholars were the translators behind the Septuagint. The Septuagint was translated in the third and second centuries BC in Alexandria, Egypt. As Israel was under the authority of Greece for several centuries, the Greek language became more and more common. By the second and first centuries BC, most people in Israel spoke Greek as their primary language. For this reason, the effort was made to translate the Hebrew Bible into Greek so that those who did not understand Hebrew could have the Scriptures in a language they could understand. The Septuagint represents the first major effort at translating a significant religious text from one language into another.

> Thus far we have considered the Hebrew noun, olam, and the Greek noun, aion (which appears in both the singular and the plural form in the LXX and the New Testament). We now come to the word that was used by the LXX and the authors of the New Testament in place of olam as the adjective form of the noun aion: aiónios. As the adjective form of aion, aiónios should best be understood to mean "belonging to, or lasting for, an eon." Hence it is rendered "age-abiding" in Rotherham's Emphasized Bible, "age-during" in Young's Literal Translation, and "eonian" in the Concordant Literal New Testament. Just as "color" is to "colorful," "length" is to "long," and "day" is to "daily," so aion is to aiónios. And just as "daily" can never mean "yearly" (because its limit is defined by the noun "day" from which it is derived), so aionios can never refer to something other than an aion or "eon." Because aion is not used in Scripture to mean "eternity,"

the adjective form of the word (aionios) should not be understood to mean "eternal."[15]

The Jewish scholars who translated the Old Testament into Greek picked a specific word–aionios–to replace the Hebrew word olam. Therefore, it is important for us to know whether olam means eternal. Hebrew scholars state the following:

> The simple, basic truth is that Classical Hebrew, the Hebrew of the Old Testament Scriptures, has no term that carries the concept of "eternity." There are phrases that carry this concept, such as "without end," but there is not a single word that carries the concept of eternity as there is in English.
>
> To focus on the meaning of the term for ever, here are some things to be kept in mind.
>
> First, the Hebrew word is *olam*. The word itself simply means "long duration," "antiquity," "futurity," "*until the end of a period of time.*" That period of time is determined by the context. Sometimes it is the length of a man's life, sometimes it is an age, and sometimes it is a dispensation.
>
> The second thing to keep in mind is that there are two Hebrew forms of *olam*. The first form is *le-olam*, which means "unto an age." And the second form is *ad-olam*, which means "until an age." However, neither of these forms carry the English meaning of "forever." Although it has been translated that way in English, the Hebrew does not carry the concept of eternity as the English word "forever" does.
>
> The third thing to keep in mind is that the word *olam, le-olam,* or *ad-olam,* sometimes means only up "to the end of a man's life." For example, it is used of someone's lifetime (Ex. 14:13), of a slave's life (Ex. 21:6; Lev. 25:46; Deut. 15:17), of Samuel's life (I Sam. 1:22; 2:35), of the lifetimes of David and Jonathan (I Sam. 20:23), and of David's lifetime (I Sam. 27:12; 28:2; I Chr. 28:4). While the English reads forever, obviously from the context it does not mean "forever" in the sense of eternity, but only up to the end of the person's life.
>
> The fourth thing to keep in mind about the meaning of *olam* is that it sometimes means only "an age" or "dispensation." For example, Deuteronomy 23:3 uses the term for ever but limits the term to only ten generations. Here it obviously carries the concept of an age. In 2 Chronicles 7:16, it is used only for the period of the First Temple. So, again, the word for ever in Hebrew does not mean "eternal" as it does in English; it means

---

15. Welch "Eternal or Eionion?" Part Five (The Greek Adjective Aionios)," Para. 1.

up to the end of a period of time, either a man's life, or an age, or a dispensation.[16]

The word *olam* comes from the root *alam* meaning "to be hidden" and is often used in the sense of hiding to a place where one cannot be seen. Because Hebrew words for time are also used for space we can say that *olam* literally means "a place hidden beyond the horizon" or "a time hidden beyond the distant time."[17]

When looking off in the far distance it is difficult to make out any details and what is beyond that horizon cannot be seen. In other words, olam, and its corresponding Greek word aionios, have to do with seeing as far as we can see, but not seeing beyond that. Aionios is therefore "age-lasting" until we can see no longer. But as I have shown, there are ages upon ages yet to come according to scripture, not just two ages (life on earth, life in heaven). We cannot see beyond this age. We cannot even begin to fathom the age yet to come, yet Infernalists treat this as if it goes on forever and ever in the same condition without end. Had the scholars translating the Septuagint thought of olam as eternity, they surely would have used aidios instead of aionios.

God is ever beyond the horizon of our understanding. The aion to come, and the aionios life which will be lived within it will be an age of growing ever closer to God, yet always perceiving Him as being beyond the horizon. To come to the end of a journey means there is no more horizon. Yet in God, there is always the eternal lying beyond a horizon which we shall approach but never arrive at. He is the mystery of love ever enduring for our joy and blessing unto ages of ages.

The root of olam is Ah.L.M and means "to conceal," hence you can easily see the connection between being "beyond the horizon" and "being concealed." In the Bible, when owlam, like aion and aionios, is used to describe the eternal attributes of God, then of course owlam means forever, everlasting or eternal, as correctly translated in these verses. But only as it is being used as an adjective. The root meaning remains and cannot be changed to suit the interpreter's fancy. Now, let us give some examples to show you that owlam, depending on its context, can also mean age or age-lasting even though most Bible versions always translate it to mean "forever, everlasting or eternal."

---

16. Fruchtenbaum, "How Long is Forever?" Para. 2.
17. Benner, "Ancient," Para. 3

Genesis 17:13 "He who is born in your house and he who is bought with your money must be circumcised, and My covenant shall be in your flesh for an everlasting (owlam) covenant."

We can be sure that in this verse owlam means an "age-lasting" covenant, even though it is translated in the NKJV version above, and other versions of the Bible, to mean everlasting covenant. In Isaiah 24:5, the Mosaic Covenant given to Israel has been translated to mean an everlasting covenant. However, we know from the New Testament, in Hebrews 8:13, that the Old Covenant of the Law under Moses has now been superseded by the New Covenant of Grace under Jesus Christ. So, the Bible itself confirms that owlam, depending on its context, does not always mean everlasting, but it can also mean "age or age-lasting." The Old Covenant lasted until the end of the age, which took place in AD 70.

The scripture Jonah 1:17 clearly tells us that Jonah was in the belly of the great fish for only three days and three nights: "Now the LORD had prepared a great fish to swallow Jonah. And Jonah was in the belly of the fish three days and three nights."

However, according to most Bible versions, in their translation of the scripture Jonah 2:6, Jonah was in the belly of the great fish forever, thus contradicting Jonah 1:17 above. Three days and three nights in the belly of the great fish may have seemed like forever to Jonah, but the point we are making is that owlam in the Bible does not always literally mean forever.

There are other places in the Old Testament where it can be clearly seen that owlam does not mean "forever, everlasting or eternal" and that it can only mean age or age-lasting, which can vary from a very short period of only a few days, as in the case of Jonah, up to a very long period of thousands of years.

This mistranslation is found in another OT verse which is appealed to as proof that there is an everlasting hell: Daniel 12:2 "And many of them that sleep in the dust of the earth shall awake, some to everlasting life, and some to shame and everlasting contempt."(KJV)

Versions of the Bible which support the doctrine of hell, translate owlam in this verse to mean "everlasting life," and "everlasting contempt." As in the case of Matthew 25:46, which we have already discussed in this chapter, this verse is similarly mistranslated.

Daniel 12:2 "And many of those who sleep in the dust of the earth shall awake, some to age-to-come (owlam) life, some to shame and age-lasting (owlam) contempt."(YLT)

Age-to-come life is the glorious life in Christ, which Christians will receive when they rise from the dead in resurrection. However, age-to-come contempt is also just age-lasting, which all unbelievers will receive when they

THE ETERNITY OF HELL FROM THE CHURCH FATHERS AND SCRIPTURE 109

rise from the dead in resurrection. This is when they will be condemned to the lake of fire during the Great White Throne Judgement Age, and they will become ashamed of their sin of unbelief, repent and believe the true Gospel through God's refining corrective judgement. Both conditions will last through the next age until another age begins. Remember, it is "ages upon ages," which are to come after this life, not a single final age called eternity.

Apart from Daniel 12:2, there is little in the Old Testament which can be misunderstood or mistranslated in support of the doctrine of hell.

My friend's paper then moves to Matthew 18:7 in another attempt to prove that there is an eternity of suffering in an everlasting fire.

> Matthew 18:7 Woe unto the world because of offences! for it must needs be that offences come; but woe to that man by whom the offence cometh! 8 Wherefore if thy hand or thy foot offend thee, cut them off, and cast them from thee: it is better for thee to enter into life halt or maimed, rather than having two hands or two feet to be cast into everlasting fire.

Same problem. Bad translation. Here is the Young's Literal Translation of the Greek, which I have come regard as an accurate translation of the Greek:

> Matthew 18:7 Woe to the world from the stumbling-blocks! for there is a necessity for the stumbling-blocks to come, but woe to that man through whom the stumbling-block doth come! 8 And if thy hand or thy foot doth cause thee to stumble, cut them off and cast from thee; it is good for thee to enter into the life lame or maimed, rather than having two hands or two feet, to be cast to the fire the age-during. (aionios)

Why am I repeating myself here? Because my interlocutor conveniently has forgotten the end of the chapter. This chapter is a teaching on offenses and forgiveness. Let's look at the last teaching in it.

> Matthew 18: 21 Then came Peter to him, and said, Lord, how oft shall my brother sin against me, and I forgive him? till seven times? 22 Jesus saith unto him, I say not unto thee, Until seven times: but, Until seventy times seven. 23 Therefore is the kingdom of heaven likened unto a certain king, which would take account of his servants. 24 And when he had begun to reckon, one was brought unto him, which owed him ten thousand talents. 25 But forasmuch as he had not to pay, his lord commanded him to be sold, and his wife, and children, and all that he had, and payment to be made. 26 The servant therefore fell down, and

> worshiped him, saying, Lord, have patience with me, and I will pay thee all. 27 Then the lord of that servant was moved with compassion, and loosed him, and forgave him the debt. 28 But the same servant went out, and found one of his fellow servants, which owed him an hundred pence: and he laid hands on him, and took him by the throat, saying, Pay me that thou owest. 29 And his fellow servant fell down at his feet, and besought him, saying, have patience with me, and I will pay thee all. 30 And he would not: but went and cast him into prison, till he should pay the debt. 31 So when his fellow servants saw what was done, they were very sorry, and came and told unto their lord all that was done. 32 Then his lord, after that he had called him, said unto him, O thou wicked servant, I forgave thee all that debt, because thou desiredst me: 33 Shouldest not thou also have had compassion on thy fellow servant, even as I had pity on thee? 34 And his lord was wroth, and delivered him to the tormentors, *till he should pay all that was due unto him.* 35 So likewise shall my heavenly Father do also unto you, if ye from your hearts forgive not every one his brother their trespasses.

In this parable, the lord to whom is owed a great debt is a figure of God the Father. The debt of our sins is as unpayable as the thousand talents would be to a common laborer living in Israel at that time. The debt of the fellow servant is minor in comparison, yet the first servant acts with cruelty. This is a picture of our cruelty to our fellow man when we ignore the poor, let the hungry starve, indulge the rich, steal, rape, murder and do all the other sins that are acts against mercy and love for our fellow man. As a result, the lord is enraged and has the man delivered to tormentors until all that was due was paid.

Now note this: it does not say forever, does it? Oh, it will feel like forever to the one paying off this enormous debt to God's justice! I easily imagine murderous tyrants like Mao, Hitler, Mussolini, Stalin, Lenin, and a whole host of other unpleasant characters are just beginning what is going to be a prolonged stay in God's remedial and corrective justice. And this is nothing to laugh about or make fun of, as some do when warned of the justice of God. I cannot imagine, nor can you, the sheer horror of them facing the reality and truth of what they did here on earth. They were not saviors of their country, noble men fighting for a noble cause, or any of the other nonsense they told themselves as they murdered millions. The sheer, stark terror of the truth of what they did is now a full-blown torment which they are experiencing.

Please do not think that anyone believing in apokatastasis has any such idea as I have heard from ignorant detractors when they say, "Oh, so you think you can live any way you want and just go to heaven!"

Absolutely not!

If anything, we should all be doing all we can in prayer and sharing the truth about Christ's love to the wicked to bring them to repentance and keep them from this terrible fate! It shows a distinct lack of love on our parts that we do so little to warn the wicked of the terrible consequences that await them except they repent. We as believers should run from sin, pray much for ourselves and others, and do all that the Lord has commanded us so that we are not included in this dismal chorus of wailing and gnashing of teeth.

But it does end, according to verse 34. It would be unjust of God to extract from any soul one ounce more in torments than justice requires. For God, who is love and just in all His dealings, to do such a thing should be unthinkable to us. The Calvinist idea of predestination unto damnation, of God willing the creation of a multitude of souls who would not be saved, but whose entire purpose of being was only to suffer forever to display His eternal glory, is a teaching which should make you sick at your stomach!

> Matthew 3:7 But when he saw many of the Pharisees and Sadducees come to his baptism, he said unto them, O generation of vipers, who hath warned you to flee from the wrath to come? 8 Bring forth therefore fruits meet for repentance: 9 And think not to say within yourselves, we have Abraham to our father: for I say unto you, that God is able of these stones to raise up children unto Abraham. 10 And now also the axe is laid unto the root of the trees: therefore, every tree which bringeth not forth good fruit is hewn down, and cast into the fire. 11 I indeed baptize you with water unto repentance: but he that cometh after me is mightier than I, whose shoes I am not worthy to bear: he shall baptize you with the Holy Ghost, and with fire: 12 Whose fan is in his hand, and he will thoroughly purge his floor, and gather his wheat into the garner; but he will burn up the chaff with unquenchable fire.

Two things about this passage. John the Baptist is acting as prophet in the same manner Christ does in Matthew 21:33–46. Note what happens when the Pharisees and Sadducees appear. He warns them sternly to repent and tells them what will happen if they do not repent–they will be hewn down as bad trees and thrown into the fire. When did this happen? I believe the Parable of the Wicked Husbandmen in Matthew 21, and the destruction of Jerusalem, spoken of in Matthew 23–25, give us the answer. It happened in AD 70!

What happened to the bodies of the dead who were killed by the Romans? They were thrown into the fire of the Valley of Ghinnom (Gehenna) where the worm dieth not and there is fire unquenchable. It is dishonest to try to make the word "unquenchable" mean "eternal." The word is simply an adjective for a fire which cannot be put out. This was the description of the fires in the trash dump of Jerusalem, which burned night and day. The worms in the pit had an ongoing feast. This is yet another example of reading into the text that which some have been preconditioned to believe.

THE APOCALYPSE OF JOHN–REVELATION 14 AND 20.

My friend then presents another popular proof text for the existence of eternal hell. But is it? Let's examine the text in question. Maybe it is speaking of something else.

> Revelation 14:9–11 And the third angel followed them, saying with a loud voice, If any man worship the beast and his image, and receive his mark in his forehead, or in his hand, 10 The same shall drink of the wine of the wrath of God, which is poured out without mixture into the cup of his indignation; and he shall be tormented with fire and brimstone in the presence of the holy angels, and in the presence of the Lamb: 11 And the smoke of their torment ascendeth up for ever and ever: and they have no rest day nor night, who worship the beast and his image, and whosoever receiveth the mark of his name.

I believe a compelling case can be made that the Revelation of John is specifically written about the end of the Old Covenant, the covenant with national Israel which made them the special and chosen people of God. With the death of Christ, the covenant was ended, as shown by the rending of the Veil of the Temple from top to bottom. That action corrupted the Holy of Holies by exposing it to human eyes, thus making it unfit for further use. No Holy of Holies means no Yom Kippur, and no Yom Kippur means no covenant. If this is so, then Revelation is a writing which further explains Matthew 24, the destruction of the Temple, and the end of the Old Covenant. For this to be true, Revelation must have been written before 70 AD as a prophecy of the coming destruction.

> Revelation was written before 70 AD
> Revelation 1:1 The Revelation of Jesus Christ, which God gave unto him, to shew unto his servants things which must shortly come to pass.

1. The time statements refer to soon events of cataclysmic Jewish importance. If it was written in 96 A.D., there are no events soon from that time that could even remotely fit. If, however, it was before 70 A.D., then the destruction of Jerusalem rises to the occasion as both Jewish and cataclysmic. The time statements demand we look here.
2. The second century Syrian version of the book has the title of "John the Evangelist in the Isle of Patmos, where he was thrown by Nero Caesar." Nero, of course, was dead by 68 A.D.
3. Some versions have a few manuscripts that have the number of the beast as 616, instead of the Hebrew 666. (You can find this stated in almost any Study Bible). What is shocking is that using gematria Caesar Nero's name would add up to 616 in those versions, but in Hebrew, 666. This is very strong evidence that Caesar Nero really was the one being referred to as the beast and that the change from 666 to 616 in some manuscripts was intentional for that very reason. It is nearly impossible to find another person's name in that time frame that would do this!
4. According to the epistles to the churches, there were still Judaizers (Revelation 2:9; 3:9) presenting problems in the churches. This, would be ridiculous after 70 AD.
5. The temple and the city were apparently still standing in Revelation 11, because John is sent to measure them. This would not be possible after 70 AD. And if John is referring to some rebuilt temple in the far distant future, and he is writing in 96 A.D., then his complete silence about the destruction of the temple in 70 A.D. is deafening!
6. There were "other apostles" still around according to Revelation 2:2. Tradition has it that all the apostles were dead before 70 AD and John was the only original surviving past that time.
7. The 6th king in Revelation 17 is the one that persecutes the saints. Roman emperors are (1) Julius, (2) Augustus, (3) Tiberius, (4) Caligula, (5) Claudius, then (6) Nero. Nero was the first and only Roman Caesar of the Julian line to persecute Christians. Nero's death ended the Julian dynasty. The one ruling after him reigned only a little while . . . Galba, 6 months. If the 6th king is indeed Nero, he would be the one that "now is" according to the prophecy, and this would date the writing before 68 A.D. when Nero supposedly committed suicide. Nero also persecuted Christians for 42 months as is stated in the prophecy.

8. Caesar Nero's name in Hebrew gematria adds up to 666. Since this was written about soon events, no other person can be found within this time scope whose name fits this requirement and description. Especially none can be found in the soon future of 96 AD.
9. What purpose would it serve for John to tell the first readers of his prophecy to "calculate" the number of the name of the beast if he was not to be born until 2000 years later? This would be completely ridiculous. This implies that the beast was living at the time of this writing, thus proving not necessarily the pre-70 A.D. writing, but definitely the "at hand" time statements of the book.
10. The 7th king of Revelation 17 is not yet here. If Nero is the 6th, then the book was written before Galba, i.e., before 70 A.D.
11. In Revelation there seems to be only 7 churches in Asia. Historically, there seems to be many more than that after 70 A.D. as Christianity began to grow very rapidly.
12. The incredible parallels of Matthew 24 and Revelation, which Jesus said would happen in "this generation" and "when Jerusalem (is) surrounded with armies." Most of that generation were dead in the time of 96 A.D. and Jerusalem was surrounded with armies in 70 A.D.[18]

Revelation is very deep in what is called Jewish Apocalyptic Language. The current understanding of Revelation is that it is a mysterious book which is about the end of the world. Most Christians believe the events mentioned in it have yet to take place, especially the last three chapters which speak of Christ sitting on a white throne of judgment and the casting of the death and hell into the lake of fire. It would certainly be easy to think this as the events here sound like the end of all things, especially when the book ends using the phrase "forever and ever." That phrase has become an idiom for eternity. But is it the correct translation of the Greek?

> Many English-speaking peoples have heard and used the English expression "forever and ever." This phrase has become an idiomatic expression meaning to most English-speaking people "eternity, perpetuity or everlasting." This is an English rendering of several different phrases found in the Greek New Testament. However, if one told the original writers of the Greek New Testament that by this phrase one meant "eternity," they would say that you are not using an "idiomatic" expression, but an "idiotic" one. They would not recognize our "forever and ever" as

18. Kiser, "Revelation was Written Before 70 A.D."

anything remotely representing what the Greek actually meant to them and they would tell you that the Greek behind our "forever and ever" is not a Greek idiomatic expression meaning "eternity." You see, the Greek construct of this term would make it extremely difficult for a first century Greek to see how we moderns ever concocted "forever and ever" from these Greek phrases and words. Let me explain.

The English idiom "It's raining cats and dogs" only makes sense to us because we have been taught to associate the meaning, "It's raining heavily" with those words. Should a Chinese person just beginning to learn English read "it's raining cats and dogs," their natural instinct would first be to take the phrase literally. There is no way they could determine the "idiomatic" meaning of that phrase unless someone explained to them they were reading an idiom and then gave them its meaning. An idiom is an expression peculiar to a particular people or language the meaning of which is not apparent to those outside that group. Most languages have them. American English is filled with them. "I'm hip," "that's cool," "far out, man" "I dig you," are some examples. (I say "American" English because many idioms of the United States are not idioms of other English-speaking countries.)

We have a rather unique situation with this expression "forever and ever." It has come to be an English idiom meaning "eternity." However, it is supposed to be a literal translation of the New Testament Greek, not an idiomatic expression. This article will prove this phrase it is neither a literal translation of the Greek nor an idiom representing the true first century Greek language. Its meaning is so far removed from the early Greek, that first century Greeks could not possibly be able to determine how a modern English-speaking person got these Greek phrases to mean "eternity." They would think the English "forever and ever" was as crazy as "It's raining cats and dogs" would be to a Chinese person. To the first century Greeks, our English "forever and ever" would not be a literal translation of the Greek, nor would they consider it an idiomatic expression. They would consider it simply idiotic!

Many Bible translations contain the words "forever and ever." It sounds nice because we have heard and read this expression thousands of times. Once a tradition is set into the language or customs of a particular people, it is difficult to remove. Just because a tradition has been around a long time and has been assimilated by a large group does not make it true. There are more traditions in this world based upon pure falsehood and superstition than our libraries could possibly contain. Santa, the Christmas tree, and the Easter Bunny are examples of how pagan myths and superstitions have entered Christendom. Many of our Bible translations contain material as far off from reality as is the Easter Bunny. The phrase "forever and ever" is one of them.

The phrase "forever and ever" is a traditional phrase which has been around in English-speaking nations for several hundred years. It has been accepted as a true rendering of the Greek New Testament for a long time by millions of people. Nevertheless, this "tradition of the elders" is false. Furthermore, it is a tradition that has cause great havoc and produced many contradictions in our English Bibles. Even more significantly, it is a tradition that besmears the character of the God of Christianity to such an extent that the original writers of the Bible would not recognize this God as the one they were inspired to write by in the first place!

For example:

Revelation 20:10 is one of several places where we find the English phrase "forever and ever."

In the original it is written:

kai okarnos tou basanismou auton eis aionas ton aionon anabainei

and smoke the torment of them into eons of the eons is ascending.

Please note: Our English word "ever" appears in the singular form. We have no plural form for "ever." Putting another "ever" next to an "ever" does not add anything to the meaning. It's a nonsensical thing to do. We merely do it because of the tradition of the elders we have swallowed without thinking it through.

We get our English word "eon" and its plural "eons" from the Greek word "aion" and its inflections. Note that our English "eon" does have a plural form "eon" unlike our English word "ever."

In the Greek, both words which were translated "ever" are in their plural form. (aionas, aionon) "Ton aionon" is in the genitive form meaning "of" or "belonging to" or "what comes out of" the aionon.

The Greek word for "and" is "kai," not "ton." Why did some of the leading translations replace the Greek "of the" with "and?" There is no linguistic reason for them to do so. "Of the" works perfectly fine and many English translations contain such rendering in the very text itself and many others show it in the margins, footnotes or appendixes.

Given this information, we see that if the King James Bible and its cousins wanted to translate the Greek word "aion" as "ever," and stay true to the Greek forms of speech, they should have come up with the following rendering:

"And the smoke of their torment is ascending for the evers and evers."

As we can plainly see, this is getting pretty messy. But it gets much more messy than that. Any beginning Greek student knows that the Greek word for "and" is "kai," not "ton." So why do many modern English Bibles use the expression "forever and ever?" There is only one answer—tradition!

There are many English Bibles who have broken the "tradition of the elders" in this regard in order to bring forth the true meaning of the Greek. They have translated this Greek phrase "aionas ton aionon":

"for the eons of the eons." Concordant Literal New Testament

"for the ages of the ages." Young's Literal, and others

"for the aeons of the aeons." The New Covenant by Dr. J.W. Hanson

"unto the ages of the ages." Rotherham's Emphasized, and others

"through the ages of the ages." The Holy Bible in Modern English

The Greek word "aion" in its form in this verse is in the plural both times. So we have "eternities" (plural) and more "eternities" (plural). Are there more than one "eternities?" Does adding one "ever" to another produce eternity? Would "evers and evers," double plurals make eternity longer? You see, dear reader, when we look at the original Greek construction behind our English phrase "forever and ever," it becomes quite plain to a rational person that this phrase found in many of our leading English Bible translations, comes from the same place that Santa Claus and the Easter Bunny come from.

Simply put, we have a plain manipulation of the Greek word "aion" twice in this text and a mistranslation of the Greek word "ton," which basically means "of the." "Ton" never means "and," unless, of course, one is translating according to tradition rather than by proper translation methods.[19]

In Revelation, John speaks of the coming ages, not of eternity! To me this means that what has just come to pass in the earlier chapters of the book

---

19. Amirault, "Questions and Answers," Para. 1–21.

is describing the end of one age and the beginning of another. Notice what happens at the end. The New Jerusalem descends from above. Why would there be a new Jerusalem except that the old Jerusalem had been destroyed? The heavenly Jerusalem, the church, has replaced the former Jerusalem. The time element here is all wrong for those who believe this passage is speaking of the end of all time. It would mean that the age of the Old Covenant continued going right up to the time that Christ returns to end all things. If this passage in Revelation is speaking of the end of time, it means that the church, the New Jerusalem, comes down to earth at the same time Christ comes to wrap all things up. This is impossible.

WHILE WE ARE ALIVE ON EARTH IS THE TIME FOR TESTING, NOT AFTER DEATH.

My friend continues her paper in the same problematic vein of scriptural inaccuracy, for which I cannot really blame her. Centuries of distortion, bad theology, and wretched translations are not her fault. As a faithful Roman Catholic, she has accepted what she has been taught, believing her church to be without error. This idea of ecclesial inerrancy come from a self-serving translation of 1 Timothy 3:15, in which St. Paul states that the church is the "pillar and ground of truth." Roman Catholicism has taught for centuries that this means the Roman Catholic Church and truth are synonymous.

What does it mean to be a pillar? It means to hold something up. A pillar is a foundational structure which holds up the main body or building which rests upon it. The church therefore is a pillar which holding up the truth. And what is truth, according to the Bible? "I am the way, the truth, and the life . . . " Jesus the Christ, Savior of the world and all mankind. The church holds up the One who is Truth. Somehow, holding up Jesus as the truth morphed into "We are the truth."

Unfortunately, over many centuries, the Roman church became a model more political than ecclesiastic.[20] I believe that to maintain control over her people, this verse was changed to mean that only in Rome are the teachings true and faithful, and anyone who opposes them will surely go to an eternity of burning fire to be tormented forever. The church in Rome

---

20. If you wish to understand the changes which took place in the Roman Church which caused it to meld together religion and politics, I recommend Father John Strickland's informative podcast series, Paradise and Utopia. You may find it at https://www.ancientfaith.com/podcasts/paradiseutopia. Without bias he presents the overall history of Christianity, beginning before the Filioque controversy up through the conversion of Russia.

is now teaching doctrines which would make the early fathers of the first millennium shake their heads in disbelief.

There is another thing I would like to ask my friend. What is meant by the time on earth is a time of testing? Testing for what? Does the all-knowing God really need to test an individual to know the depths of a person's heart? Our sorrows and our response to them do not show God what we are. He already knows, so no testing is of any avail as far as His omniscience goes. The sorrows and trials of this life are to test us so we become aware of what we are and can repent. Life is filled with self-delusion. The trials of life can strip this all away, taking away our dependence upon ourselves and showing us–sometimes to our great shame–what we really are. This gets us ready for eternity–if we prepare wisely.

There is no place in the Bible, other than the Book of Job, where it is taught that we are being in some manner tested. And even Job's testing was not unto salvation or damnation, but that Job obtained a much clearer understanding of who he was and who God is. The warnings in the Bible are about examining our lives and preparing to meet God.

PERSECUTIONS FORETOLD

Once again, my friend turned to Matthew 24 in her paper, along with a mixture of other verses, trying to make a link between persecution and eternal hell. As noted, Matthew 24 is Christ's warning to the Jews who heard him speak at in the first century. The entire chapter is about the destruction of Jerusalem and the persecutions which were coming. In numerous places we see Christ tell His disciples clearly what to expect:

> Matthew 24:9–12. The incredible parallels of Matthew 24 and Revelation, which Jesus said would happen in "this generation" and "when Jerusalem (is) surrounded with armies." Most of that generation were dead in the time of 96 A.D. and Jerusalem was surrounded with armies in 70 A.D.[21]

Matthew 24: 9 "Then shall they deliver you up to be afflicted, and shall kill you: and ye shall be hated of all nations for my name's sake. 10 And then shall many be offended, and shall betray one another, and shall hate one another. 11 And many false prophets shall rise, and shall deceive many. 12 And because iniquity shall abound, the love of many shall wax cold. 13 But he that shall endure unto the end, the same shall be saved."

---

21. Kiser, "Revelation was Written Before 70 A.D." Para. 13

Multitudes of people place the events of Matthew 24 in this century. By putting these events into the future, expecting a Great Tribulation and the Anti-Christ to come, the word "saved" is transformed from being saved out of the destruction of Jerusalem to being eternally saved. There is also the problem of assuming that being saved, wherever it is mentioned in the Bible, automatically means that you are saved from eternal hell. This is again reading into the text. With the persecutions coming, it could mean being saved from them. It could mean, as is my personal belief, the word "saved" in Matthew 24, means being saved from being killed when the Roman armies of Titus destroyed Jerusalem. It could also refer to being saved from corrective punishment in the next age after AD 70.

Matthew 16:24 "Then Jesus said to his disciples, 'Whoever wants to be my disciple must deny themselves and take up their cross and follow me. 25 For whoever wants to save their life will lose it, but whoever loses their life for me will find it. 26 What good will it be for someone to gain the whole world, yet forfeit their soul? Or what can anyone give in exchange for their soul? 27 For the Son of Man is going to come in his Father's glory with his angels, *and then he will reward each person according to what they have done.*'"

Precisely! Therefore, we who have come to know our Lord's rich and kind mercy should make efforts to warn people of the day which is coming to every life when the works we have done will decide what shall happen to us. For those who have done well in this life there will be rewards equal with the degree of their good. I have no doubt the monks of Mount Athos, the martyrs who gave testimony with their lives, and all who have done the works of charity our Lord told us to do, shall have a far greater reward than those who approached the Christian life in a lazy and self-indulgent manner. In like manner, the chastening fire of God's love will torment the wicked in proportion to the evil they have done. But there is no work which deserves an eternity in suffering and torment. That is not justice at all, yet how fond the Infernalists are of rebuking our universal hope by saying, "Oh, but God is just, you know!" Yes! And justice means you get what you deserve and not one second more.

We also get what we do not deserve, which is God's abundant mercy to turn us from our self-delusion and see the evil we have done. Many sinners fancy themselves as wonderful people without any need of God in their lives. In eternity, the truth will show them their utter nothingness outside of a relationship of love with Christ. In truth, all of us will get what we need to be healed and brought into a state of full humanity.

Revelation 2:21 "I have given her time to repent of her immorality, but she is unwilling. 22 So I will cast her on a bed of suffering, and I will make those who commit adultery with her suffer intensely, unless they repent of her ways. 23 I will strike her children dead. Then all the churches will know that I am he who searches hearts and minds, and I will repay each of you according to your deeds."

Yes, this verse could perhaps be used as a proof text that we are given only this life in which to repent and turn to Christ. But even if so, the reward is *according to our deeds*, not according to some warped idea of divine justice in which God delights in the torment of the wicked (according to Aquinas).

THERE IS A DEFINITIVE MOMENT OF JUDGMENT THAT COMES AFTER DEATH

Revelation 20:11–15. The Dead Are Judged.

> Revelation 20:11 Then I saw a great white throne and him who was seated on it. The earth and the heavens fled from his presence, and there was no place for them. 12 And I saw the dead, great and small, standing before the throne, and books were opened. Another book was opened, which is the book of life. The dead were judged according to what they had done as recorded in the books. 13 The sea gave up the dead that were in it, and death and Hades gave up the dead that were in them, and each person was judged according to what they had done. 14 Then death and Hades were thrown into the lake of fire. The lake of fire is the second death. 15 Anyone whose name was not found written in the book of life was thrown into the lake of fire.

The Revelation of John is a difficult book to read and understand. The symbols and language are alien to our understanding. Being centuries from reading it as a believing Jew familiar with the OT makes it even harder. Many people have speculated on it, some of them making very odd observations. I am no better than they. All I can do is give you my opinion on what is being said here.

Here is the exegetical problem with Revelation. People read it as if it is a book about the end of all time, the consummation of the age, and the end of all things. This is the way it has been understood and taught for centuries. I don't believe it is. The Bible from Genesis to Revelation is the book which is about God–God in creation and God in restoration. The book is about a covenant made, broken, and restored as the New Covenant in which all people are part of the Kingdom. The Bible begins with the fall of man and ends with the restoration of the Kingdom. Instead of seeing Revelation as the end of all things, I believe it should be read as a book about the end of the Old Covenant and the opening of the Kingdom of God to all.

Beginning with Revelation chapter 18, we see the destruction of Jerusalem. Only of Jerusalem could it be said, "And in her was found the blood of prophets, and of saints, and of all that were slain upon the earth." This statement correlates with what Jesus said to the Pharisees in Matthew 23:

> Matthew 23:29 Woe unto you, scribes and Pharisees, hypocrites! because ye build the tombs of the prophets, and garnish the sepulchres of the righteous, 30 And say, if we had been in the days of our fathers, we would not have been partakers with them in the blood of the prophets. 31 Wherefore ye be witnesses unto yourselves, that ye are the children of them which killed the prophets. 32 Fill ye up then the measure of your fathers. 33 Ye serpents, ye generation of vipers, how can ye escape the damnation of hell? 34 Wherefore, behold, I send unto you prophets, and wise men, and scribes: and some of them ye shall kill and crucify; and some of them shall ye scourge in your synagogues, and persecute them from city to city: 35 *That upon you may come all the righteous blood shed upon the earth, from the blood of righteous Abel unto the blood of Zacharias son of Barachias, whom ye slew between the temple and the altar.* 36 Verily I say unto you, all these things shall come upon this generation.

Upon this generation. The ones standing right there listening to Jesus, not people living in the 21st century. Making this comparison between the passages in Matthew and Revelation, we have another compelling evidence that Revelation is pointing to the destruction of Jerusalem. People who point to Matthew 23–25 as somehow prophesying a future Great Tribulation two thousand years or more from Christ are not paying attention!

THE FIRST RESURRECTION.

> Revelation 20:4 And I saw thrones, and they sat upon them, and judgment was given unto them: and I saw the souls of them that were beheaded for the witness of Jesus, and for the word of God, and which had not worshiped the beast, neither his image, neither had received his mark upon their foreheads, or in their hands; and they lived and reigned with Christ a thousand years. 5 But the rest of the dead lived not again until the thousand years were finished. This is the first resurrection. 6 Blessed and holy is he that hath part in the first resurrection: on such the

second death hath no power, but they shall be priests of God and of Christ, and shall reign with him a thousand years.

Revelation is a book rich in Jewish Apocalyptic Language and symbolism. To attempt a literal translation of the words in it is to wander off the rails and into theological weeds. This is what happened in the last months of the year nine hundred ninety-nine. Everyone thought Christ was soon to come because a thousand years were about to end.

I believe the number one thousand used here is symbolic of the completeness of God's rule before all things are placed under the Father. Those who die in faith "live" in the sense of being with Christ rather than in the corrective scourging of the lake of fire. Remember, to be alive is to be in union with God, as Adam and Eve were before they fell. Once they ate of the tree, they were "dead," not in the physical sense, for they lived for hundreds more years, but in the sense of separation from God.

And what of the second resurrection unto the lake of fire? Infernalists place this thousands of years later, at the end of the world. I see no reason to do this in the text. Second does not necessarily mean second in time, but rather designates a different class of people. These people remain "dead" because they have no union with Christ. They have died intoxicated with sin, in love with wickedness, and thus they must go into the smelting furnace of God's love to be cleansed. Only after they are cleansed will they be united to Christ and truly be alive. All who are in a state of sin are dead.[22]

What is the difference between the first and second resurrection? Dying in faith. All who die in faith take part in the first resurrection because, being in Christ, they take part in Christ's resurrection, the first among men to be raised from the dead. Only those who are in Christ can do this, therefore, there is for all others a resurrection which is unto the lake of fire.

> Revelation 20:12 "And I saw the dead, small and great, stand before God; and the books were opened: and another book was opened, which is the book of life: *and the dead were judged out of those things which were written in the books, according to their works.* 13 And the sea gave up the dead which were in it; and death and hell delivered up the dead which were in them: and they were judged every man according to their works. 14 And death and hell were cast into the lake of fire. This is the second

---

22. First Timothy 5:6 But she that liveth in pleasure is dead while she liveth. The father of the Prodigal Son said, "For this my son was dead, and is alive again. . ." The Prodigal was never physically dead. He was separated from his father. Adam and Eve died when they ate of the fruit, but they remained physically alive for several hundred more years. People who are living in a state of sin are literally walking dead men. They are alive physically, but dead spiritually, being separated from union with Christ.

> death. 15 And whosoever was not found written in the book of life was cast into the lake of fire."

For Infernalists, this section is speaking about the end of the world and throwing sinners into eternal hell. If you take the events chronologically, something happens after this passage which throws everything out of order for them.

> Revelation 21:1 And I saw a new heaven and a new earth: for the first heaven and the first earth were passed away; and there was no more sea. 2 And I John saw the holy city, new Jerusalem, coming down from God out of heaven, prepared as a bride adorned for her husband. 3 And I heard a great voice out of heaven saying, Behold, the tabernacle of God is with men, and he will dwell with them, and they shall be his people, and God himself shall be with them, and be their God. 4 And God shall wipe away all tears from their eyes; and there shall be no more death, neither sorrow, nor crying, neither shall there be any more pain: for the former things are passed away. 5 And he that sat upon the throne said, Behold, I make all things new. And he said unto me, Write: for these words are true and faithful. 6 And he said unto me, It is done. I am Alpha and Omega, the beginning and the end. I will give unto him that is athirst of the fountain of the water of life freely. 7 He that overcometh shall inherit all things; and I will be his God, and he shall be my son. 8 But the fearful, and unbelieving, and the abominable, and murderers, and whoremongers, and sorcerers, and idolaters, and all liars, shall have their part in the lake which burneth with fire and brimstone: which is the second death.

Verse 1 In Jewish Apocalyptic Language, "heaven and earth" are a reference to the Old Covenant kingdom passing away. As discussed earlier in the book, the reference is to the Temple in Jerusalem, the very heart of the Kingdom of Heaven. This is precisely what happened in 70 AD, prophesied by Christ when He spoke the parable of the fig tree in Luke 13:1–9. The fig tree, national Israel, had borne no fruit. The owner of the vineyard gave it one more year to bear fruit, then it would be cut down. The added year ended in 70 AD with the destruction of Jerusalem, which according to Matthew 21:33–46, was the end of national Israel as the special husbandmen of the vineyard of God, the kingdom on earth. Not understanding Jewish Apocalyptic Language, it was not too long before Greek and Roman Christians began seeing this as a prophecy of the destruction of the visible earth and the heavens above us.

Verse 2 Some important wording here is totally missed. The New Jerusalem comes down from heaven. What is this New Jerusalem? The verse itself tells us. It is the bride. Who is the bride of Christ but the New Covenant church? God gives to the world the church in all Her beauty to bring salvation to us. How can the church come down to the world if this is the end of all things? The church came down to the world in fullness on the day of Pentecost.

Verse 3 The tabernacle is the dwelling place of God among men. Everything is changing now with the end of the Old Covenant. There is a new Jerusalem, the church, come down to be among men. Within each parish of the church is a tabernacle where God dwells in the Eucharist. Everything Judaism had is found new in Christianity.

Verse 4 This could be one of those "Ah hah! Gotcha!" verses for those who believe this is speaking of the end of all things. In discussing verses six and seven, I will show you why this is impossible. Those who believe that this chapter is speaking of the eschatological end of all things will snidely ask, "No pain? No sorrow? Who are you kidding? Look around you!" At first, I was a bit stumped by this until I realized that this passage is speaking of the celestial view of reality and not of this illusory life. For the Christian, there really is no pain or sorrow. We have been redeemed. Our 21st century lazy and self-indulgent lives have entirely missed what it means to be a Christian. This verse is speaking of the spiritual reality for the believer. Death no longer has dominion over us. Look at the joy of the martyrs as they die with hymns of praise on their lips. Truly suffering has no hold over them.

Verse 6 This verse has a time indicator showing that this passage cannot be the end of the world. At the end of all things, according to Infernalists, your eternal state is settled. Either you are in Christ, and thus not thirsty, or are separated from Him, and will be thirsting but will get nothing to drink forever. This is not what the verse says. It says those who are thirsting may come and drink freely. This cannot be a believer, since he already has rivers of water flowing from within, quenching his spiritual thirst. It can only mean the unbeliever who comes to recognize his thirst for the living water of Christ and appeals for a drink. This is the promise of the Gospel, which went out to all the world and made millions of converts. The message of God's love made men and women thirst to experience that love. If this passage in Revelation is about the end of all things, this invitation is ridiculous because the wicked, according to Infernalist teaching, will never have their desire (thirst) for God satisfied.

Verse 7 Another time indicator showing this is about things that are yet to come. How does Jesus say "he that shall overcome (future tense) shall inherit all things" if this passage is about the end of the world, and the issue of inheriting eternal life or being disinherited is completely settled? If you think this is the end of the world, then there is no "shall inherit" because those who are in heaven with Christ have already inherited and those who you assume are in hell forever cannot inherit. The way Infernalists read Revelation 20, everything is finished, and you are either redeemed with Christ or damned in the eternal lake of fire, with no opportunity to overcome. Instead, here is an invitation open to all: overcome your passions, overcome the sin that binds you, and you shall inherit that which has been prepared for all my children from the beginning of all things.

Verse 8 Infernalists teach that this verse is speaking about casting sinners into an everlasting fire of hell. It is not. It is a warning to those who shall remain stubbornly attached to sin. They shall not only experience the first death, that of their physical bodies, but also the second death of being cast into the smelting furnace, described here as the lake of fire. Again, remember that we are speaking of symbolic language here. It is not a literal fire as described by the warped imaginations of some Western theologians. There is only one fire in the next life and in the ages of ages to come–the passionate fire of God's love, of which early fathers such as St. Isaac the Syrian spoke. Our God is a consuming fire, and what is consumed is all that is His enemy–death, the grave, and all evil. We are not His enemies. We are all of us His children. Some have been, and many are to this day, extremely sick with evil, but that does not make them not His children. It makes them sick and in need of bitter medicine to become well. We can either take it now, or take it later, which will be much, much more unpleasant. The choice is yours!

Reading the rest of chapter 21 verifies this. From verse ten on we see a description of the church as the bride of Christ. We are given a description of how it appears as a celestial reality. And notice that the gates of it are never shut. The Gospel invitation remains open to all, even after death. The only restriction is that in this beautiful celestial city, no one may enter who is defiled with sin. This is the whole purpose of the fire of God's love. It is to cleanse the impurities and bring the soul to repentance. This is the splendor of God's love.

I will need to answer one more objection which I already can hear from those Infernalists who are determined to make this book a book of God's eternal condemnation of sinners. It is from the closing chapter of Revelation.

Revelation 22:10 "And he saith unto me, Seal not the sayings of the prophecy of this book: for the time is at hand. 11 He that is unjust, let him be unjust still: and he which is filthy, let him be filthy still: and he that is righteous, let him be righteous still: and he that is holy, let him be holy still.

12 And, behold, I come quickly;[23] and my reward is with me, to give every man according as his work shall be."

God insists to John that the wicked remain wicked and the just remain just. Infernalists will point to verse eleven as a proof text that there is no repentance after death. But in their zeal to damn souls, they cruise right by yet another crucial time indicator which shows a shift in the action. Here the action returns to earth away from visions of the heavenly city. Christ speaks to John in the here and now with instructions about the coming destruction of Jerusalem. The time is *at hand*, coming quickly–not two thousand years down the road. At hand. Quickly. These are important adjectives which show that the time for all this was about to happen. The focus of Christ has shifted back to what is about to happen to Jerusalem.

And what is about to happen to those in Jerusalem whose future is destruction? Christ says let the wicked remain wicked. They are going to reap the reward of their evil and there will be no turning from it. This is the true meaning of election. Jesus spoke about the Pharisees as having been blinded by God so that they might not see what He was teaching and be saved. He goes on to say that this is not from some dreadful decision of God made before the foundation of the world, but because this is what they have chosen and now God honors that choice and does not give them ears to hear and eyes to see. It is not about some plan of God to damn people out of the mystery of his will, but about the choices we make.

This is a fearful pronouncement that all should take to heart. Just like Pharaoh, there comes a time when God says, after you have refused and refused and refused to listen, "Okay. Have it your way. Reap what you have sown." After the Crucifixion, national Israel was symbolically given one more year as the fig tree to repent, turn to Christ, and bear fruit. Not only did they utterly fail, but they also filled up the measure of their fathers who killed the prophets by persecuting to death Christ's people. Now the full reward for their evil would be given, starting with their deaths in Jerusalem and their falling into the chastening hands of God. There would be no turning back. God now declares their hearts shall be hardened just as Pharaoh's heart was. Behold I come quickly, Christ says, and to give every man in this wretched nation what they have earned according to their deeds.

The only mercy of this terrible proclamation is that God's justice is not eternal conscious torment. As discussed before, in lex talionis, you are scourged in proportion to what you have done. Once your measure is filled up, justice is served.

23. In Greek, the word is tachý, takh-oo' and means quickly, speedily (without delay). 2,000 years of waiting for the coming of the Lord hardly meets the qualification of quickly or speedily.

Matthew and Revelation, so often quoted as proof-texts for a future Great Tribulation and eternal damnation of souls, are about national Israel. The focus of Christ is on the coming destruction. His warnings on how to be saved are focused on this event. He warns both the nation and individuals of what will happen if they repent–and what will happen if they do not. He weeps over Jerusalem, His beloved city as He has come to realize their stubbornness has sealed the fate of this once magnificent city. Yet the last book of the Bible closes with the promise of something even greater. The New Jerusalem appears to all, her gates never to be shut, and the eternal invitation is this: "Come all you who thirst, and drink freely of the water of life."

Revelation closes and completes this wonderful story–the redemption of all creation and the victory of God over evil. In Genesis the way back into the Garden, a symbol of God's presence, is blocked. In Revelation, the Garden of His love is opened and shall never be shut. All may enter in. Some will in this life, finding the fullness of that entrance after death. Others, after dying, will have a long journey of repentance, filled with the cleansing fire of our Father's corrective love. But the invitation is ever extended, the mercy of God never fails, the will of God to save all shall be accomplished. This is the Good News of the Gospel.

PEOPLE FALL INTO TWO DIVISIONS–THE SAVED AND THE DAMNED.

My friend's paper goes on to present more Bible verses with the same errors I have already answered. For instance, I am presented with the Parable of the Wheat and the Tares as a proof that God separates humanity into two classes of people at the Judgment. I remind you that these parables of separation have to do with the end of the age; the destruction of Jerusalem which brought the age of the Old Covenant of Judaism to a close. Several other passages are mentioned from scripture, all of which are answered by the same answers I have given before; therefore, I decline to repeat myself. They do prove her point of being a separation of the righteous from the wicked, but they do not prove in any way an eternity of torment for the wicked.

On page thirty-eight of the paper, however, a statement is made that really leaves me speechless. The writer states: "In the book of Revelation some have the mark of the beast and some have the Father's name on their foreheads. A person either belongs to God or the devil."

This is such a horrendous distortion of the salvation Christ accomplished on the Cross that I am dismayed that any intelligent person would believe in it. Yet this is the common belief of so many today, that the devil owns the wicked. They forgot exactly what Christ our God accomplished with His death on the Cross.

Mark 3:27 "No man can enter into a strong man's house, and spoil his goods, except he will first bind the strong man; and then he will spoil his house."

Satan is the usurper. Christ entered this strong man's house, and by His death, burial, and glorious resurrection, bound him. In Orthodoxy we refer to this as the Harrowing of Hell, celebrated on Holy Saturday. Not only did Christ enter Hades to bind Satan, but scripture says that He preached to the souls who were formerly disobedient in the days of Noah. Satan has been stripped of the authority which he stole in Eden's garden, has been bound, and nothing belongs to him anymore. Christ entered his house and took back all the stolen goods (souls) which are rightfully his. The usurper has been defeated and he owns *nothing!*

To say a person belongs to the devil, in the sense of being a permanent possession of the devil, is to deny the efficacy of the Cross. Romans 5:18 says: "By the act of one man, Adam, all were condemned. By the act of one man, Christ, all have been redeemed," which means they are no longer under the dominion of death. Yes, men may sell themselves to do evil. They may even, in their insane delusion, think they have the devil as their father and protector. At death they will go to be in the presence of God, for God rightfully owns all which he has created. I dismiss this statement as vain and unthinking nonsense!

ONLY THOSE WHO ARE IN UNION WITH GOD CAN ENTER HEAVEN. SOME PEOPLE CHOOSE TO REJECT THE GRACES OF GOD.

As an Orthodox believer, I would modify this to say only those who are in union with God can enjoy being in the presence of God. Remember, Orthodoxy teaches all go to be in the presence of Christ, but not all enjoy it. The love of God is experienced as torment to the wicked until the justice of God is met. We are at least in partial agreement here. There is no union with God, no experiencing of His love until the soul bows to the Lordship of Christ in obedience and repentance.

This is really saying there will be people who will choose to reject God even in eternity, yet there is not one single verse of scripture which says this. We do not know exactly what happens to the soul after death. From the fabulous Orthodox conjecture about toll houses to the fatuous purgatorial claims of the Catholics, we have a plentitude of vain imaginations about life after death when Christ Himself was silent about it.

The greater question for me is this: why do so many people object to the idea of God's mercy and His power being so great as to allow for corrective discipline and restoration of souls after death?[24] Is it the misunderstanding of horribly mistranslated scriptures which gives force to this desire? Is it a desire for revenge, thinking that surely certain people do not deserve to ever be forgiven? Maybe it is a lack of really meditating on what "God is love" really involves. Whatever it is, I find it odd for people to not eagerly accept this truly good news of God's immense and restorative love, but instead opt for the delight of being a holy and righteous soul watching with glee sinners get fried in the fires of hell they deserve.

I also wonder, as I write this, how many people might read these answers and realize the teaching of an eternal hell is a smear on the character of God, a political lie done by men who sought control of others by fear, and certainly not consistent with the verses which teach mercy for all. I do realize that after fifteen hundred years of being pounded with the divine wonderfulness of eternal torment, such a change is more than a little hard, yet for me, after considerable thinking on the subject, it is the only thing to make sense.

Scripture says the will of God is for all to repent and come to the truth. To not allow a soul to repent after chastisement is to create a schizophrenic God who works against what He has willed. The will of God cannot be thwarted. It will come to pass, either in this life or in the ages of ages yet to come.

WARNINGS ABOUT THE HORRORS OF HELL (THERE IS NO MENTION OF LEAVING IT OR BEING RECONCILED TO GOD AFTER DEATH)

There is also no mention of the Monophysite and Monothelitism controversies, how the two natures of Christ, exist in the one person of Jesus of Nazareth, is there? There is no mention of many of the issues which were discussed in the seven ecumenical councils of the church. In other words, my devout Catholic friend has suddenly morphed into a Protestant sola scripturalist, the kind that says, "If I don't find it in the Bible, I don't believe it." I find this kind of amusing in a sad way. In debating, this logical fallacy is called The Argument from Silence. What we do have in the Bible,

---

24. And honestly, some people really get their knickers in a knot when you suggest universal restoration in their presence!

plainly spelled out for us in unmistakable wording, is the will of God to save all. It is the will of God that all be saved (1 Timothy 2:4), that God will have mercy on all (Romans 11:32), that in Adam all die, in Christ all live (Romans 5:12–19), that Christ died for all and not just some "elect of God." (2 Corinthians 5:14–15). I have shown that the original texts in Greek have been massively and horrifically mistranslated into Latin and then to English. I turn this around on my friend. There is no mention in the Bible of an eternity in fiery torment if you read the Scriptures translated correctly! The only way to make this case is a continuous and stubborn determination to believe what has wrongly been taught for fifteen hundred years.

My conclusions:

1. There is no biblical support for an eternal hell. The idea of hell as a place of torment was not known to the Jews of Christ's day. It came from paganism and the darkness of men's minds laboring under the idea of God as Roman Courtroom Judge rather than Great Physician and Healer of Souls. The first five hundred years of the church saw a great multitude of people who taught and believed in apokatastasis.

2. There is no Orthodox support for this idea. Those Orthodox who do support such an idea are usually Western converts to the Orthodox faith who are bringing theological baggage with them. Orthodoxy has yet to have an ecumenical council to once-and-for-all-times discuss and settle this issue. The theologoumenon of those in the Orthodox Church, even priests and bishops, does not override the authority of an ecumenical council. And as I have shown A.) there is no evidence of any council anathematizing apokatastasis and B.) those canons of Constantinople II which appear to do so are bogus.

3. Constantinople II cannot be quoted in support of this. The council was started improperly, run improperly, and the will of Justinian was imposed by threat of violence. The fifteen canons against Origen have been found to be of questionable nature by modern scholarship and are not even mentioned by Catholic sources.

4. Proper textual criticism and investigation shows the verses speaking of condemnation and punishment properly belong to the destruction of Jerusalem and the end of the age. The Bible is the story of creation and redemption, not condemnation. The doors of the New Jerusalem never shut.

5. Visions, dreams, private interpretations, and any Roman Catholic council held after the schism of 1054 AD are not authoritative sources, especially when they conflict with either the Bible or the early fathers.

Neither are the theological and soteriological errors of any early father, including and especially Augustine, whose errors have polluted Western thinking.

6. It is profoundly dishonest to selectively choose what you like of the Scriptures and ignore the rest which speak of God's will to save all. It is also dishonest to avoid philosophical questions about this issue by suddenly becoming a sola scripturalist when the discussion goes to places you do not like and do not wish to discuss.

Part Four

Using Reason and Intellect to Understand God

THE PURPOSE OF THIS section will be to probe deeper into our limited understanding of who God is. By this I mean, as a sentient Being with a will, how does He act? To what can we compare Him? How do we understand His actions? What clues do we have of this from the intellectual capabilities we have which set us apart from even the highest thinking of the animal kingdom? What role does our understanding of language and the analogies we have from Sacred Scripture play in coming to a proper understanding?

I once read a comment which intrigued me. It said that Abraham knew God intimately before any Bible existed. The believer in sola scriptura thinks you can only way to properly find and understand God is in the Bible. Yet Abraham knew God intimately, so intimately, in fact, that he feels comfortable remonstrating with God over the destruction of Sodom. Abraham felt he could approach God in the manner he did, forcefully, but with humility. He begs God down to the necessity of just five righteous people being found in Sodom to save it, and there is no sign that God goes away steaming under the collar, thinking Abraham disrespectful.

The Bible therefore cannot be the only and exhaustive means by which we know God. At the same time, it is important to realize that the Bible does give us a much clearer understanding of God than the blindness of our imagination. Scripture itself speaks of the Holy Spirit working in the hearts of men without them so much as even having heard of Jesus Christ or the Gospels. But another reality is also true. Like Lewis's dwarfs in The Last Battle, men can be either blind, or at best seeing through a glass darkly.

To understand the ability of mankind to produce the idea of a God who tortures His creatures without mercy nor end, it is important to understand the ground into which this seed of thought was planted.

The fertile ground of such a diabolical understanding is the natural blindness of man's mind, a blindness which persists unless the Holy Spirit brings light to the soul. The Bible describes man as spiritually blind, his understanding darkened, and that this is our natural state because of the fall in the garden of Eden:

> Proverbs 2:12 To deliver thee from the way of the evil man, from the man that speaketh froward things; 13 Who leave the paths of uprightness, to walk in the ways of darkness;
> Proverbs 4:19 The way of the wicked is as darkness: they know not at what they stumble.
> Matthew 6:23 But if thine eye be evil, thy whole body shall be full of darkness. If therefore the light that is in thee be darkness, how great is that darkness!
> First John 2:11 But he that hateth his brother is in darkness, and walketh in darkness, and knoweth not whither he goeth, because that darkness hath blinded his eyes.
> John 12:35 Then Jesus said unto them, yet a little while is the light with you. Walk while ye have the light, lest darkness come upon you: for he that walketh in darkness knoweth not whither he goeth.
> Ephesians 4:17–18 This I say therefore, and testify in the Lord, that ye henceforth walk not as other Gentiles walk, in the vanity of their mind, 18 Having the understanding darkened, being alienated from the life of God through the ignorance that is in them, because of the blindness of their heart.

See the common theme? Darkness is the natural condition in which men stumble about, not knowing the light of truth.

The establishment of the church, and the giving of the Holy Spirit, did not somehow magically remove this darkness from those who were baptized. Paul reprimands Peter for his hypocrisy, Ananias and Sapphira try to pull a fast one over the Apostles (and experience severe consequences for this sin), and Paul writes scolding epistles to places like the Corinthian church, which was celebrating rather than mourning incest within its membership. If pure light and truth were given to each convert upon baptism, we would never have such stories. Christianity is the struggle to grow in the light of truth right up until the moment of our death. Each Christian you meet is at a certain stage in this growth, and this fact does not exempt priests or bishops. This we know from history as we see whole countries, with their bishops and priests, deceived by the heresy of Arias, who insisted Christ was not one in essence with the Father and the Holy Spirit. This darkness of the ecclesiastical mind continued with the Chalcedonian controversy and the schism which came from it. Further on down the road, we see baptized Frankish bishops daring to change the Creed by adding the words "and the Son," and then refusing to submit to correction when confronted. Baptism and membership in the church offer no protection against error as we work our way out of our natural blindness.

Because we do not think as God thinks, nor love as He loves, it seems to me that the natural response to either seeing a wrong or having a wrong done to us is to seek revenge. Sometimes mere restitution of lost goods is not enough. There is a streak in us that wants to see the guilty party suffer, as if the suffering would somehow teach the guilty one not to do such a thing again. In many years of watching online discussions of salvation and the treatment of sinners, I come away with a distinct sense that there is a psychology of punishment among Christians, with the attendant idea that sinners really do deserve any pain God would unload on them here on earth, but more especially in an eternal hell of suffering. I would be hard pressed to recall the multitude of times I have seen Christians on Facebook and other social media talk about the wicked in the most hateful language imaginable, rather than expressing deep concern for the state of their souls and offering prayers that they might be converted. And yes, I have been guilty of this myself. During the most recent Lenten season, I have been especially concerned to pray to God about this shortcoming in my charity, as well as deliberately offering prayers for the many wicked politicians who are promoting dreadful policies such as abortion and infanticide. May God have mercy on their souls!

This darkness of our sinful state was pierced by the light of the Living Word who came to walk among us. Yet even when He who brought the light of truth to the world did astounding miracles such as raising the dead, certain people preferred darkness to His light. The bestowal of titles, of clerical robes, the saying of long prayers, or any other theological activities, does not guarantee walking in the light with clarity of understanding. From the Orthodox monk Seraphim Rose to Thomas Aquinas, I am constantly besieged with writings which I am supposed to accept as a perfect understanding of God. One can almost hear the gasp of horror when I oppose some of the theological fluff men like them put out as truth. When Orthodox priests speak of the tollhouses, I find nothing from Christ at all about this most important event which supposedly takes place after death. When Aquinas speaks of the state of man's soul after death, I am likewise chagrinned to see that what Jesus said vs what Aquinas said creates a serious conflict.

Beware especially of those whose speech always draws your attention away from the revelation of God in scripture to what they personally think. Beware of those who have uncritically accepted traditions handed down without sufficiently testing them. Beware of those whose apologia is a thoughtless repetition of nostrums handed down from century to century. And even beware of me writing this book. Test everything, read, research, and above all, pray for enlightenment.

To begin to understand the incomprehensible, unsearchable, mysterious God, we must set a foundation in what we have been divinely given and can know. This would be the revelation of God found in Jesus Christ and the Scriptures about Him. This revelation is the basis upon which I will build this reflection. For me, all arguments are subject to one foundational truth:
God
Is
Love

THE ARGUMENT FROM LOVE

This understanding of God is from the Bible; for the Christian it is therefore the basis of every approach to God. Unfortunately, most Christians parrot this verse without taking the time to unpack these three short words and meditate deeply on what this means for mankind. This is compounded by the word love being commonly misused in a variety of ways which have nothing to do with a proper understanding of love. We must begin therefore by correctly defining what love is. To do this, let us turn to the Bible.

Not far into the first Gospel of the New Testament, we find Christ giving a definition which must have burned the ears of those who heard Him:

> Matthew 5:43 You have heard that it was said, 'Love your neighbor and hate your enemy.' 44 But I say unto you, love your enemies, bless them that curse you, do good to them that hate you, and pray for them which despitefully use you, and persecute you; 45 that you may be children of your Father in heaven. He causes his sun to rise on the evil and the good, and sends rain on the righteous and the unrighteous. 46 If you love those who love you, what reward will you get? Are not even the tax collectors doing that? 47 And if you greet only your own people, what are you doing more than others? Do not even pagans do that? 48 Be perfect, therefore, as your heavenly Father is perfect.

Hate your enemies. Jesus acknowledges that this the way the world thinks, the accepted mode of behavior in a world of sinners. Someone offends me, I'm gonna git him . . . and git him good! Jesus turns this upside down. Love your enemies. What does this mean? Does it mean to muster up some sort of good feeling about them? Jesus gives the most challenging definition of love we could imagine. Bless those who hate you and do good to them. Love is action. It is the action of doing that which is best for the other, despite his offense against us. According to verse forty-eight, this is the very action of God towards them who hate Him. He gives a multitude of blessings and good things to those who carelessly used His name as a curse word. His love is extended to those who burn Bibles and churches. This is the same God who loved His enemies to the point of asking the Father to forgive those who had just driven the nails into his wrists after unimaginable torture.

When we say God is love, we must have this proper definition in mind. He actively does good to all. God, who is love, is not to be thought of as a deity who smiles benignly upon humanity, looking down on us like an ancient doddering old grandfather. Love is a robust action of self-emptying which actively seeks the good of the other. The love of God repeatedly calls all to Himself, offering the riches of life with Him. It is love which beckons us to love our enemies because that is precisely what He does. The love of God does not stop when a person dies. The fantastic homiletic imaginations of Jonathan Edwards and others who picture God as ever angry with mankind are delusional. I believe they come from a darkened intellect and pagan influence.

Love is self-emptying. It is concerned with the happiness and well-being of the object of its love. In a beautiful scene from the movie, What Dreams May Come, Dr. Chris Nielsen, played by Robin Williams, dies and goes to heaven, only to discover that his wife has committed suicide and will not be with him. He decides if he cannot have heaven with his wife, he will go be with her in hell, no matter what unknown horrors wait there. That is love. Not the mushy, emotion-filled sentimentality which passes for love in our world, but is gone at the first sign of trouble. Real love says of its beloved, "I will go through anything for your sake. I cannot imagine for one second being without you. I will give everything I am and have to not only have you with me, but to make you whole."

Is this not the very essence of salvation? This is the heart of God, who indeed as the Living Word, set aside everything He had with the Father–His glory, His authority, a multitude of angels to serve His will–to come for mankind and rescue us. Unlike Dr. Chris Nielsen in the movie, Christ knew exactly the horrors which would face Him on the Cross. Like Dr.

Nielson–He did not care. He was undeterred by them. This is the love we are called to. It is the self-emptying love of God. As I recently read in a Christian commentary on this self-emptying love of God: try imagining yourself becoming a slug.

In his CD series on The Theology of the Body, Christopher West speaks of the change which took place after the fall. Before the fall, Adam and Eve looked upon each other with a longing to give to each other in love. After the fall, mankind's focus went from this self-giving love to a "love" based exclusively on what can be gotten out of it for the self. It is the kind of love a child has when he says, "I love ice cream." It is centered strictly around what gives pleasure to the self–and this includes others. If a woman's body gives me pleasure, I will use it and then move on. If I desire your possessions because I will enjoy them, I will take them, either by force or by subtlety.

West says this is the reason Adam and Eve covered their nakedness. Each realized the other was looking not with a gaze of self-giving love, but with a look which expressed a desire to use the other as an object. No one is exempt from this. Even the most generous of human loves has some of this corruption in it. Sin has made it impossible for mankind to understand love in the manner of a self-giving, sacrificial absorption with the happiness and good of the other. Consequently, we transfer this distorted idea of love to all others, and especially to the God who has created us to unite with Him in love. Depending on the degree of darkness in our intellect, we assign to Him the values, character, and intentions we fallen human beings have. Some of the darkest and most perverse visions of God have come from pagan myths created by men who reasoned from a place of complete spiritual and intellectual darkness.

To say God would act in any other way than in a manner which aims to do the highest good for the objects of His love–all Creation and all beings in it–is to superimpose on God our flawed idea of love. The proper understanding of love from both an intellectual and scriptural basis is that because God is love, He can only act according to that which is the good. This was shown to us in the greatest act of love ever seen when God took upon Himself human flesh and endured a death painful beyond our comprehension in order that all things be restored.

On this basis alone I should be able to say this issue is settled, rejecting completely the wretched Western ideas found in such lurid tales as Jonathan Edwards' infamous Sinners in the Hands of an Angry God sermon. Edwards' description of human beings as "loathsome spiders held over the fires of hell" is no description of how God views mankind. In Edward's imagination, God is not viewed as loving Father, but as disconnected third party with no emotional stake in the outcome of the sinner. Such a view not from a heart of love, but from Edward's intellectual and spiritual darkness. A man whose intellect is this darkened is in no way capable of giving a correct understanding of our heavenly Father who is love. I feel the same must be said of the many Roman Catholic visions in which God is always portrayed as angry and ready to pounce upon sinners. Such people have religion and are very devoted to the practices found in it. Watching their devotion infers that they are close to God and know of Him intimately. I would beg to differ. There is a great deal of psychology invested in religious devotion, and some of it is not from a position of being psychologically healthy.

I remember an incident which made a considerable impact on me. After a revival meeting at the Baptist church I was attending, a few of us were chatting in the narthex. The issue of pagans in Africa came up in the discussion. I can't recall the exact words now, but the response of one of the men was along the lines of, "Well, too bad for them if they don't find Christ." I went away disturbed, feeling this was a rather cold-hearted response regarding people who as pagans were most certainly going to the eternal hell we feared. But we had our salvation, our safety was secured, and because we were Baptists of the right kind, we knew that anything that happened to those who were not with us was deserved.

As I recall the many years of participating in social media and debates online, this psychology of punishment seems to be deeply ingrained in the human heart. I have watched two Baptists debating online soundly condemn each other to hell over a small difference in how baptism should be done. Fundamentalists of all stripes are eager to heap coals of hellfire on anyone who does not belong to their denomination or church. And by fundamentalists, I don't just refer to the common American understanding which is found in Anabaptist Fundamentalism. Fundamentalist Orthodox are quick to send all non-Orthodox into the fires of hell, especially Roman Catholics. Traditional Latin Roman Catholics make the same statements about all who are not of their brand of Catholicism. I read their posts online, long-winded screeds about the lack of grace in the other side, and I go away shaking my head in disbelief. Neither side will acknowledge the amazing miracles and the great saints which exist in their opponent's history.

What psychology lies behind this false image of God? I believe it is shame-based. In his book, Healing Your Wounded Soul, Father Joshua Makoul, says that in our broken world, many Christians find their spiritual progress hindered or stalled by psychological wounds from their past. Trauma creates shame in us. There is shame over guilt, which is a proper and true shame, and then there is shame over just being ourselves because we have been made to feel unworthy, unlovable, and a mistake of being. It is a shame born from being traumatized, unwanted, unappreciated, unloved.

I believe we feel this same shame before God. We sense our being is wrong, but rather than seeing God as loving Father who waits to heal us, we feel condemned.

> Our inner lives are often quite noisy. Highly selective memories ladened with emotions and colored with varieties of shame combined with a cultural bombardment of noise, engineered to excite the passions, serve as a layered cocoon beneath which is the self, often unattended and little recognized. Instead, we "identify" with the stuff. We work with the noise in an effort to make it more bearable, both for ourselves and for those around us.[1]

One of the ways in which we work with inner noise of self-condemnation is by adopting the defense of perfectionism. Perfectionism is a safe niche in life where the conscience can be muted. It is a small step from there to find a group of like-minded people in which we can together drown out the voice of our shame by intensely living the path we have chosen and looking down on the rest of Christianity as not being worthy of God's love because they have not accepted our beliefs. Those of us who struggle with this shame have come to believe that God loves us for what we are doing to be perfect Christians. We are perfect in belief, in our worship, in how we act in the world, and how we treat our fellow man. All who do not agree with us are deserving of eternal punishment because they are not doing exactly what God wants.

Shame and the corresponding perfectionist drive it creates give birth to religious fundamentalism. Everything about God is seen through the lens of the behavior we have perfected, a behavior which drowns out the inner noise of our shame. Having lived up to the standard we have set for ourselves, we assure ourselves of God's love, not based on free grace, but on our performance.

If God loves others in their brokenness, then this poses a real threat to me, for I can no longer silence the voice of my shame before God by being perfect in all I do. If God accepts them as they are, then I must be who I am before Him also, and my shame will not let me do this. People who bear shame from childhood trauma cannot believe they can be loved for being who they are, therefore, they must be constantly doing something to earn love and to feel worthy. I honestly believe this is at the heart of the psychology of eternal punishment. This need for personal affirmation overrides the reality that God is love–a love so rich, so deep, so unimaginable that we cannot understand it when it loves even its enemies. Perfectionist religious habits and judging others can make us feel we are good and worthy of God's

---

1. "Freeman, God and the Mystery of Self." Para. 12

love, while those who are not practicing our religious perfections are certainly worthy of hell. In other words, I am better than you and therefore, God accepts me. This is a deception, one born out of the darkness in which we struggle, not understanding the fullness of the mercy of God.

Far worse than this are the centuries of abuse and evil produced by such a distorted theology. Let's take Augustine's views on God and man as an example. If God is the punishing Judge who sends men into an eternal hell of torment, then it means God cares not for humanity, and freely torments without the slightest qualms of conscience or mercy:

> Thomas Aquinas: "In order that the happiness of the saints may be more delightful to them and that they may render more copious thanks to God for it, they are allowed to see perfectly the sufferings of the damned. So that they may be urged the more to praise God. The saints in heaven know distinctly all that happens to the damned."[2]

> Jonathan Edwards: "The sight of hell torments will exalt the happiness of the saints forever. Can the believing father in heaven be happy with his unbelieving children in Hell? I tell you, yea! Such will be his sense of justice that it will increase rather than diminish his bliss."[3]

Someone who delights in the pain and suffering of another is not a saint, but a sociopath! If this is a correct vision of God, and for far too many people it is, it then becomes but a small step for a leader in the church (pope, metropolitan, bishop, pastor, etc.) to mimic what they believe to be God's eternal actions by commanding similar treatment of heretics here on earth. Bad theology always turns into bad practice somewhere down the road. Aquinas called for their extermination.[4] After all, if heretics or pagans are not "one of the elect of God," then they are God's enemy, and since God burns His enemies for eternity, we should treat them in similar manner here on earth. Killing those who do not follow our interpretation of God or the

---

2. Aquinas, "Of the Relations of the Saints Towards the Damned."
3. Edwards, "The Eternity of Hell Torments"
4. "With regard to heretics two points must be observed: one, on their own side; the other, on the side of the Church. On their own side there is the sin, whereby they deserve not only to be separated from the Church by excommunication, but also to be severed from the world by death. For it is a much graver matter to corrupt the faith which quickens the soul, than to forge money, which supports temporal life. Wherefore if forgers of money and other evil-doers are forthwith condemned to death by the secular authority, much more reason is there for heretics, as soon as they are convicted of heresy, to be not only excommunicated but even put to death." (Thomas Aquinas ST II:II 11:3 corpus)

scriptures, who are going to go to an eternal hell of fire anyway, is not seen as violating the commandments of Christ to love our enemies, but is instead commended as "protecting the flock from error" or "saving souls from hellfire." This kind of thinking led the Puritan leader, Governor Winthrop of the Massachusetts Bay Colony, to delight in the murder of some three hundred Native American women and children because they were pagans, and as such, deserved to fall under the just condemnation of God, which Winthrop, being a good and devout Christian, was only too happy to administer as God's agent on earth!

This same thinking pervaded the Roman Catholic Church when it put to death Orthodox Christians and those who were outside the church of Rome, such as the Cathars, the Albigensians, and others. Funny thing about that, I don't find any instructions from Jesus or St. Paul regarding the killing of heretics! Something I do remember was about loving your enemies and doing good to them. Perhaps the popes of the Middle Ages missed that little detail in their haste to conquer the world for the Roman Catholic Church.

To create sentient beings, capable of pain and suffering, with no intention of them ever experiencing anything else other than suffering for all eternity, can in no way be said to be an act of love, based on the definition of love as doing that which is best for the object of one's love. This would mean that all who end up damned forever were never objects of God's love, but of hatred. Because God is love, it is impossible that the Creation be anything other than an act of love. Therefore, in creating mankind with foreknowledge of the fall and the entrance of sin, to have done this without having a complete plan of redemption, that is, without knowing in advance all things that would happen and having a remedy which would meet the need of even the hardest of hearts, to go forward with such an act, knowing that the outcome would be the eternal misery of billions, could in no way be called an act of love. It would be, in fact, an act of the most vicious and cruel malice ever known. Infernalists not only do not wish to admit this (for it destroys any argument they have) but try to avoid the reality of this by placing the blame on man's free will turn from God.

At the same time, I do not want to appear to turn the love of God into sentimentalism. There is a tough side to love. My wife and I had to administer tough love to our oldest son when his drug abuse overwhelmed him. For his own good, we managed to get him into our van. Surrounded by friends who kept him from escaping once he realized what was going on, we placed him in a highly recommended therapy program. All this was against his will. To him, this must have seemed like a punitive and mean treatment, but the happy end was his freedom from drug abuse. That which was seen by him as a torment turned out for his ultimate good.

In like manner, the fires of God's love, that which the church fathers called hell, are only for the good of the soul. They cannot be for anything else because love can only do good to the object of its affection. This is the goal of love, that the other may be blessed–even if it costs me everything. The problem with our understanding of love is that it is cheap. It stops when the price becomes too great. If that had been the attitude of Christ, He would have simply declared as forgiven a few chosen, forgiven them, and let the rest of the world go to hell forever. His horrendous passion was the ultimate price, the giving of everything He had, that all might be saved. And when you really begin to understand love like that, you will understand why apokatastasis must be true. You do not pay such an expensive price that it might go to waste!

ARGUMENT FROM THE SACRIFICE OF LOVE

What is the efficacy of the Cross? Is it fifty percent? Seventy-five percent? Or will only five percent of all those ever created in the womb by the hand of God receive salvation, with the rest to be damned forever, as St. Lawrence of Port Maurice and other Roman Catholic clergy and mystics have insisted? To properly understand the Cross, one must first understand Creation.

> It is not the way of the compassionate Maker to create rational beings in order to deliver them over mercilessly to unending affliction in punishment for things of which He knew even before they were fashioned, aware how they would turn out when He created them–and whom nonetheless He created.[5]

This is the point of David Bentley Hart his book That All Shall Be Saved. Hart testifies that he learned from fathers such as St. Isaac, Origen, Gregory, and Maximus that protology is eschatology.

> Perhaps the first theological insight I learned from Gregory of Nyssa is that the Christian doctrine of *creatio ex nihilo* is not merely a cosmological or metaphysical claim, but also an eschatological claim about the world's relation to God, and for that reason a moral claim about the nature of God in himself. In the end of all things is their beginning, and only from the perspective of the end can one know what they are, why they have been made, and who the God is who has called them forth

---

5. St. Isaac of Ninevah, "Ascetical Homilies"

> from nothingness. Anything willingly done is done toward an end; and anything done toward an end is defined by that end.[6]

> The cosmos will have been truly created only when it reaches its consummation in 'the union of all things with the first Good,' and humanity will have truly been created only when all human beings, united in the living body of Christ, become at last that "Godlike thing" that is 'humankind according to the image.'[7]

When I first understood what Hart was saying it blew me away! I believe many of us think that the cosmos will reach its end when the saved are in heaven and sinners in hell. In Hart's view, he sees it as incomplete until all are saved because that was the end unto which God created. The creation was not done and finished in Genesis, it is ongoing, precisely because the end in view at creation is the deification of all mankind and the submission of all things in Christ to the Father, so that God may be all in all. Only then will creation find its proper end and perfection.

God created toward an end, and if that end includes the damnation of people created in God's image (in some theological traditions majority of people are damned), then what shall we say of God's goodness? What can we say of His perfection? And what shall we make of biblical claims such as "Where sin increased, grace abounded all the more, so that, as sin reigned in death, even so grace would reign through righteousness to eternal life through Jesus Christ our Lord" (Romans 5:20–21).

The efficacy of the Cross therefore must be one hundred percent and no less. The purpose of the Cross is the restoration of all things, the achieving of the end which creation was intended. Scripture says even creation itself groans awaiting the redemption. The purpose of the Cross must be the total undoing of every bit of destruction done by the fall of Adam. Here is a question you must answer for yourself: if even one soul is lost forever, much less billions, can it really be said the Cross was a victory for God? I have asked this question of some Infernalists with whom I was debating online. They inevitably feel they can hold their position of billions being in hell forever in tandem with the idea that nonetheless God achieved a monumental victory over Satan.

Now if the intention of God in creation was only to save a few and let all others suffer forever, then you could indeed claim the Cross as victory. I cannot see it as such. And neither does the Bible.

---

6. Hart, "That All Shall Be Saved," Page 68
7. Hart, "That All Shall Be Saved," Page 68

> Second Corinthians 5:14 For the love of Christ constraineth us; because we thus judge, that if one died for all, then were all dead: 15 And that he died for all, that they which live should not henceforth live unto themselves, but unto him which died for them, and rose again.

The Orthodox Church is not exempt from this theological schizophrenia. During Pascha members of the Orthodox Church joyously sing the refrain, "Christ is risen from the dead, by death He conquered death, and to those in the tombs, He granted life." But that is not the eschatological reality of many Orthodox laity and clergy. If you believe that billions go into the permanent state of death called hell, you must say death won. You must say that even the love of Christ is not strong enough to take all from the grasp of death, and that God is not wise enough to find a way to guarantee that even the most wicked and hardened of sinners can be brought to repentance without violating that soul's will. In short, you have to say love failed and death won. Saving five percent of all the people ever to be created, while the rest suffer eternal misery, is not my idea of some monumental victory, nor of Christ's death conquering death! If you believe in eternal hell and an eternal state of death, then stop singing the Paschal Hymn you Orthodox folks! You are trying to have it both ways, and it doesn't work.

ARGUMENT FROM LOVE AND JUSTICE

A frequent response to saying that God is love and love simply does not act in such a fashion, is "Oh, but God is just." Well, I agree, but only if we properly understand what it means to be just. In the Roman courtroom mentality of the West, when the word "just" is used in theological conversations, it understands God rolling up His sleeves and administering a beating.

What is justice? What does it mean to act justly?

> Justice, in its broadest sense is the principle that people receive that which they deserve; with the interpretation of what then constitutes "deserving" being impacted upon by numerous fields, with many differing viewpoints and perspectives, including the concepts of moral correctness based on ethics, rationality, law, religion, equity and fairness.
>
> Consequently, the application of justice differs in every culture. Early theories of justice were set out by the Ancient Greek philosophers Plato in his work The Republic, and Aristotle in his Nicomachean Ethics. Throughout history various theories have been established. Advocates of divine command theory

argue that justice issues from God. In the 1600s, theorists like John Locke argued for the theory of natural law. Thinkers in the social contract tradition argued that justice is derived from the mutual agreement of everyone concerned.[8]

Based on the definition above, what is it that we justly deserve and how do we arrive at that conclusion? How does it relate to love? The problem with the Western view of God and His dealings in justice is that they are based on a retributive model rather than a restorative model.

In the retributive model, if someone does something wrong, we must respond by punishing for the committed action itself, regardless of what outcomes punishment produces. Wrongdoing must be balanced or made good in some way, and so the criminal deserves to be punished. It says that all guilty people, and only guilty people, deserve appropriate punishment. This matches some strong intuitions about just punishment: that it should be proportional to the crime, and that it should be of only and all of the guilty. However, it is sometimes argued that retributivism is merely revenge in disguise. However, there are differences between retribution and revenge: the former is impartial and has a scale of appropriateness, whereas the latter is personal and potentially unlimited in scale.[9]

Two questions come from these definitions: what do human beings, created in the image of God, deserve, and how does retribution balance things out to make all things right? For the woman who is raped, how does putting the rapist to death make things right again? There is never any way that she will be unraped or have the horror of what happened erased. Putting the rapist to death may be a suitable way to show potential rapists that rape will not be tolerated, but it does not undo the crime. Nor does it change the ontological being of the rapist, who will rape again if allowed out of prison because he is not changed in heart. In like manner, how does eternal suffering undo the sin that was done? If it cannot undo or repay the sin, then to what purpose it is, other than revenge. Yet we are not called to revenge, are we? The demand of Christ in Matthew is that we become like our Father in heaven by forgiving our enemies. In relation to an eternal, unforgiving hell, does God hold us to a standard that He does not keep?

Humanity bears the image of God, even the most depraved. Does the image of God deserve the treatment of an eternal, fiery punishment which makes no change in the ontological makeup of the soul, but instead locks it

8. "Justice," Para. 1–2.
9. "Justice,," Para. 30

in a state of sin forever? Would love do that? Or does love look beyond the offense to see the value of the image of God and seek to remove all that is corroding and distorting it so that it can be what it was created to become?

Love looks beyond the offense to restoration, that is, the offense is dealt with in a manner which acknowledges the wrongdoing but does so in a manner which looks to change the wrongdoer, so the offense does not happen again. This is restorative justice and is as different from retribution as black is from white.

Here is an example of restorative justice. A young boy steals from a shop owner. He is caught. The judge makes the young man restore the value of the goods taken by working for the store owner on weekends. The owner, being a good man, treats the offender with forgiveness and mercy, even though the young boy is often sullen and defiant.

One day, when sweeping the floor, the young boy overhears the store owner talking with a friend about a locket which contained a picture of his grandmother. The locket was part of the theft. The picture is gone forever, and the store owner begins to weep because the locket had deep sentimental value. For the first time, the boy deeply understands the wrong he has done. Crying, he comes to the store owner to tell him how sorry he is. His heart is changed, and he vows such hurt done to another human being, will never be part of his life again.

Now take this to the Judgment Seat of Christ. The soul sees God in all His goodness and kindness. It sees how churlishly it has treated this One who is only love and only good. All the kindness of God is made known to the soul in that instant. In contrast, the soul, stripped of all illusion and falsity, understands for the first time the depth of its offense against pure love. It is a moment of clarity in which the soul comes to repentance. The fiery love of God enters the soul and burns away everything that is not like Christ, cleansing the soul as if in a smelting furnace, and making it fit to eternally receive the love of God.

This is restorative justice. "But where is the punishment?" you may ask.

> I also maintain that those who are punished in Gehenna are scourged by the scourge of love. For what is so bitter and vehement as the punishment of love? I mean that those who have become conscious that they have sinned against love suffer greater torment from this than from any fear of punishment. For the sorrow caused in the heart by sin against love is sharper than any torment that can be. It would be improper for a man to think that sinners in Gehenna are deprived of the love of God. Love is the offspring of knowledge of the truth which, as is commonly confessed, is given to all. The power of love works

in two ways: it torments those who have played the fool, even as happens here when a friend suffers from a friend; but it becomes a source of joy for those who have observed its duties. Thus I say that this is the torment of Gehenna: bitter regret. But love inebriates the souls of the sons of Heaven by its delectability.[10]

There will also be loss of reward in the next life. For those who opened themselves to God and obeyed in this life, there will be great rewards. There is no way I expect the honors and rewards that will be given to men like the monks of Mount Athos. These are men who spent their entire lives in prayer and fasting seeking God, and through their ascetic struggles became models of God's love to humanity. Surely, they have earned a great reward in heaven. I do believe that part of the justice of God is the loss experienced by those who pursue evil here and now. Of them, Christ said they have their reward.

Justice does not stand free from love. It is a component of love. It gives to each what is deserved. Let me use another analogy. Suppose within the walls of a great building being demolished, a once thought to be lost painting is discovered. It is an invaluable masterpiece by a famous artist. It is now moldy, paint has chipped off the canvas, and is covered with dust and plaster. Would it be thrown away or taken to a trash yard to be burned? Of course not. The greatest experts in the world would be given the task of restoring its original beauty and value.

Yet we are supposed to think that the image of God in each man is not worth restoration. The idea of deserving eternal, fiery torment comes from the idea of man being nothing more than a worthless pile of dung. Blame Augustine. His terrible anthropology is foundational to the Calvinist idea of mankind (individual sinners) being born in a state of "total depravity." In Western anthropology, we are worthless and deserve nothing. I hear this over and over in discussions on the Internet, that we deserve hell. Really? We may deserve justice for our choices, but the idea that we, by the simple fact of our existence as beings who have fallen into error, somehow deserve endless torment, should be repulsive to anyone who has the heart of Christ for His creation.

In justice, love does not violate its own standards. The standard of God is lex talionis–the punishment fits the offense. Infernalists have yet to come up with a good explanation of the sin which deserves endless torment. I have no doubt that some especially wicked men even now have been in God's scourging fire for centuries and have centuries to go before justice is fully met. But there is no sin which calls for the eternal tormenting of a soul.

---

10. St. Isaac the Syrian, "Homily 72: On the Vision of the Nature of Incorporeal Beings, in Questions and Answers"

The idea that sin is an eternal offense against the dignity and honor of God and therefore deserves an eternal punishment is from Medieval Feudal Law. The Kingdom of God is not a feudal kingdom, it is a fatherly kingdom, and He will bring all His children back home.

Here is one last thing regarding love and justice. Think of the man or woman who meets their murderer in heaven. The soul of the murderer, now seeing the reality of its being and what it did, is now consumed with grief for its actions. The murdered person comes to the murderer and says "Father, forgive him, for he did not know what he was doing." This beautiful act of forgiveness does several things. It deepens the repentance of the murderer's soul. It also brings, after the sorrow, the union of the two souls in the love of God, which is a forgiving love. But most importantly, it makes the soul of the murdered one to be like Christ, who while being murdered said to His Father, "Father, forgive them, for they know not what they do." This action of praying for one's murderers has been the testimony of millions of martyrs throughout the ages. It is Christ in them, acting through them, displaying His loving forgiveness for the world to see. There is no revenge in heaven, despite what the Infernalists say. The forgiveness of God is greater than we can wrap our minds around. The martyrs are but a small picture of this immense, forgiving love which we barely understand.

This is not to make lightly of the sins we commit here on earth. It is God taking an evil and turning it into a good for the benefit of both parties.

Love and justice are not opposed to each other. Justice is love manifested.

ARGUMENT FROM LOVE AND GOD'S SOVEREIGNTY

Question: What does sovereign mean?

> God's sovereignty is one of the most important principles in Christian theology, as well as one of its most hotly debated. Whether or not God is actually sovereign is usually not a topic of debate; all mainstream Christian sects agree that God is preeminent in power and authority. God's sovereignty is a natural consequence of His omniscience, omnipotence, and omnipresence. What's subject to disagreement is to what extent God applies His sovereignty—specifically, how much control He exerts over the wills of men. When we speak of the sovereignty of God, we mean He rules the universe, but then the debate begins over when and where His control is direct and when it is indirect.[11]

11. Houdmann, "What Does it Mean that God is Sovereign?" Para. 1

It is God's sovereignty, made possible by His omniscience, omnipresence, and omnipotence, which assures His divine will cannot be thwarted. In short, unlike man, who makes plans only to come to a point where he utters curses in the frustration of being unable to accomplish what he has set as a goal, God's will shall be done. In the Christian realm, there is no argument with this, and in fact, many of the highly anticipated but failed plans of men are written off with precisely this comment: "It was not God's will." Some may respond in this manner in anger and frustration, others in acceptance, but the fact remains and is true–God oversees the outcomes of all that happens in this life following an ultimate plan of which we know practically nothing.

Let try using an analogy: suppose I set a goal of driving to San Francisco, California from Richmond, Virginia. San Francisco is the goal. I look on the map and I see that Interstate 80 runs across the entire country.

Driving north to Harrisburg, Pennsylvania, which is on the way to New Columbia, where we will pick up I-80 and head west, I decide to change my plans and instead go west on I-76, the Pennsylvania Turnpike. I do this because the weather channel has informed me of severe weather in New Columbia and dangerous driving. I drive to Pittsburgh and decide to continue west on I-70 until Indianapolis, where my new plan is to go north on I-74 and catch I-80 just east of Davenport, Iowa.

But, in Indianapolis, my children decide they want to go to St. Louis and see the famous St. Louis Gateway Arch. A check of the Internet shows the weather to be much nicer there, so I decide that going south would be good and we go to St. Louis and stay there for three days. After three days, we head west, trying to reconnect with I-80. But alas, another freak storm has created ten-foot snow drifts in Wyoming. The wise choice, eschewing the opportunity to be an automotive pinball on icy I-80, is to head south as far as possible. We pick up I-25 in Denver, go all the way down to I-19 in New Mexico, where we pickup I-40 west outside of Albuquerque. From there we complete our trip without further problems.

Did we make the intended end? Yes. Did we do it exactly as planned? Not exactly. But the point is not the trip. The point is the end, the telos. Likewise, the end is that which was planned by our loving God from before the creation of all things. For mankind, it is to become fully human by entering full union with Him. Christ is the prototype, the Man who is fully human. From the beginning the intention of God was for us to become by grace what He is by nature.

What Infernalists do not allow is that this journey is different for each one of us. No two journeys are identical, even if they may be close, such as a group of monks on Mount Athos. Each is an individual and each will have a specific and special experience of God along the way. God is everywhere present and in all things. St. Paul said that in him we live, move, and have our being. There is no escaping Him, either here in this world or in the ages of ages. And this is true for those of us who do not enter so fully into the ascetic life.

Using my road trip analogy, Infernalists do not want to allow that some will go through purging and repentance after death. The trip of salvation must be the same for everyone, even to the point of belonging only to a specific religious body which is special to God. For them, the only journey one can take to heaven is here and now. Yet there is no proof of this, other than their claim to some private visions of the most depraved kind,[12] visions which I find curiously suspect. All these visions of sinners in the hands of an angry God come from the West–the legal courtroom of punishment rather than the East, where salvation is seen as medicinal and healing. I believe it is culture influencing the psychology and belief of people, even to the point of psychological impairment, manipulation of feelings, and visions that are more of a slander on God's character than a true depiction of His unfathomable love for all mankind.

> In the majority of the apparitions considered, children or adolescents were the sole or main visionaries, making it likely that an element of child psychology might well be involved. For a thorough evaluation of the visions and messages, it would be necessary to know a great deal more about the children—what kind of religious art they had been exposed to, what sermons they had listened to, what teaching they had received at school and catechism classes, and what religious books they had read.[13]

Moving on from here, I need to say that I am a child treading in deep theological waters. Men far more brilliant than I have discussed and debated the issue of God's sovereignty for centuries. I have nothing to add to their thinking on the subject. What follows is just me thinking aloud and trying to figure this out for myself, something I will not do on this side of the grave.

> God is described in the Bible as all-powerful and all-knowing (Psalm 147:5), outside of time (Exodus 3:14; Psalm 90:2), and responsible for the creation of everything (Genesis 1:1; John 1:1). These divine traits set the minimum boundary for God's

---

12. A popular vision of perdition is as a physical place of fire and brimstone, extraordinary torments and monsters. Many artists added their own ideas, such as Hieronymus Bosch, who in the 15th century painted a highly original vision of hell, a tableau of violence and excruciating tortures

13. Lambouras, "The Marian Apparitions: Divine Intervention or Delusion?" Para. 37.

> sovereign control in the universe, which is to say that nothing in the universe occurs without God's permission. God has the power and knowledge to prevent anything He chooses to prevent, so anything that does happen must, at the very least, be "allowed" by God.[14]

Yes, but why? In relation to mankind and the creation in which we exist, it must go back to the very beginning and to a plan which has a goal. Hart's meditation on creatio ex nihlo sets forth only two choices in regards to mankind: either creation was made with the sovereign goal that despite the entrance of sin, there will be a wonderful working out of all this for the good and the restoration of all things and all people or, as the Calvinists teach, creation was done for the purpose of showing the power and majesty of God, with the goal that some are chosen to eternal life and others to eternal damnation. In either scenario, God achieves this goal. He is sovereign and the goal will be met.

> At the same time, the Bible describes God as offering humanity choices (Deuteronomy 30:15–19), holding them personally responsible for their sins (Exodus 20:5), and being unhappy with some of their actions (Numbers 25:3). The fact that sin exists at all proves that not all things that occur are the direct actions of God, who is holy. The reality of human volition (and human accountability) sets the maximum boundary for God's sovereign control over the universe, which is to say there is a point at which God chooses to allow things that He does not directly cause.[15]

I question this statement. To say there is a boundary for God's control infers there could be some action taken somewhere that is no longer under His control. This would mean He is not sovereign over all things.

> The fact that God is sovereign essentially means that He has the power, wisdom, and authority to do anything He chooses within His creation. Whether or not He actually exerts that level of control in any given circumstance is actually a completely different question. Often, the concept of divine sovereignty is oversimplified. We tend to assume that, if God is not directly, overtly, purposefully driving some event, then He is somehow not sovereign. The cartoon version of sovereignty depicts a God who must do anything that He can do, or else He is not truly sovereign.
>
> Of course, such a cartoonish view of God's sovereignty is logically false. If a man were to put an ant in a bowl, the

---

14. Houdmann, "What Does it Mean that God is Sovereign?" Para. 2
15. Houdmann, "What Does It Mean that God is Sovereign?" Para. 3.

"sovereignty" of the man over the ant is not in doubt. The ant may try to crawl out, and the man may not want this to happen. But the man is not forced to crush the ant, drown it, or pick it up. The man, for reasons of his own, may choose to let the ant crawl away, but the man is still in control. There is a difference between allowing the ant to leave the bowl and helplessly watching as it escapes. The cartoon version of God's sovereignty implies that, if the man is not actively holding the ant inside the bowl, then he must be unable to keep it in there at all.

The illustration of the man and the ant is at least a vague parallel to God's sovereignty over mankind. God has the ability to do anything, to take action and intervene in any situation, but He often chooses to act indirectly or to allow certain things for reasons of His own. His will is furthered in any case. God's "sovereignty" means that He is absolute in authority and unrestricted in His supremacy. Everything that happens is, at the very least, the result of God's permissive will. This holds true even if certain specific things are not what He would prefer. The right of God to allow mankind's free choices is just as necessary for true sovereignty as His ability to enact His will, wherever and however He chooses.[16]

Notice the one thing not spoken of in this article–love. In discussions with those who go into theological spasms of rapture discussing the sovereignty of God, I have found that they are captivated by His power. God has the power to do all His holy will and no created being can stop that will from taking place. This is true. Now take that sovereignty and apply it to redemption. Will any created thing be strong enough in rebellion to hold out against the sovereign love which sent Christ to the Cross? Love seldom enters discussions of God's sovereignty. He is the all-powerful God who, if you offend Him, will roll up His sleeves and administer a beating. Sovereignty for them is not about forgiveness, it is about power. The church needs to get back to an all-powerful love that will not be thwarted.

Isaiah 46:9 "Remember the former things of old: for I am God, and there is none else; I am God, and there is none like me, 10 Declaring the end from the beginning, and from ancient times the things that are not yet done, saying, My counsel shall stand, and I will do all my pleasure."

This is true sovereignty, that God will do all His good pleasure. If any hand could stop Him, then He would not be sovereign. That good pleasure, according to 1 Corinthians 15:28, is that God will be all in all. This is the end to which all things in the beginning were made. It could have been

---

16. Houdmann, "What Does It Mean that God is Sovereign?" Para. 4–6.

accomplished without Adam's fall. But the point is that it still will be accomplished. It is the love of God which directs His sovereign power.

The problem I have with the usual Christian presentation of God's sovereignty is that it is one of raw, terrifying power which can just as easily turn against us as towards us. It is all up to Him, and we have no control over whether He shall bless us or curse us. I believe this is why one can find so many Christians who are deeply fearful. They understand God is all-powerful. They forget this power is ruled by love. It cannot be any other way, for the Divine Being is love. It is not that He chooses to love, which would mean He is also free to choose to hate, but that He is love. God cannot be anything other than what He is. Therefore, neither can His actions or His sovereign will be expressed in any other manner than love. The Calvinist idea of a God who easily and with no qualms chooses a vast majority to torment forever before they are even born is a sick caricature of God, a description which is akin to the pagans and their understanding of a divine power neither particularly friendly nor fatherly. True sovereignty means that love wins, for ultimate power is ruled by the love which is its foundation.

Is sovereignty limited by a love that allows the other to assert itself and its will? Does sovereignty mean that as a sovereign being, you do things exactly the way I want them done–or else! Such a threatening posture may be the sovereignty of power, but it is not the sovereignty of love. We are back to the ontology of God being love. Love which grants to the object of its affection a freedom which will return to it. Raw power finds a way to brutalize others into submission. Sovereign love finds the way that the beloved is drawn by the irresistible attraction of love. There have been earthly kings who have been served because to oppose them meant losing one's head. And there have been kings who were so kind and loving to their subjects that the people of his kingdom would have willingly died for him. In both cases, the subjects were obedient, but in one, not of love but fear. Which is our God?

To genuinely love another cannot be forced. It is a response of the will, a choice made by the person. God as Person can only love us because love is what He is. The choices we make in this life have consequences. God uses those consequences to train us so we see clearly how evil is not our friend, is not in our best interest, and is not good for others. Those who learn this lesson in this life, like the man whose blog piece I quoted, turn willingly from their sin and increasingly see the beauty of Christ. As their spiritual eyes open, they are drawn to Christ, not by force or coercion, but by love. True sovereignty is the power to irresistibly draw us to God through the overwhelming beauty of love. In sovereignty, nothing is ever out of control of God, no matter how things may look to us as we wander loose in the fool's paradise of our own choosing.

A Summary–Context Is Everything

IN THE MANY DISCUSSIONS I have about apokatastasis, in the end, the argument always seems to come back to this:

"Look, the Bible says that there is hell and it is everlasting, and that settles that."

Well, actually, no it doesn't. Just pointing to a verse in the Bible and creating an entire doctrine around it is what Jehovah's Witnesses do. Religious cults are built by taking one verse and building an entire religion around it, interpreting everything else in the Bible according to that seminal idea. This is what the Seventh Day Adventists have done with the commandment to keep the Sabbath holy, ignoring the larger context of the Bible in which Exodus 31:6 states that the Sabbath is part of the Old Covenant, which has passed away.

We are back to looking at aionios one last time. Infernalists insist that this word must mean eternal. It has been dutifully translated as such in the West for centuries.

> Apart from the Platonic philosophical vocabulary, which is specific to few authors, aiónios does not mean "eternal;" it acquires this meaning only when it refers to God, and only because the notion of eternity was included in the conception of God: for the rest, it has a wide range of meanings and its possible renderings are multiple, but it does not mean "eternal." In particular when it is associated with life or punishment, in the Bible and in Christian authors who keep themselves close to the Biblical usage, it denotes their belonging to the world to come.[1]

Like many adjectives, the word aionios carries multiple meanings. For example, if I simply say "red," you are left to your imagination as to which shade of red. But if I say, "a red fire engine roared by on the way to a fire," you

---

1. Ramelli, Ilaria L. E. & Konstan, David, "Terms for Eternity."

immediately know what kind of red I am talking about. I have just narrowed things down to a specific shade of red, that of a fire engine. There is only one red which is traditional to fire engines.

Therefore, the setting of the word determines the meaning of the word. In the Bible, we have several contexts which are completely ignored by Infernalists in their determination to send people to eternal torment.

FIRST CONTEXT–JUDAISM.

One of the popular verses Infernalists rely upon for their defense is Matthew 25:46. To look to this verse as a proof text for eternal hell is to completely ignore the context of Matthew 23–25. The context is the coming destruction of Jerusalem in AD 70, which would be the final covenant ending destruction of national Israel as God's specific people, replacing this nation with the Jewish/Gentile church. Jesus made prophecy of this in Matthew 21: 33–46, He wept over this destruction as He foretold it in Matthew 23. It was the coming of the end of the age–the age of the Old Covenant with national Israel. The KJV has erroneously translated this passage in such a manner to make it look like the end of the world. It is not. Look at the proper translation of Matthew 24:1–3, which shows us exactly what is about to happen:

> Matthew 24:1. Jesus left the temple and was walking away when his disciples came up to him to call his attention to its buildings. 2. "Do you see all these things?" he asked. "Truly I tell you, not one stone here will be left on another; every one will be thrown down." 3. As Jesus was sitting on the Mount of Olives, the disciples came to him privately. "Tell us," they said, "when will this happen, and what will be the sign of your coming and of the end of the age (aion)?"

The false translation of this passage has completely messed up the entire context of the Gospel of Matthew, as well as the rest of the Scriptures. Matthew is the Gospel to the Jews. Everything about has to do with being a Jew. Right from the very beginning in Matthew 1, where the genealogy of Christ is laid out, a thing which would be important to those Jews expecting the Messiah, but would mean nothing to a Gentile, Jesus comes to offer Himself to national Israel as the Promised One. But after three years of hardening their hearts to Him, the prophecies turn to a warning that the age of Israel will end and a new age will begin.

It is in this context Jesus speaks in Matthew 24 of entering the age to come with its blessings–or missing it and entering a punishment which will last for the duration of the next age. This verse is a warning of another age coming, which in turn is one of many ages yet to come. Infernalists do not see this. They approach the Bible as if there is life now and then death and either eternal life or eternal hell, and that's it. Yet St. Paul spoke of the coming of ages and ages.

Multiple ages are yet to come. We have no idea how many, nor how long they last, until at the end, our Lord hands the Kingdom over to the Father and God is all in all.

In the context of the end of the age, in the context of warning His listeners to repent of their unbelief and believe in Him, Jesus is not speaking about eternity. Those who wish to make Matthew 23–25 speak about anything other than the end of the age have not paid close attention.

There is another interesting witness against Israel which I have discovered in my research. It is the Song of Moses:

God told Moses to write a song as a witness against Israel.

> 'Now therefore, write down this song for yourselves, and teach it to the children of Israel; put it in their mouths, that this song may be a witness for Me against the children of Israel. When I have brought them to the land flowing with milk and honey, of which I swore to their fathers, and they have eaten and filled themselves and grown fat, then they will turn to other gods and serve them; and they will provoke Me and break My covenant. Then it shall be, when many evils and troubles have come upon them, that this song will testify against them as a witness; for it will not be forgotten in the mouths of their descendants, for I know the inclination of their behavior today, even before I have brought them to the land of which I swore to give them.' Therefore, Moses wrote this song the same day, and taught it to the children of Israel. (Deuteronomy)

Moses told the elders the song was for the latter days. This is a covenant warning. In making covenant, both parties in the covenant swear binding oaths which contain self-maledictory sanctions which will befall the one breaking the vows. When a covenant oath is broken, there must be witnesses against the oath-breaker so that the sanctions can be carried out. The Song of Moses is the warning which shall be the witness against Israel.

> 'For I know that after my death you will become utterly corrupt, and turn aside from the way which I have commanded you. And evil will befall you in the latter days, because you will do evil in the sight of the LORD, to provoke Him to anger through the work of your hands.' Then Moses spoke in the hearing of all the

assembly of Israel the words of this song until they were ended:" (Deuteronomy)

In the song Moses says He can see that their end will be a faithless and perverse generation. Is this an absolute promise, or a warning that the nation of Israel could have heeded and avoided destruction? Because God is love, I must think the latter. St. Paul says "But to Israel he saith, All day long I have stretched forth my hands unto a disobedient and gainsaying people."

> And He said: "I will hide My face from them, I will see what their end will be, for they are a perverse generation, Children in whom is no faith."

Now it gets interesting. We find Jesus calling His generation faithless and perverse. And where does this occur? It is in the gospel to the Jews– Matthew, the gospel which I have insisted ends with the destruction of Jerusalem and the end of the Old Covenant with the Jewish nation.

> Then Jesus answered and said, "O faithless and perverse generation, how long shall I be with you? How long shall I bear with you? Bring him here to Me."

Jesus states Jerusalem is the one who kills the prophets and then pronounces judgment on Jerusalem.

> "O Jerusalem, Jerusalem, the one who kills the prophets and stones those who are sent to her! How often I wanted to gather your children together, as a hen gathers her chicks under her wings, but you were not willing! See! Your house is left to you desolate;"

From Matthew the progression of events goes to John's vision in the Apocalypse where John sees a sign of the seven angels having the seven last plagues, and those who have victory over the beast singing the Song of Moses and of Jesus.

> Then I saw another sign in heaven, great and marvelous: seven angels having the seven last plagues, for in them the wrath of God is complete. And I saw something like a sea of glass mingled with fire, and those who have the victory over the beast, over his image and over his mark and over the number of his name, standing on the sea of glass, having harps of God. They sing the song of Moses, the servant of God, and the song of the Lamb, saying: "Great and marvelous are Your works, Lord God Almighty! Just and true are Your ways, O King of the saints!"

The judgments are then poured out on Jerusalem. These are the covenant sanctions which fall upon national Israel for killing their Messiah.

> Then the third angel poured out his bowl on the rivers and springs of water, and they became blood. And I heard the angel of the waters saying: "You are righteous, O Lord, The One who is and who was and who is to be, Because You have judged these things. For they have shed the blood of saints and prophets, And You have given them blood to drink. For it is their just due."

Conclusion: The wrath of God and judgments spoken of in the book of Revelation were directed at first century Jerusalem. Revelation is a more detailed presentation of Matthew 23–25. The is nothing beyond Revelation except that which St. Paul spoke of when Christ turns the Kingdom over to the Father and God becomes all in all. That–and not some fatuous "Rapture of the church" or other such folderol–is what we should be expecting. In the meantime, the New Jerusalem offers entry to anyone who will enter, and her gates shall never be shut. Not now, not after death, never!

SECOND CONTEXT–THE CHARACTER AND INTENT OF GOD IN SCRIPTURE

To say aionios means eternal, thus giving weight to the idea of never-ending torment, causes numerous problems with the rest of the Bible. When I was a fine little fundamentalist, I was taught the Bible cannot contradict itself. If you have a contradiction, you need to do further research to find out where you made the error and reconcile the opposing verses. I see wisdom in this, especially when it comes to descriptions of God's interaction with human beings.

Infernalist belief in an eternal torment is a contradiction to several passages in scripture which speak of God's will to save all:

> First Timothy 2:4: "Who will have all men to be saved, and to come unto the knowledge of the truth." Will His desire come to pass, or is it just a weak wish? Sovereignty. Is God all-powerful or not? Would love ever give up, especially the love of One who is sovereign over all things? This is the character of love, that all people shall come to enjoy His love.
> First Corinthians 15:22: "In Adam all die, in Christ, all live." One of the strongest verses I have seen to declare that God leaves none of His children behind to be devoured by the evil one,

even the most wicked and worst of His kids is included. (Yes, Virginia, even Adolf Hitler!)

Colossians 1:20: "And, having made peace through the blood of his cross, by him to reconcile all things unto himself; by him, I say, whether they be things in earth, or things in heaven." All things. All things. All things. Say it over and over and over until the light comes on and you say to yourself "Wow. All things are reconciled to Christ through the Cross."

First Corinthians 15:22: "For as in Adam all die, even so in Christ shall all be made alive."

Many more verses besides, seventy-six in total, indicate the salvation of God is extended to all people. None are excluded. This is what love does. To say the will of God from before creation was to create sentient beings capable of knowing pain and suffering, with the will for most of them to be in torments forever without respite, is to smear the character of God and certainly not to understand at all what love is. Such character assassination makes our loving Father appear more like the pagan gods of antiquity, who in the pagan mind, needed blood sacrifice in appeasement. No wonder David Bentley Hart expresses a certain indignation at theologians and philosophers who casually describe our God in such a manner.

> As far as I am concerned, anyone who hopes for the universal reconciliation of creatures with God must already believe that this would be the best possible ending to the Christian story; and such a person has then no excuse for imagining that God could bring any but the best possible ending to pass without thereby being in some sense a failed creator.[2]

It is therefore quite reasonable, given the context of scripture which points to the will of God being to save all people, to insist the translating aionios as "eternal" simply does not fit. To translate it properly as "age-lasting," means hell–the chastisement of the wicked–will end and has a goal. The goal is will of God to save all, spoken of in the Bible.

THIRD CONTEXT–THE GENERATION TO WHICH CHRIST SPOKE

In reading the Scriptures, another problem is that each generation does not hear the words of Christ as a first century Jew would. For instance, what newly baptized Christian would read chapter one of Matthew and be

---

2. Hart, "That All Shall Be Saved," Page 66

inspired? Answer: a Jewish convert in the first century after Christ's resurrection. He would find in the long genealogy ample proof Jesus was the Promised One, the Messiah of Israel. To us, the reading is a big yawn. The context of the time in which our Lord spoke is especially important. It puts proper understanding to the words He spoke.

As I mentioned before, when Christ speaks in multiple places of Gehenna, a Jew listening to Him would think of the garbage dump outside of Jerusalem, a place where the fire never went out and the worm never died. The garbage and dead bodies of criminals dumped there kept the fires and worms going without cease. No Jew listening to Christ speak would have gone away thinking of Dante's Inferno.

Red does not mean green. Words mean things, and it was patently dishonest of the translators of the Scriptures not to use the exact Greek word Gehenna, instead of the word hell, in Mark 9:43 and the many other passages where it is used. The use of this word pointed to the destruction of Jerusalem in AD 70. It was a warning those listening they would wind up corpses on the garbage dump if they did not repent. When Jerusalem did fall to the Roman armies of Titus, a multitude of the Jews who had heard Christ and ignored those warnings wound up exactly there.

The same translation problem occurs in the OT as well with the misuse of the word "Sheol" to mean hell. To get the flavor of the time in which Christ spoke, let us examine some Jewish sources:

> In classical Judaism death closes the book. As the anonymous author of Ecclesiastes bluntly put it: "For the living know that they will die, but the dead know nothing, and they have no more reward" (Eccles. 9:5). The death of human beings was like that of animals: "As one dies, so dies the other. They all have the same breath, and man has no advantage over the beasts . . . all are from the dust, and all turn to dust again" (Eccles. 3:19–20). Life alone mattered: "A living dog is better than a dead lion" (Eccles. 9:4). Even Job, whose questioning at times verges on subverting Yahwist doctrine, ends up endorsing the official creed: "Man dies, and is laid low . . . As waters fail from a lake, and a river wastes away and dries up, So man lies down and rises not again; till the heavens are no more he will not awake, or be roused out of his sleep" (Job 14:10–12).
>
> Yet such views were far from universal. The archaeological record suggests that the various racial elements assimilated to form the Jewish nation each had brought to the new community its own tribal customs, often based on beliefs in an afterlife. Both Moses (Deut. 14:1) and Jeremiah (Jer. 16:6) denounced

> mortuary practices taken to imply such beliefs. Necromancy, although officially forbidden, was widely practiced, even in high places. Saul's request to the witch of Endor to "bring up" the dead prophet Samuel for him (I Sam. 28:3–20) implied that the dead, or at least some of them, still existed somewhere or other, probably in Sheol, "the land of gloom and deep darkness" (Job 10:21). In Sheol, the good and the wicked shared a common fate, much as they had in the Babylonian underworld. The place did not conjure up images of an afterlife, for nothing happened there. It was literally inconceivable, and this is what made it frightening: death was utterly definitive, even if rather ill-defined."[3]

From this entry in Brittanica/Judaism, it appears there was no concept of a place of eternal torture in the Jewish mind prior to the first century. By the first century, at the time of the destruction of Jerusalem, this appears to have changed:

> Flavius Josephus, the Jewish historian of the 1st century ad, recorded in Bellum Judaicum (History of the Jewish War) how doctrinal disputes about death, the existence of an afterlife, and the "fate of the soul" were embodied in the views of various factions. The Sadducees (who spoke for a conservative, sacerdotal aristocracy) were still talking in terms of the old Yahwist doctrines, while the Pharisees (who reflected the views of a more liberal middle class) spoke of immortal souls, some doomed to eternal torment, others promised passage into another body). The Essenes held views close to those of the early Christians.[4]

It does not speak well for the defenders of eternal, conscious torment that it was the Pharisees who promoted eternal torment in the first century. Remember, it was these same Pharisees who, in spiritual blindness, crucified their Savior, bringing upon them the destruction of their nation. I would not consider spiritually blind people to be a good promotion for any doctrine I want to promote!

In addition, religious history records the influence of Platonic thinking upon the Jews of the first century and later Christian writers such as Augustine, an ardent defender of the idea of eternal hell. One must wonder just how much Plato's Myth of Er influenced him to believe in eternal hell. There is a serious lack of theological purity to the musings of the early church. I am not talking about the decisions of the councils, which canons

---

3. "Death—Judaism," Para 6–7.
4. "Death—Judaism," Para 12.

are binding on me as an Orthodox Christian. I am speaking of the theologoumenon of some of the writers of the early church. This is why councils had to be called to sort out truth from falsehood. It is a shame eschatology was not addressed along with the Christology they had to work out.

> The subject of death is treated inconsistently in the Bible, though most often it suggests that physical death is the end of life. This is the case with such central figures as Abraham, Moses, and Miriam.
>
> There are, however, several biblical references to a place called Sheol (cf. Numbers 30, 33). It is described as a region "dark and deep," "the Pit," and "the Land of Forgetfulness," where human beings descend after death. The suggestion is that in the netherworld of Sheol, the deceased, although cut off from God and humankind, live on in some shadowy state of existence.
>
> While this vision of Sheol is rather bleak (setting precedents for later Jewish and Christian ideas of an underground hell) there is generally no concept of judgment or reward and punishment attached to it. In fact, the more pessimistic books of the Bible, such as Ecclesiastes and Job, insist that all of the dead go down to Sheol, whether good or evil, rich or poor, slave or free man (Job 3:11–19).[5]

The Jewish eschatological vision does not support the idea of Jesus teaching there is an eternal hell. As an Orthodox Jew, Jesus would have believed as a classical Jew, believing Sheol as the place where all mankind goes. But as God in the flesh, He would have had a deeper insight than His contemporaries. He would have known that He was going to go through the portal of physical death down to Sheol, where He would tear down the gates, preach the Gospel Good News to those waiting there, and free the prisoners.

Christ's dealing with Sheol is summed up by the beautiful hymns we sing during Holy Week from the Holy Week prayer book (p. 415) used in Greek Orthodox churches:

> Today Hades cried out groaning: "Would that I had not received the One born of Mary; for He came upon me and loosed my power. He shattered the gates of brass; the souls, which I held captive of old, as God He raised up." Glory O Lord to Your Cross and Your Resurrection.
>
> Today Hades cried out groaning: "My authority is dissolved; I received a mortal, as one of the mortals; but this One, I am powerless to contain; with Him I lose all those, over which, I

---

5. Rose, "Heaven and Hell in Jewish Tradition." Para. 2–4.

had ruled. For ages I had held the Dead, but behold, He raises up all." Glory O Lord, to Your Cross and Your Resurrection.

Today Hades cried out groaning: "My power had been trampled on; the Shepherd has been crucified, and Adam He raised up. I have been deprived of those, over whom I ruled; and all those, I had the power to swallow, I have disgorged. He, who was crucified has cleared the tombs. The dominion of Death is no more." Glory O Lord, to our Cross and Your Resurrection.

For Orthodox Christians Hell is not a fearful place of torment and punishment, but rather a battlefield where a great battle was fought and our Hero Christ triumphed over the enemy Death (1 Corinthians 15:20–26).[6]

THE GREATEST CONTEXT OF ALL–LOVE

To me, love is the greatest context of all, a great light which sheds itself over all the world in the glory of God. It is the context of the Cross, the complete and final victory of God over death. To say God would give to the enemy, death, even a small measure of victory by allowing it to hold eternally billions of souls created for Him, is to make the Cross not the greatest act of God humanity shall behold for all eternity, but either a dismal failure or an obscene mockery of love and justice.

It is the Cross which overshadows everything. Without the Cross, there is no meaning to life, nothing to look forward to, and the Jewish understanding of death is true—a somber place of darkness and isolation. The Cross has freed mankind, even though in this world of sorrows and trials it is often hard to see this as truth.

In this final context, bring every objection to the Cross. Stand before the Cross and ask yourself if this agony was done only to fail to have a plan to bring even the most hardened of sinners home to the Father? Ask yourself if this intense act of love was only intended for a small minority of the "elect?" Observe Christ suffering indescribable agony, and ask if He would really submit to such a thing for only a few to be restored to wholeness out of billions who would ever live? Ask yourself if a limited atonement was really the plan of God from the beginning? What would be the purpose of such love if that love, big enough to endure such agonies, was not also big enough to encompass the entire world and all who would ever live?

I honestly don't think that Infernalists take the time to realize what a slander it is on the character of God to think that God would create ex nihlo

---

6. Arakaki, "Holy Saturday and the Harrowing of Hell," Para. 6–9.

and without obligation of any kind, sentient creatures with the sole intention of seeing them suffer eternally. Nor do I think they reason through the issue of the truncation of Christ's victory on the Cross if only a ridiculously small percentage of people obtain eternal felicity.

In closing this section, I want everyone reading to take a moment and remember, if you experienced it, a love that meant everything to you and yet that you somehow lost. Perhaps it was an engagement that was broken, a summer vacation that became a relationship continued by letter until the other disconnected, or a beloved relative who died and left you grieving for years. In any case, the outcome was the same, a deep longing that the end never happened and an extended period of regret and desire that the relationship could be restored and continued.

Now take these feelings and put them into the infinite and unending love of God which drove Him to the Cross and enabled Him to endure it for the joy that was set before Him. Could such love have joy knowing that billions of His deeply loved children would never be brought home to enter the beauty of His love? Could such love simply turn to hate and abandon the children His love created, no matter how sick with sin, or how, like the Prodigal Son to his father, they insulted Him to His face? I simply cannot get my mind around how one could say that God is love and in the same breath attribute to Him a behavior, which if we saw it in humans, would leave us aghast.

It makes no sense when you stand at the foot of the Cross.

If This is True, Why Even Bother?

ONE OF THE MORE frequent objections to the teaching of universal salvation is that it gives no reason to people to repent. If everyone is going to heaven anyway–why bother? Just live life, do whatever you want to, and then at the end, you get the Pearly Gates and the streets of gold. As a Jewish friend of mine used to say, "Such a deal!"

Proponents of eternal conscious torment warn that teaching it sends souls to hell, believing that people will engage in sin without fear of punishment. This is an understandable concern, given mankind's penchant for finding excuses to sin. Both our Lord and St. Paul warned that we shall receive rewards for both the good and the evil we have done in this life. My wish is that books on universal salvation would remind people of this fact and warn them that evil behavior will reap a bitter consequence in the next life. I have a great concern that as this teaching of God's universal salvific love is becoming more openly taught, many sinners may use it as excuse to not turn to Christ and instead, live as their selfishness demands, then curse us in the next life as they inherit the painful chastening which they have earned by doing evil works.

Sin is not a thing to take lightly. There are many warnings in the Bible which point to great losses which will be experienced by those who turn from God's gracious offer of salvation and instead indulge their passions.

THE CONSEQUENCES OF REFUSAL–WHY EVANGELIZE?

TO SAVE PEOPLE FROM TORMENT IN THE NEXT LIFE.

What person is so cold-hearted that he can observe without pity the suffering of another human being? Do not all but the most hard-hearted and indifferent want to run to the aid of another human being who is suffering? If we could see the suffering of souls in the next life, how they cry out for mercy, how the reality of their sins torments them, we would strive to warn everyone that our sins carry a price to pay. I am sure that Hugh Hefner wishes now that he had listened to the voices which urged him to turn from his wickedness. I believe he is in despair, thinking that the torments he is suffering will never end. Do I really want that for even the worst of people? Or do I love them as God loves them, looking on them with pity and trying to warn them of the painful chastisement which lies ahead, so that hopefully they may avoid it?

In Orthodox eschatology, there is not a place called hell. All souls go to be in the presence of Christ. All experience His endless love as God. But those who have loved sin, who have turned from God and embraced sin and selfishness, will find His love is a dreadful torment, while those who have repented in this life will find His love to be a warm embrace. The condition of our souls at death determines how we experience God in the next life. It is a mercy to warn people of this fact because the torment the wicked will experience will seem endless. Even if it assuredly does end, who in their right mind would wish suffering upon another? Unlike the musings of St. Thomas Aquinas, who said that the righteous in heaven would look upon the suffering of the wicked and rejoice in it bringing glory to God, the Bible states that God takes no pleasure in the death of the wicked. Neither should we.

TO GIVE PEOPLE JOY IN THIS LIFE.

Many of the people who loudly proclaim how they enjoy their sin go home at night and weep in loneliness and misery. I have both seen this in others, when the imbibing of a sufficient amount of alcohol released true feelings, and I have personally experienced it myself. As a young man, I could not understand why I was depressed and having serious thoughts of suicide, which terrified me. I was having fun, at least, according to the world's idea of fun. I did drugs, which made my body feel pleasure, engaged in free-wheeling sexual adventures, and lived a life totally for myself. How could I be unhappy?

But I was–desperately so–and I have met people who have expressed the same thing about their former lives of sin. Sin is a lie. It is the cheese in the mousetrap. That first bite is oh, so good! But there is a terrible price to pay when down the road the spring is triggered. There is a reason those who practice sexual perversity have suicide rates three times the national average. Our actions have consequences, despite the constant drumbeat of those propagandists who tell us that we can do whatever we want with no sorrow or regret. We were made for joy, for love, for peaceful lives. Sin ruins all this in this life and leads to torment in the next until the full debt is paid.

FOR THE BENEFIT OF THE COMMUNITY.

Jesus and St. Paul both made it abundantly clear that there are consequences to our actions in this life. If walking in the love of God, which is the goal of the Christian life, brings peace to nations and between people, walking in hatred and selfishness brings nothing but misery. Sin not only ruins your life; it ruins the lives of those with whom you come into contact. Look at any action which causes destruction and sorrow in this world: constant wars (caused by lies and political selfishness), poverty (caused by the insatiable greed of the rich), divorce (caused by selfishness in the marital relationship), sexual diseases and death (caused by immoral behavior), fights, thefts, rape, murder, etc.

These sins are caused by those who have no inner moral guidance such as the Christian faith provides, and they devastate individuals, communities, and nations. Our world from the beginning has been in an almost constant state of war between nations because of the lies of politicians, the greed of kings, and the lust for power and conquest. In war, families suffer the loss of loved ones and injuries that will last a lifetime. Young women live in a rape culture because of magazines like Playboy, spawned by the Sexual Revolution of the 1960's, which taught us the lie that sex is not reserved for marriage alone, but is a fine sport for a weekend. Pornography inflames the lusts of men to seek an outlet. Rape is the result. A whole security industry has arisen because there are immoral people who will steal all your money if they can just access your personal information online.

I have read online testimonies of people who engaged in wickedness and hedonism, only to come to a place where the pleasure they found in sin had turned to dust in their mouths. Psychologists have said most people who are institutionalized for deep psychological problems are burdened with guilt for what they have done. Inappropriate or excessive guilt is listed as a symptom of depression by the American Psychiatric Association (1994).

To experience Christ, not just to know about Him, but to really experience Him, brings a deep change in the way a person lives. As one grows in Christ and in love, sin becomes less and less attractive. The good of others becomes increasingly important. Changed lives mean changed societies, and ultimately, a changed world. We as Christians need to tell people this, and more importantly, live it in front of them.

The Christian is to be a follower of Christ in a humility which prefers others to self. How would such thinking affect the behavior of people in the public venue? Would we see the hatred of racism, the grinding down of the poor, the political and theological lies we see which mold our lives to hate one another as enemies instead of looking to others in a spirit of love and friendship? Sin brings a terrible cost with it, and those who are not being transformed by the Holy Spirit into Christlikeness will in some way or the other fall into its trap.

In the first century Roman Empire, Christians stood out because of the love they had for others. In an empire in which women were chattel property, slaves were raped and beaten with impunity, war was common, and punishments for crimes were excessive, the Christian community was a beacon of light in a darkened world. In every country where the message of Christ went, pagan nations were turned from darkness and selfishness to self-giving love. Man in his natural state cannot achieve this. No number of political programs, wars, or coercion by violence can bring the internal and external peace the saints experienced and showed to the world by their lives. From the Roman Empire to the Aztec nation, the violent pagan nations which expanding Christianity encountered reflected the natural condition of man's heart–violence and cruelty. Submission to Christ changes this violence by changing men's hearts.

Look at the condition of the world today. Every misery you see has a foundation in the selfishness of sin. If this is what life should be, if this is what you want and enjoy, then, no, there is no need to convert. But if you believe we could have so much better, if the condition of the world distresses you because of the hatred and violence you see, then this is one very earthly reason for people to turn to Christ.

THE OFFER OF REWARDS

> Matthew 16:27 "For the Son of man shall come in the glory of his Father with his angels; and then he shall reward every man according to his works."
> Matthew 5:12 "Rejoice, and be exceeding glad: for great is your reward in heaven: for so persecuted they the prophets which were before you."
> Matthew 5:46 "For if ye love them which love you, what reward have ye? do not even the publicans the same?"
> Matthew 6:1 "Take heed that ye do not your alms before men, to be seen of them: otherwise ye have no reward of your Father which is in heaven."
> Matthew 6:2 "Therefore when thou doest thine alms, do not sound a trumpet before thee, as the hypocrites do in the synagogues and in the streets, that they may have glory of men. Verily I say unto you, they have their reward."

I have had people tell me that eternal life is the reward we get, and they are incensed to think someone who lives a life of repentance and sacrifice would get the same reward as a desperately evil man. Searching the Bible gives us no such idea. Quite to the contrary, Jesus says that every man will be rewarded according to his works. He also says that it is possible to lose one's reward. Eternal life is the victory of Christ over death for all mankind. What we do with the offer determines what we receive in the ages of ages.

What is to be gained or lost? Here are my thoughts, which I hope you will consider.

THE REWARD OF HONOR.

John 12:26 "If anyone wants to serve me, he must follow me, and where I am, my servant will be too. If anyone serves me, the Father will honor him."

Where will the Father honor those who have been faithful servants of Christ? It must be in the ages of ages to come, in the courts of heaven.

Romans 2:10 ". . . but glory and honor and peace for everyone who does good, for the Jew first and also the Greek."

Where? Certainly not here on earth. Those who have done good have often been dishonored and suffered terribly at the hands of the wicked. I believe this honor spoken of awaits the faithful in the next life.

First Timothy 5:17 "Elders who provide effective leadership must be counted worthy of double honor, especially those who work hard in speaking and teaching."

If so on earth, how much more so in the next life?"

First Peter 1:7 "Such trials show the proven character of your faith, which is much more valuable than gold–gold that is tested by fire, even though it is passing away–and will bring praise and glory and honor when Jesus Christ is revealed."

Scripture proves my point. There is praise and glory which awaits all the faithful at the end of this life. Conversely, for those who love their sin, there will be no honor. There may even be contempt for them until they have expiated their sins. Where there is great honor, there must also be those who have lesser honor. And if Christ warned about losing our rewards and our honor, then we should take this warning seriously.

Matthew 5:19 "Whosoever therefore shall break one of these least commandments, and shall teach men so, he shall be called the least in the kingdom of heaven: but whosoever shall do and teach them, the same shall be called great in the kingdom of heaven."

Jesus said there would be those who would be called least in the kingdom of heaven. If here on earth we call men like St. John Chrysostom great, how much more will he be acknowledged in the eternal kingdom? If men sacrifice here on earth, giving up many good things to achieve earthly honors, what more should we be willing to give up for the honor which will last forever? I cannot believe that I, a man who willingly plunged himself into wickedness for years, and whose Christian life has been less than exemplary, would go into eternity and receive the same honor and glory as a monk who for fifty years lived a life of ascetic denial and faithfulness in prayer on Mount Athos. It would be unjust of God to do such a thing! And as the Infernalists like to remind us, God is just!

James 1:12 "Blessed is the man that endureth temptation: for when he is tried, he shall receive the crown of life, which the Lord hath promised to them that love him."

What then of the man who does not resist temptation? The one who is baptized into the church and then goes forth to live a life of utter sin and selfishness? Do you really think this one will also get the same crown promised to those who fight temptation, some even unto death? Those righteous souls who warred against sin in this lifetime, who practiced ascetic denial, who obeyed God in all things to the best of their ability, shall have a crown of glory which will testify to their faithfulness for all eternity. I guarantee you, if you could see the beauty and glory of the crown which awaits the faithful, you would consider sin your dire enemy and strive to do all you could to obtain that crown!

Look at St. Paul, enduring beatings, stoning, and other trials. For what?

First Corinthians 9:25 "And every man that striveth for the mastery is temperate in all things. Now they do it to obtain a corruptible crown; but we an incorruptible."

Paul knew. He understood what it was that he was striving for. Far be it from him to say "Meaaah, God is going to save all, so it doesn't really matter what I do"

Second Timothy 4:8 "Henceforth there is laid up for me a crown of righteousness, which the Lord, the righteous judge, shall give me at that day: and not to me only, but unto all them also that love his appearing."

Do you want the crown of righteousness? Then turn from sin to Christ, for only those who love Christ love the thought of His appearing. The wicked have no desire for Christ, hence, there is no crown for them.

First Peter 5:4 "And when the chief Shepherd shall appear, ye shall receive a crown of glory that fadeth not away."

A crown is a symbol of authority and honor. It is the reward of eternal honor to those who fought the good fight of faith here on earth. But it will not be given to all. Only to those who have earned it.

THE REWARD OF AUTHORITY.

Revelation 1:6 "And hath made us kings and priests unto God and his Father; to him be glory and dominion for ever and ever. Amen."

Revelation 5:10 "And hast made us unto our God kings and priests: and we shall reign on the earth."

These two curious verses in the last book of the Bible raise a question in my mind. If believers are kings, then over what do they rule? Covenant theologians see God's Kingdom as a Suzerainty kingdom. Suzerainty kingdoms existed in Abrahamic times in the Middle East. Great kingdoms which ruled over lesser kingdoms were known as Suzerainty kingdoms. They were ruled by a Great King, or Suzerain. At the time of war, he might see a neighboring kingdom, and desiring to have it as part of his kingdom, this king would send a delegation to the lesser king with terms of peace. If the lesser king refused, there would be war. If he accepted the terms, he would be brought under the protection of the Suzerain and enjoy the peace which went with being part of the Suzerainty kingdom. A treaty covenant would be cut which included loyalty oaths to the great king in return for his protection.

Who is the great sovereign of the universe?

Psalm 24:8 "Who is this King of glory? The LORD strong and mighty, the LORD mighty in battle."

Psalm 24:10 "Who is this King of glory? The LORD of hosts, he is the King of glory. Selah."

Psalm 29:10 "The LORD sitteth upon the flood; yea, the LORD sitteth King forever."

As I see it, the whole of Creation is merely a part of the Suzerainty Kingdom of God. He is the Great King, therefore, those who have accepted His offer of peace are, according to these verses in Revelation, made kings and queens unto him. Which brings us to the question: over what shall they rule?

I believe they shall rule over all who refused the offer of union with God in this life. This kingship, which is given to all who come into union with God through Christ, is one of the rewards given to the faithful. The verses I quoted in Revelation speak of God having made "us"–not all mankind, but "us"–kings and priests unto Him. Believers are the "us" of those verses. All will be happy, all will enjoy life eternal, but for those who repented and believed Christ in this life, there will be a special position of rulership and honor.

Where will they rule? Again, this is just my idea, but looking at the incredible vastness of the universe, I easily imagine an eternity of millions of earth-like planets, filled with happy people enjoying the knowledge of God. Each planet having a ruler over it, perhaps with countries like those on earth, each country being ruled by a king who is vassal to the one rewarded by our heavenly Father to be Suzerainty King over the entire planet. If this idea is true, you will lose the chance to be an eternal king by choosing sin over Christ.

Mark 9:33 "And he came to Capernaum: and being in the house he asked them, what was it that ye disputed among yourselves by the way? 34 But they held their peace: for by the way they had disputed among themselves, who should be the greatest. 35 And he sat down, and called the twelve, and saith unto them, If any man desire to be first, the same shall be last of all, and servant of all."

The Apostles thought in this manner, looking forward to a kingdom in which they would rule over others. They were arguing about who would be the greatest among them when Christ interrupts their little pride fest with His probing and embarrassing question. Look at verse thirty-five. Those who desire to be first, who lack humility, shall be last. Where? Not on this earth, for it is the proud, the arrogant, the wicked, who in so many cases rule over others, causing grief and misery.

They have the praise of others, people flattering them and seeking their favors, power and authority which comes with the positions which they have obtained, sometimes by evil or crooked means. Jesus taught their reward is here and now. So, when do they become last of all and servant of all?

In the eternal kingdom when God is all in all. Their position of servant to all will be locked in forever. They will be last of all. All their illusory glory will be stripped from them at death, and they will be given a servant's robe with no crown to wear. And the last–those humble servants of God seen as the least of all men on earth now–the holy priests, the monks and nuns, the faithful to God unto martyrdom, they shall rule and reign as promised.

Whether it is for all eternity on individual planets filled with people or only for the ages of ages in a single kingdom until all is wrapped up in God, I do not know. But whatever it is, rewards have been promised and are worth pursuing.

THE REWARD OF INTIMATE KNOWLEDGE OF THE FATHER.

Of all the rewards offered in scripture, the knowledge of our Father's love is the best. On earth we see the depth of this intimate unity depends on our response to His overtures. To each man is offered a unique relationship to God through Christ, based on whether he turns to or from the Lord. Just as a man who is addicted to pornography cannot develop a proper intimacy with his wife, neither can a human being who is in love with himself (sin), develop a deep union with God. Unlike many who boldly pronounce their deep knowledge of the next world, I do not know anything about it. But earthly realities are symbols and types of eternal truth. I think it fair to imagine exactly what my godparents told me when I was a Protestant catechumen: "Everyone will love God only to the degree they are able. Some will be like a 55-gallon drum in their ability to receive God's love, and some will be only a shot glass. But all will fully have the love of God to the degree that they can receive it."

Daniel 12:3 "And they that be wise shall shine as the brightness of the firmament; and they that turn man to righteousness as the stars for ever and ever."

How much of God's love do you want to experience in the next life? How much of His glory do you want to radiate? Do you want to be like a dying flashlight on the last breath of the batteries inside, or do you want to shine like the midday sun? Do you want to sense the Father's love from a distance, knowing it is there, but not fully experiencing it as others do, or do you want to be so filled with His love that you explode in joy throughout the universe? Yes, these questions employ hyperbole, but they are done so to make a point. There is much to gain and much to lose.

No, life in the ages to come will assuredly not be the same for everyone. Just as there are stars of various brightness in the sky, so will the brightness of our glory be in proportion to the love of God, obedience to Him, and turning from sin which we pursue here. Just as the Theotokos is the highest and most honored of all humanity created by God, so there will be various levels of honor in the next age. No woman carries the honor She does. No man carries the honor of John the Baptist. And no ordinary layperson shall carry the honor of the saints and martyrs. There is much to gain in this life, and much to lose in the next if we turn from Christ to pursue the vain illusions of this life.

THERE IS HELL TO AVOID!

In online discussions with those believing in eternal hell, I have constantly received the comment "So you believe there is no hell?" It is often expressed with what can be seen as a fair amount of sarcastic indignation. This accusation is not in line with traditional belief in apokatastasis.

> For some, perhaps many, the return of Christ Jesus in glory will ignite a gehennic conflagration in the depth of their souls. Imprisoned in their egoism and malice, they will hate the Son and with all their might will attempt to extinguish the love born in their hearts. And so they will burn. They will know the torment of hell, a torment of love, guilt, and self-condemnation. Guiding Bulgakov's reflections here are the homilies of St Isaac the Syrian, which he knew in Russian translation. He refers to the following passage several times:
>
> I say that those tormented in gehenna are struck by the scourge of love. And how bitter and cruel is this agony of love, for, feeling that they have sinned against love, they experience a torment that is greater than any other. The affliction that strikes the heart because of the sin against love is more terrible than any possible punishment. It is wrong to think that gehenna are deprived of God's love. Love is produced by knowledge of the truth, which (everyone is in agreement about this) is given to all in general. But by its power love affects human beings in a twofold manner: It torments sinners, as even here a friend sometimes causes one to suffer, and it gladdens those who have carried out their duty. And so, in my opinion, the torment of gehenna consists in repentance. Love fills with its joys the souls of the children on high. (Quoted in Bride, p. 466; emphasis mine)[1]

This is but one of many quotes of the early fathers you can find which declare that for the wicked there will be suffering. Its intensity will correspond to the degree of sin with which the soul has pleasured itself in this life. This is the Orthodox faith and eschatology. There is no place called hell. There is something far worse for the sinful–the very presence of God which strips away every lie, every self-delusion, and every falsehood.

I know this personally because I was given a minuscule taste of it after the death of my first wife. I had spent years being driven by Christian fear-mongers who threatened me with eternal fire if I did not believe correctly and did not win souls to Christ. One even went as far as to say that nothing was more important than serving Christ, even one's own family. In the grip

---

1. Kimmel, "Hell as Universal Purgatory," Para. 2–3.

of this brainwashed farce of a religion, I became driven and self-righteous. I was sure I had the correct religion, and since my family didn't share my views, I was cold and indifferent to them. I gave more time to my church and its activities than to them, desperately working to be sure God loved me and would receive me into His Kingdom rather than toss me into hell. At Thanksgiving and Christmas, I was a judgmental boor, constantly badgering people about "getting right with God" so they could go to heaven. While the message was technically correct, the insensitive way I clubbed people over the head with it was not.

It was only after Karen died that I was brought one night to see what a jerk I had become. At the urging of two friends who were Carmelite nuns, I went back to a monastery I had visited before, wondering if the life of a monk was now God's plan for the rest of my life. On my last night of a three month stay, I had an interior illumination which shook me to my core. In this illuminated moment, with clarity I remembered my poor wife, sitting alone upstairs, watching TV, without her husband there to be with her. Every night I came home, made dinner, and went downstairs to spend hours on the computer. For the first time I clearly realized how selfish this was. The knowledge of this truth was like waves of fire raining down on my conscience. I cannot begin to adequately describe in words the agony of this knowledge, but fire is a good description. That is exactly what it felt like. There was nowhere to run or hide. All I could do was weep and beg God to forgive me for what I had done. All pretense of being a good Christian was stripped away in the raw, naked truth of how selfish I had been. True Christian, self-giving love would have put aside my desires and would have given my time to Karen.

Believe me, if I could make you feel what I felt that night, you would run to your church and fall on your knees to beg God to forgive whatever sin has you in its grip with its false delights. For the deeply wicked, I cannot begin to imagine what they face when the stand in the presence of the One who is Truth. Every petty tyrant will see himself not as the bold warrior or great defender of his country he fancied himself to be, but as a murderer, thief, and beast. Every fornicator, adulterer, and sexually impure person will see the truth about himself and how he simply used others for his pleasure. It will be agonizing beyond any earthly description to face this raw truth.

Yes, there is hell, but the good news for all is that it is not just raw punishment or vengeful justice, but is designed to reform the sinner, to free him from his lusts, to change his very person into the likeness of Christ. St. Athanasius said, "God became man so that man might become god."[2] Because

---

2. Athanasius, "On the Incarnation."

of sin, the process of becoming deified is a long, arduous, and sometimes quite painful one. It can be carried out here, with difficulty and pain, or in the next age, with a suffering that anyone who tasted even a small bit of it, would run from, casting himself into the arms of Christ.

The Fram Oil Filter Corporation ran a television ad years ago in which the punch line was "You can pay me now. . . or you can pay me later." In the ad, a mechanic delivered this line, standing in front of a disassembled automobile engine. The idea was simple. Pay now for the filter and protect your engine, or pay later for a complete engine overhaul when it fails, which will be far more expensive to your wallet than a few dollars for a Fram filter now.

In Matthew 5:19–26, Jesus is teaching about sin and judgment. He ends this section of the Sermon on the Mount with this warning: "Verily I say unto thee, thou shalt by no means come out thence, till thou hast paid the uttermost farthing."

In closing, I beg of you to be wise. I am begging you on bended knee. Please believe me, you do not want to pay later for the sins you think so important in this life. Turning to Christ now is going to be a whole lot easier than having to go through the painful scourging of God's love in the next age. Pay to God what is owed now. He is owed our loving obedience, our turning from sin and self, and our faithfulness, even unto death. The cost in this life may be great, but the reward in the next life will be worth any sacrifice you make.

But above all these reasons stands one glorious reason–the splendor, the beauty, the love of our wonderful God. Jesus deserves to be loved and honored in this world with lives who worship Him, giving Him the glory, He deserves for His great love to us. The command of our Lord in Matthew 28 is "Go ye therefore, and teach all nations, baptizing them in the name of the Father, and of the Son, and of the Holy Ghost: teaching them to observe all things whatsoever I have commanded you: and, lo, I am with you always, even unto the end of the world." It is a two-fold command: a command to bring His love to people to change them for the good, and a command that He receive that honor and love of which He is so worthy.

It is for our good, the good of others, and the good of the world, that Christ gives this command to all who believe in Him–go and evangelize. Tell the good news. Tell people they don't have to be a slave to their passions. Tell them there is joy in Christ, and more importantly, live that joy before them. You don't have to live in sorrow and fear.

Closing Comments and Questions

ONE HUNDRED PLUS PAGES into my rough draft, as I go through reworking this manuscript, I find myself shaking my head and asking, "What the heck just happened here?" This was supposed to be a thorough but short answer to my friend's objections. It was never intended to be more than that. Somehow it is.

What have I learned from this investigation? A brief summary regarding the three main objections to apokatastasis is in order here:

First objection: The Second Council of Constantinople. The council as condemnation of apokatastasis fails miserably. Justinian's canons should be stricken from the records of the church, as was done in the case of the Robber's Council. The whole council, being called under threats of violence and duress, is somewhat suspect. Any appeal to II Constantinople as a proof that apokatastasis was condemned falls on my deaf ears.

Second objection: The Bible. The Scriptures have been horribly mistranslated, especially in those critical verses which are commonly used to defend the idea of eternal punishment. Honest translation from real Greek scholars, such as Dr. Illaria Ramelli, needs to bring forward a scripture text true to the original manuscripts, and all others should be corrected to reflect the proper interpretation of the original manuscripts!

Third objection: The church. I found that politics, cultural norms, and personal psychology intruded into the workings of the church. It would be wonderful if theology and the understanding of God could be of a clear and unambiguous nature, but until we see Christ face to face, the understanding of even the best among us is clouded. Even saints and holy men are not without the ability to fall into error. The history of Christianity is hardly a pure spring of unadulterated truth from the beginning. It has been a raucous fight for truth which appears to have not always succeeded.

The truth of this issue appears to me to be like a three-legged stool consisting of the revelation of God in Christ, i.e., that God is love, the revelation of scripture, and the Holy Tradition of the church. Taking any one of these three as a sole source of truth is a recipe for theological disaster. In doing my investigation and putting all three of these sources together, I believe I have good reason for a strong hope in God's ultimate restoration of all things, including all people.

This is what happens when a person gets caught up in the investigation of an interesting subject. There is so much out there, and I have barely scratched the surface of all the writings, both theological and philosophical, which exist about the teaching of apokatastasis. My investigative journey has been a most interesting one and has led me to the point that I can no longer listen to the threats of eternal conscious torment without raising a questioning eyebrow.

For those who have been kind enough to read my mental meanderings, I hope you have found in them something thoughtful, something valuable, and something that has given you a new and wonderful view of our loving God. More than that, I hope you will go from this reading to begin your own investigative journey. The riches of understanding the depths of God's love, and joy that knowledge will bring, will be worth every effort you make.

Bibliography

Amarault, Gary. "Why Can't Aionas Ton Aionon Mean Eternity?" https://tentmaker.org/FAQ/forever_eternity.html

Arakaki, Robert. "Holy Saturday and the Harrowing of Hell." https://orthodoxbridge.com/2015/04/10/holy-saturday-and-the-harrowing-of-hell/

Aquinas, Thomas. "Of the Relations of the Saints Towards the Damned," First Article, "Whether the Blessed in Heaven Will See the Sufferings of the Damned?" Summa Theologica, Third Part, Supplement, Question XCIV

"The Athanasian Creed." Christian Classics Ethereal Library. https://www.ccel.org/ccel/schaff/creeds1.iv.v.html#fnf_iv.v-p22.1.

"Augustine of Hippo." Orthodox Wiki. https://orthodoxwiki.org/Augustine_of_Hippo

Benner, Jeff. "Ancient." Ancient Hebrew Research Center. https://www.ancient-hebrew.org/definition/ancient.htm#:~:text=For%20this%20reason%20the%20same%20Hebrew%20words%20are,of%20old%2C%20I%20remember%20the%20years%20long%20ago%28%D7%A7%D7%93%D7%9D%29.

Broussard, Karlo. "Why We Can't Change Our Soul After Death." https://www.catholic.com/magazine/online-edition/why-we-cant-change-our-soul-after-death.

"Cyprian." Wikipedia. https://en.wikipedia.org/wiki/Cyprian

"Death. Judaism." Encyclopedia Britannica. https://www.britannica.com/science/death/The-fate-of-the-soul.

De Kock, Edwin and Van Wyk, Koot, "538 AD and the Transition from Pagan Roman Empire to Holy Roman Empire—Justinian's Metamorphosis from Chief of Staffs to Theologian." https://www.academia.edu/31985959/538_A_D_and_the_Transition_from_Pagan_Roman_Empire_to_Holy_Roman_Empire_Justinians_Metamorphosis_from_Chief_of_Staffs_to_Theologian_1

Drake, Harold. "The Emperor as 'Man of God.': The Impact of Constantine the Great's Conversion on Roman Ideas of Kingship." https://www.scielo.br/j/his/a/TPCJ8LW6JNCkZDRztWxY8NJ/?lang=en#aff1

Edwards, Jonathan. (Sermon). April 1739 & Discourses on Various Important Subjects. 1738

Ehrman, Bart. D. "What Jesus Really Said About Heaven and Hell." Time. May 8, 2020. https://time.com/5822598/jesus-really-said-heaven-hell/

"The Epistle of Ignatius to the Ephesians" New Advent. https://www.newadvent.org/fathers/0104.htm

"Fathers of the Church, Second Council of Nicea." New Advent. https://www.newadvent.org/fathers/3819.htm

Freeman, Stephen. "God and the Mystery of Self" Glory to God for All Things. https://blogs.ancientfaith.com/glory2godforallthings/2021/07/22/god-and-the-mystery-of-the-self/?fbclid=IwAR2QTwfUviyGCjFkz_O3GV48aInporgJn AvohZdLdOyNkDz2VDwASBQC6Qo

Fudge, Edward. "The Origin of Hell-Fire in Christian Teaching." Truth According to Scripture. https://www.truthaccordingtoscripture.com/documents/death/origin-of-hell-fire.php

"Exposition on Psalm 6." New Advent. https://www.newadvent.org/fathers/1801006.htm

Fruchtenbaum. "How Long Is Forever?" https://www.jewishroots.net/library/anti_missionary_objections/how_long_is_forever.html

Gonzales, Anthony. "The Indefectibility of the Church." http://roman-catholic.com/Roman/Articles/The%20Indefectibilty%20of%20the%20Church.htm#:~:text=Anthony%20Gonzales%20The%20Catholic%20Encyclopedia%20of%201917%20gives,will%20be%20preserved%20unimpaired%20in%20its%20essential%20characteristics.

Hanson, J.W. "Universalism the Prevailing Doctrine of the Christian Church During its First Five Hundred Years." https://books.google.com/books?id=ezURAAAAYAAJ&pg

Hara, Edward. "God's Hand & Our Free Will" the reluctant heretic. https://http4281.wordpress.com/2017/07/03/gods-hand-our-free-will/

Hart, David Bentley. "Saint Origen" https://www.firstthings.com/article/2015/10/saint-origen

———. "That All Shall Be Saved." Yale University Press 2019

"Hell." Catechism of the Catholic Church.https://www.vatican.va/archive/ENG0015/__P2O.HTM

"Hell." Encyclopedia Americana. https://archive.org/details/encyclopediaame28unkn goog/page/n108/mode/2up

"Hell." New Advent. https://www.newadvent.org/cathen/07207a.htm.

Houdmann, S. Michael. "What Does It Mean that God is Sovereign?" Got Questions. https://www.gotquestions.org/God-is-sovereign.html

Hughes, Philip. Constantinople II, 553. https://www.ewtn.com/catholicism/library/constantinople-ii-553-10319.

Kimel, Aiden. "A Glimpse Into the Enigma that is Fr. Aiden Kimel." Eclectic Orthodoxy https://afkimel.wordpress.com/2021/01/10/a-glimpse-into-the-enigma-that-is-fr-aidan-kimel/

———. "Did the Fifth Ecumenical Council Condemn Universal Salvation?" Eclectic Orthodoxy https://afkimel.wordpress.com/2020/05/31/did-the-fifth-ecumenical-council-condemn-universal-salvation/

———. "Dogma, Damnation, and the Eucatastrophe of the Jesus Story." Eclectic Orthodoxy https://afkimel.wordpress.com/2020/08/17/dogma-damnation-and-the-eucatastrophe-of-the-jesus-story/

———. "Hell As Universal Purgatory." Eclectic Orthodoxy. https://afkimel.wordpress.com/2019/09/19/hell-as-universal-purgatory-2/

"Indefectibility." Catholic Culture. https://www.catholicculture.org/culture/library/dictionary/index.cfm?id=34157

Kiser, Greg. "Revelation was Written Before 70 A.D." https://tentmaker.org/articles/revelation_written_before_70AD_Kiser.htm#:~:text=This%20short%20article

%20gives%20a%20small%20example%20and,servants%20things%20which%20 must%20shortly%20come%20to%20pass.

Ladouceur, Paul. "On Ecumenoclasm: Anti-Ecumenical Theology in Orthodoxy" St. Vladimir's Theological Quarterly, 61, 3 (2017), Page 345. https://www.academia.edu/35500142/_On_Ecumenoclasm_Anti_Ecumenical_Theology_in_Orthodoxy_St_Vladimirs_Theological_Quarterly_61_3_2017_323_355

Lambouras, Miriam. "The Marian Apparitions: Divine Intervention or Delusion?" http://orthodoxinfo.com/inquirers/marian_apparitions.aspx

Livermore, Jeremy. "Augustine." Apologetics.com. 2009. https://apologetics.com/blog/jlivermore/augustines-philosophical-theology-a-neoplatonism/

Nemes, Stephen. " Illaria Ramelli, The Christian Doctrine of Apokatastasis: A Critical Assessment from the New Testament to Eriugena" Journal of Analytic Theology. Vol 3. May 2015 https://jat-ojs-baylor.tdl.org/jat/index.php/jat/article/view/jat.2015-3.181913130418a/271.

Penley, Paul. "When Heaven and Earth Passed Away: Everything Changed." https://www.reenactingtheway.com/blog/when-heaven-and-earth-passed-away-everything-changed87942018717985315018

Percival, Henry. "Nicene and Post-Nicene Fathers, Second Series, Vol. 14." Wm. B. Eerdmans Publishing 1956.

"Roman Law." Wikipedia. https://en.wikipedia.org/wiki/Roman_law

Rose, Or N. "Heaven and Hell in Jewish Tradition." My Jewish Learning. https://www.myjewishlearning.com/article/heaven-and-hell-in-jewish-tradition/#:~:text=Like%20other%20spiritual%20traditions%2C%20Judaism%20offers%20a%20range,biblical%20model%2C%20which%20focuses%20on%20life%20on%20earth.

"St. Justinian on Universalism." Classical Christianity. https://classicalchristianity.com/category/bysaint/st-justinian-the-emperor-ca-483–565/

Sanidopoulos, John. "The Synodikon of Orthodoxy." 2010. https://www.johnsanidopoulos.com/2010/02/synodicon-of-orthodoxy.html

Schaff, Philip. " Anathematisms of the Emperor Justinian Against Origen." https://www.ccel.org/ccel/schaff/npnf214.xii.x. html

———. "Encyclopedia of Religious Knowledge." Schaff-Herzog, 1908, Volume 12, Page 96

———. "Excursus on the Genuineness of the Acts of the Fifth Council." https://www.ccel.org/ccel/schaff/npnf214.xii.iii.html

"Second Council of Constantinople." New World Encyclopedia. https://www.newworldencyclopedia.org/entry/Second_Council_of_Constantinople.

"Second Council of Constantinople—553 A.D." Papal Encyclicals Online. https://www.papalencyclicals.net/councils/ecum05.htm

Synodikon of Orthodoxy. Serbian Orthodox Church. http://www.spc.rs/eng/synodikon_orthodoxy_0

Talbot, Thomas. "Mercy on All, Free-will Theodicies of Hell." https://www.mercyonall.org/posts/free-will-theodicies-of-hell

Thompson, Silouan. "The Fifteen Anathemas Against Origen." https://silouanthompson.net/2019/09/anathemas-against-origen/

Turner, Reid. "'Torn Among the Boars': St. Hildegard's Frightful Vision of Purgatory." The Five Beasts, April 7, 2015. https://thefivebeasts.wordpress.com/2015/04/07/torn-among-the-boars-st-hildegards-frightful-vision-of-purgatory/.

Wallace, Warner. "What Did The Early Christians Believe About Hell?" https://coldcasechristianity.com/writings/what-did-early-christians-believe-about-hell/

Ware, Timothy. "The Orthodox Church: An Introduction to Eastern Christianity." Penguin Books 2015.

Welch, Aaron. "Eternal or Eonian? Part Five (The Greek Adjective Aiónios). https://thathappyexpectation.blogspot.com/2015/01/eternal-or-eonian-part-five.html

www.ingramcontent.com/pod-product-compliance
Lightning Source LLC
Chambersburg PA
CBHW050801160426
43192CB00010B/1593